RESEARCHING LOCAL HISTORY
YOUR GUIDE TO THE SOURCES

RESEARCHING LOCAL HISTORY

YOUR GUIDE TO THE SOURCES

STUART A. RAYMOND

Pen & Sword

FAMILY HISTORY

First published in Great Britain in 2022 by
PEN AND SWORD FAMILY HISTORY
An imprint of
Pen & Sword Books Ltd
Yorkshire – Philadelphia

ISBN 978 1 52677 942 7

A CIP catalogue record for this book is
available from the British Library

Typeset in 10/13 Palatino by SJmagic DESIGN SERVICES, India.
Printed and bound in the UK by CPI Group (UK) Ltd.

Pen & Sword Books Ltd incorporates the Imprints of Aviation, Atlas,
Family History, Fiction, Maritime, Military, Discovery, Politics, History,
Archaeology, Select, Wharncliffe Local History, Wharncliffe True Crime,
Military Classics, Wharncliffe Transport, Leo Cooper, The Praetorian Press,
Remember When, Seaforth Publishing and Frontline Publishing.

For a complete list of Pen & Sword titles please contact

PEN & SWORD BOOKS LTD
47 Church Street, Barnsley, South Yorkshire, S70 2AS, England
E-mail: enquiries@pen-and-sword.co.uk
Website: www.pen-and-sword.co.uk

Or
PEN & SWORD BOOKS
1950 Lawrence Rd, Havertown, PA 19083, USA
E-mail: Uspen-and-sword@casematepublishers.com
Website: www.penandswordbooks.com

CONTENTS

INTRODUCTION

When I began to study English local history back in the 1970s, I was inspired by W.G Hoskins' *Local History in England*. I soon, however, realised that I needed more information on sources than Hoskins provided, and turned to W.B. Stephens' *Sources for English local history*. Both of these books are still useful, but they badly need updating (especially Stephens). Many more source materials have become easily available in the last few decades. Stephens did not even mention Lloyd George's valuation survey, one of the key sources for early twentieth-century history. The internet now enables me to easily read millions of probate records from the comfort of my own study. A huge range of other sources have been digitised for the internet, so much so that it is easy to forget that a much wider range of sources lying on record office shelves remain undigitised.

The aim of this book is to make the English[1] local historian aware of the wide range of written sources available in record offices, libraries and on the internet. Like Stephens' book, its aim is to pose the questions which ought to be asked, and then to identify the specific sources which are likely to answer those questions. I have attempted to explain how and why particular sources were created, the uses to which they can be put, and the limitations of the information they provide.

In a book of this length, it is not possible to deal with all the sources and topics that might be of interest to local historians. Nor is it possible to provide the detail that might be thought desirable. That detail is, however, provided in the numerous guides (many online) to specific sources that I have cited. I have tended to concentrate on sources relevant to parish history, although not, I hope, entirely neglecting the wider context. Some topics, for example, prisons, military history, political history, witchcraft, prices and wages, and oral history, landscape history, have been barely mentioned or dealt with cursorily. Archaeology is very important to local historians, but only very rarely is it likely to provide written sources. For other topics, of course, there is a paucity of sources. The further back in time you go, the fewer written sources are likely to be available.

ACKNOWLEDGEMENTS

This book is entirely dependent on countless local historians, and especially those whose works it cites. My thanks to them, to the librarians at Trowbridge library who obtained many of their publications for me, and to those who read my manuscript in draft. One of my former Pharos students and Simon Fowler have both made useful suggestions and saved me from errors. My thanks too to my wife Marjorie, who drags me away from the computer when I have been staring at the screen too long.

A Note on Counties
The counties mentioned in this book are those which existed before the 1974 local government reforms.

ABBREVIATIONS

FFHS	Federation of Family History Societies (now Family History Federation).
Short Guides 1.	Munby, Lionel, ed. *Short Guides to Records*. Historical Association, 1972;
Short Guides 2.	Thompson, K.M. *Short Guides to Records. Second Series, guides 25–48*. Historical Association, 1997.
TNA	The National Archives
VCH	*Victoria County History*

Chapter 1

WHAT IS LOCAL HISTORY?

History is a seamless web. Local historians are frequently concerned with family history, economic history, social history, or religious history. A good knowledge of English history, and indeed, British, European and worldwide history, is needed by anyone who wishes to research the local history of England and Wales. English history is the history of some 12,000+ parishes, and of how they relate to each other. Urban history is also important. Local historians may know their own localities best, but nevertheless need to know about *Domesday Book*, the plague, the Reformation, Royalists and Parliamentarians, nonconformists, the British Empire, the census, and the Home Front in two world wars.

Local history has a dual focus. It is local, focused on a specific place. It is history, focused on people, and on their communities. The place may be a parish, a town, or some larger region. It is likely to be in a rural area, as that is where most people lived prior to 1851.

Some places have had a continuous existence for thousands of years. That applies to many mentioned in *Domesday Book*. At that time, the manor was probably the most important institution in people's lives, and provided their sense of identity. However, its importance even then was in decline, as local churches were being built. These churches served specific areas, known as parishes. Parish boundaries were established between *c.*900 and *c.*1200, and determined where people attended church. Attendance at church defined communities for most of the last millennium, hence the importance of the parish, and of its church as the hub of the community.

Parish boundaries were not, however, confining. Most people crossed them regularly. The relationship between local communities and the region was important. Markets and fairs catered for regions, not for just one parish. Blacksmiths needed coal mined in Newcastle. Farmers needed to sell their wool at Blackwell Hall in London. Young men found their brides in neighbouring parishes. Vagrants travelled hundreds of

The church and graveyard at St Levan, Cornwall, the centre of the community.

miles in search of work, or, at least, subsistence. Trade and industry relied on transport links. The local historian must examine sources created in places other than his own parish. Parish registers and pauper records of neighbouring parishes sometimes provide useful information. The apprenticeship records of London companies identify apprentices from most English parishes. Probate records identify family members and creditors who lived at great distances from their relatives and debtors.

Some communities were not parish based. The gentry liked to think of themselves as county gentry. Nonconformist and Roman Catholic communities extended far beyond parish boundaries. The boundaries of Methodist circuits, and of Quaker meetings, frequently changed. Twentieth-century immigrant communities have created their own 'boundaries'. The boundaries of a community study should be determined by social realities, not administrative boundaries.

The local historian's research must begin by examining local topography. The physical landscape is a historical landscape. Over the centuries, our predecessors adapted it to their own purposes, and in the process totally changed its appearance. Roman soldiers built their fortress at Isca (Exeter) because it was at the head of the estuary of the River Exe. The River Severn brought much trade to Gloucester. Millers diverted rivers to power their mills. Bridges were built to connect communities separated by water. Rivers were dredged to accommodate shipping. Engineers dug numerous tunnels to accommodate canals, railways and roads. Landscapes were scarred in the search for minerals. Great expanses of the Fens, and of Sedgemoor, were drained for agriculture. Dams were built to supply water to cities. Landowners created parks and gardens, and diverted roads that interfered with their views. Millions of houses, ranging from hovels to palaces, have been built. Christians have built innumerable churches. The topography of every English parish has been drastically affected by human intervention. The buildings, the hedges, the fields, the roads, the waterways, even the woodlands, have all been created by human activity.

Topography, archaeology and architecture, are primarily dependent on evidence in the landscape rather than documents, and are therefore outside of the scope of this book. Their study demands a good pair of boots and a large-scale Ordnance Survey map. Useful guides include:

- Hoskins, W.G., *Fieldwork in Local History.* 2nd edition. Faber & Faber, 1982.
- Hoskins, W.G., *The Making of the English Landscape.* [Revised edition] Introduction by Christopher Taylor. Hodder and Stoughton, 1988.
- Welsh, Tom, *Local History on the Ground.* History Press, 2009.
- Rackham, Oliver, *The History of the Countryside.* Weidenfeld & Nicholson, 1995.

Bude Canal, built to transport sea sand to be used as fertiliser.

Archaeology is a specialised discipline. Local historians should not engage in excavation without professional supervision. For background, consult: Adkins, Roy & Lesley, & Leitch, Victoria. *The Handbook of British Archaeology.* [Revised edition] Constable, 2008.

Local historians will usually be concerned primarily with written evidence, although the archaeological evidence must be integrated with it to see the full picture. The documentary evidence does, however, require interpretation. Why were documents written? What processes were used to create them? How reliable are they? What are their limitations? Two examples may be given here. Many wills were written primarily to make provision for younger children. The fact that an eldest son was given a token bequest of one shilling does not indicate family disputes; rather, it suggests that provision had already been made for him.

Another example is provided by taxation records. They list everyone who paid tax – but not those who managed to avoid the assessor. Pre-modern administrators were frequently inefficient, corrupt, and/or weak.

Even the nineteenth-century census has many problems. It relied on householders filling in their household schedules correctly, enumerators copying that information into enumerators' books, and London clerks checking and counting the information provided. Illiterate householders misunderstood the questions asked, or did not know the answers; they sometimes answered questions that were not asked. There was plenty of room for error to creep in. Modern census indexes are not 100 per cent accurate, leaving even more room for errors when using digitised images.

Most historical sources were not compiled with the historian in mind. They had their own purposes, derived their information from diverse sources, did not necessarily include the information we would expect, and were written by men and women who all had their own idiosyncrasies, and who were not necessarily competent at their task. Historians must be aware of the original purposes of historical texts, and of how they were compiled, before the value of their evidence can be assessed.

The prime task of local historians is to use these sources to show how life was lived in the past. A number of questions define the agenda: When and why were settlements established? How did they grow and/or decline? How many people lived here? Who were they, how did they relate to each other, and how did they relate to the landscape? How did they earn their living? How were they governed? How did religion affect their lives? How typical is the area in its region and nationally? And what are its unique features? These are some of the questions which may be put to the sources discussed below.

Of course, not every question can be answered. The records are too fragmentary for that. For some topics, and some periods (especially recent centuries), there is no problem in finding information. For others, records are simply not available. Medieval households have left very limited traces. However, a little ingenuity may enable rough guesses to be made about at least some topics for which sources are limited. For example, the number of houses depicted on an eighteenth-century estate map may suggest how many householders there were. A comparison of signatures and marks on post-1753 marriage registers may give a rough indication of literacy.

Local history is a jigsaw puzzle, with an infinity of pieces. Many pieces have been lost, and not all of those which remain are to be found locally. Nevertheless, it is usually possible for the historian to paint a picture which provides interesting information about past times.

Further Reading:
The best introduction to researching local history is:

- Tiller, Kate. *English Local History: An Introduction.* [Revised edition]. Alan Sutton Publishing, 3rd edition. Boydell Press, 2020.

For a detailed exposition of the questions local historians should ask, see:

- Rogers, Alan. *Approaches to Local History.* Longman, 2nd edition. 1977.

Local history is firmly placed in its national context by:

- Campbell-Kease, John. *A Companion to Local History Research.* Alphabooks, 1989.

Hoskins' classic introduction is still worth reading:

- Hoskins, W.G. *Local History in England.* 3rd edition. Longman, 1984.

A number of Open University volumes are worth consulting:

- Finnegan, Ruth, and Drake, Michael, eds. *From Family Tree to Family History.* Cambridge University Press, 1994.
- Pryce, W.T.R., ed. *From Family History to Community History.* Cambridge University Press, 1994.
- Golby, John, ed. *Communities and Families.* Cambridge University Press, 1994.

See also:

- Phythian-Adams, Charles. *Re-thinking English Local History.* Occasional Papers 4th series, 1. Leicester University Press, 1987.
- Marshall, J.D. *The Tyranny of the Discrete: A Discussion of the Problems of Local History in England.* Scolar Press, 1997.

For encylopaedic treatment, see:

- Hey, David, ed. *The Oxford Companion to Family and Local History.* Oxford University Press, 2008.

See also:

- Richardson, John, ed. *The Local Historian's Encyclopedia.* 3rd edition. Historical Publications, 2003.

The *Local Historian* has published many articles on the discipline. See in particular:

- Tiller, Kate, & Dymond, David. 'Local History at the Crossroads', *Local Historian*, 37(4), 2007, p.250–57.
- Sheeran, George & Yanina. 'Opinion: No Longer the 1948 Show: Local History in the 21st Century', *Local Historian*, 39(4), 2009, p.314–23. A controversial article. See also responses in subsequent issues.

If you are writing a book, read:

- Dymond, David. *Researching and Writing History: A Guide for Local Historians.* 4th edition. Carnegie Publishing, 2016.

The most useful older guides to sources are:

- Stephens, W.B. *Sources for English Local History.* 2nd edition. Cambridge University Press, 1981.
- Carter, Paul, & Thomson, Kate. *Sources for Local Historians.* Phillimore, 2005.

The Open University's course guide to sources is excellent:

- Drake, Michael, & Finnegan, Ruth, eds. *Sources and Methods for Family and Community Historians: A Handbook.* 2nd edition. Cambridge University Press, 1997.

Records at TNA are the prime focus of:

- Riden, Philip. *Record Sources for Local History*. B.T. Batsford, 1987.

Extensive listings of published sources are included in:

- West, John. *Village Records*. 3rd edition. Phillimore & Co., 1997.

For specific periods, see:

- Aylmer, G.E., & Morrill, J.S. *The Civil War and Interregnum: Sources for Local Historians*. Bedford Square Press, 1979.
- Lord, Evelyn. *Investigating the Twentieth Century: Sources for Local Historians*. Tempus, 1999. This lacks any guidance on religious records.

Guides to forty-eight specific sources are included in:

- Munby, Lionel, ed. *Short Guides to Records*. Historical Association, 1972. [Guides 1–24].
- Thompson, K.M. *Short Guides to Records. Second Series,* Historical Association, 1997. [Guides 25–48].
  (References to these below are abbreviated to *Short Guides 1 & 2*).

Most sources used by local historians are also used by genealogists, and the numerous published guides to genealogy are useful to local historians too. The most comprehensive is:

- Herber, Mark. *Ancestral Trails: The Complete Guide to British Genealogy and Family History*. 2nd edition. Sutton Publishing/Society of Genealogists, 2004.

For a more up-to-date but much briefer introduction, see:

- Raymond, Stuart A. *Introducing Family History*. 2nd edition. Family History Federation, 2020.

Chapter 2

PRELIMINARIES TO RESEARCH

Local historians depend on books, libraries, record offices and the internet. This chapter explains where to look for information, and identifies some of the problems that may arise.

A. Books and Libraries

The first step in researching local history is to consult the work of other local historians. The *Victoria County History* (referred to hereafter as the *VCH*) **www.history.ac.uk/research/victoria-county-history** is a particularly important ongoing work. In addition to parish histories, it includes county volumes covering topics such as local government, religious history and economic history. Most volumes are digitised at British History Online **www.british-history.ac.uk**. Early *VCH* researchers compiled slips detailing all the original sources they could discover. If your patch has not yet been covered by *VCH*, it may be worthwhile to consult these slips, which are held locally.

Antiquarian works of the nineteenth century and earlier, both published and unpublished, are important. Coverage is narrow by modern standards, but classics such as Carew's *Survey of Cornwall* and Dugdale's *Antiquities of Warwickshire* contain much useful information, as do travellers' accounts such as those of John Leland, Celia Fiennes, Daniel Defoe and William Camden. See:

- Currie, C.R.J., & Lewis, C.P., eds. *English County Histories: A guide.* Alan Sutton, 1994.

For an early bibliography, see:

- Anderson, John P. *The Book of British Topography.* W. Satchell & Co., 1881.

Urban history is covered by:

- Gross, Charles. *A Bibliography of British Municipal History, including gilds and Parliamentary representation.* 2nd edition. Leicester University Press, 1966. Originally published 1897, but with a new introduction by G.H. Martin.
- Martin, G.H., & McIntyre, Sylvia. *A Bibliography of British and Irish Municipal History. Vol.1. General Works.* Leicester University Press, 1972. No more published.

Regular listings of new books are published in the *Local Historian*, and, for urban history, in *Urban History* (formerly *Urban History Yearbook*).

Histories of specific places can be identified in library catalogues. The catalogues of local studies libraries are a good place to start, although it may also be useful to consult union catalogues such as Worldcat **www.worldcat.org** or Library Hub Discover **https://discover.libraryhub.jisc.ac.uk**. Also consult the *British National Bibliography* **www.bl.uk/bibliographic/natbib.html** (which aims to list everything published in the UK since 1950), and the catalogues of major research libraries such as the British Library **www.bl.uk**.

The Vision of Britain website **https://visionofbritain.org.uk** covers every parish in Great Britain. It includes extracts from gazetteers and from the works of prominent travel writers, together with census data, maps and other information. The Gazetteer of British Place-Names **www.gazetteer.org.uk** provides a useful guide to places. Archi UK Maps **www.digital-documents.co.uk** is an archaeological gazetteer, with many maps, and a database of 200,000+ archaeological sites. Wikipedia **https://en.wikipedia.org** sometimes has detailed histories of particular places.

You need to be aware of local history activity across your county. Every county has its own local history societies – frequently many of them. Many publish newsletters and journals; the journals of countywide organisations such as the Yorkshire Archaeological and Historical Society and the Wiltshire Archaeological and Natural History Society frequently carry authoritative articles on local topics. Some have substantial libraries. Many are concerned with both archaeology and local history, and can offer the local historian useful advice on archaeological matters.

Local societies are listed on the website of the British Association for Local History **www.balh.org.uk**. This association enables you to keep in touch with local history activities throughout the UK. Its quarterly *Local History News* has brief articles, news reports, and notes on the activities of record offices, societies and museums. Its journal, the *Local Historian* (formerly the *Amateur Historian*), publishes authoritative articles. Past issues are available online.

Record societies are particularly important. Their annual volumes usually print specific sources, for example, Robert Bearman's edition of the *Charters of the Redvers Family and the Earldom of Devon, 1090–1217* (Devon & Cornwall Record Society, 1994) or Ivor Slocombe's *Wiltshire Quarter Sessions Order Book 1642–1654* (Wiltshire Record Society, 2014). They contain a huge amount of information likely to be of interest. The publications of national record societies, such as the British Record Society and the Catholic Record Society should not be neglected. Even if the actual documents printed tell you nothing about your specific locality, the introductions of record society volumes should be read; many provide excellent guides to sources. These publications are widely available in research libraries, and fully listed by:

- Royal Historical Society: National and Regional History
  https://royalhistsoc.org/publications/national-regional-history

Between 1870 and 2003, the Historical Manuscripts Commission (sometimes referred to as the Royal Commission on Historical Manuscripts) published many reports on archival collections outside London. These contain a huge amount of information for local historians. See:

- *A Guide to the Reports on Collections of Manuscripts of Private Families, Corporations and Institutions in Great Britain and Ireland …* 2 parts in 3 vols. HMSO, 1914–38. Continued by Hall, A.C.S. *Guide to the Reports of the Royal Commission on Historical Manuscripts, 1911–1957.* 2 parts in 4 vols. HMSO, 1977–73. See also the Wikipedia article at **https://en.wikipedia.org/wiki/Royal_Commission_on_Historical_Manuscripts**

County historical bibliographies identifying the vast majority of local publications are available for most counties. The present author's series of county genealogical bibliographies, although aimed primarily at family historians, is likely to be of use to local historians as well. Twenty-two counties are covered. Many other county bibliographies can be identified in library catalogues. For an older listing, see:

- Humphreys, A.L. *Handbook to County Bibliography, Being a Bibliography of Bibliographies Relating to the Counties and Towns of Great Britain.* 1917.

The Bibliography of British and Irish History **https://royalhistsoc.org/publications/bbih** identifies numerous books and journal articles which place local history in its wider context. It may also be useful to consult *Historical Abstracts*, which has international coverage, but is less in-depth. Both titles are only available through libraries with subscriptions. There is, unfortunately, no up-to-date bibliography specifically devoted to local historical sources, although the bibliography in Moore's work on demography (p.56) is much wider than the word 'demography' might suggest.

For older works, consult:

- Graves, Edgar B. *A Bibliography of English History to 1485*. Clarendon Press, 1975. This is continued for later centuries by *A Bibliography of British History*, in five volumes, by various authors.

Two specialist bibliographies include much of interest to local historians:

- ADS: Archaeology Data Service Library
  https://archaeologydataservice.ac.uk/library
- Ideas [Bibliography of Economic Literature]
  https://ideas.repec.org

Theses are also important. Many are devoted to local topics. A full listing of pre-1970 history theses compiled in British universities is available at **www.british-history.ac.uk/no-series/theses-1901–70**, continued to 2014 at **/theses-1970–2014**. Doctoral theses from most British universities (apart from Oxford and Cambridge) can be downloaded from the British Library's Ethos service **https://ethos.bl.uk**.

Books listed in catalogues and bibliographies can usually be found in libraries. Most public libraries run a separate local studies library, sometimes in conjunction with the local record office. These are likely to hold most local books.

It may be useful to visit your local university library. Universities frequently hold substantial collections of interest to local historians and usefully supplement local authority libraries. For example, they are likely to hold fairly complete sets of calendars issued by the National Archives (TNA hereafter), together with record society publications and county journals from many counties, providing invaluable comparative materials. Most university libraries are open to the public, but check their websites for access details.

A variety of other libraries also cater for local historians. The great majority of books published in the UK are held by the British Library **www.bl.uk** (although readers are expected to demonstrate that they cannot consult the items they need anywhere else). For Wales, the

National Library of Wales **www.library.wales** is a must. TNA has an extensive library in addition to its archival holdings. Reference has already been made to libraries run by local societies. The Society of Genealogists **www.sog.org** has an extensive library, including many record society publications and local society journals. There are also a number of independent libraries, such as the William Salt Library in Stafford, and the Devon & Exeter Institution in Exeter, which sometimes have important local history collections.

Local historians should work their way systematically through the library and note all mentions of their chosen place that they find. It is important not only to note that information but also to cite the source. At a minimum, note the title (from the title page, not the cover), the name of the author or editor, the publisher and the date of publication, together with page numbers. Then you (or your readers) will be able to check the information again, if you need to.

Local studies libraries are the subject of:

• Winterbotham, Diana, & Crosby, Alan. *The Local Studies Library: A Handbook for Local Historians*. British Association for Local History, 1998.

In recent years, many out of copyright books have been made available on the internet in digitised format. That includes most of the older books cited below. There are far too many such sites to list here; however, a useful guide to them is provided by:

• The Online Books Page
  https://onlinebooks.library.upenn.edu/search.html

The most useful digitised book websites are:

• Internet Archive
  https://archive.org
• Hathi Trust Digital Library
  www.hathitrust.org

B. Archives and Record Offices

Books differ from archives. Many copies were printed. Archives, by contrast, are unique, and must therefore be treated with greater care than books. Over the centuries, archives have survived many hazards – flood, fire, vermin, damp, ill treatment. A few are so damaged that, although they are catalogued, access to them is restricted until they can be properly conserved. Great care must be taken when consulting archives. The use of pen and ink in the search room is banned. Pencils, or perhaps computers and digital cameras, must be used.

It is crucial to be aware of the vast range of institutions which may hold written sources relevant to the history of particular places. Ecclesiastical records, for example, are found not just in the parish chest, but also amongst diocesan archives, at TNA, and perhaps in Lambeth Palace Library. The archives of substantial landowners may be deposited in a single repository, despite the fact that their property lay in many different counties. Other local documents may have strayed to a university or college archive, a local history society collection, the British Library, or a wide range of other record repositories. It is therefore important to use online union catalogues to locate stray documents. The holdings of over 2,500 archives are partially catalogued by:

- National Archives: Discovery
  https://discovery.nationalarchives.gov.uk

This is complemented by TNA's annual surveys of new accessions, covering *c*.200 repositories:

- Accessions to Repositories
  www.nationalarchives.gov.uk/accessions

Universities and colleges hold substantial archival collections. The Bodleian Library (Oxford) and Cambridge University Library have collections of national importance. The archives of Oxbridge colleges, whose estates are scattered throughout the country, are particularly worthy of note. Other institutions also have significant holdings. Keele University, for example, holds the estate records of the Sneyd family, who owned much property in North Staffordshire. The collections of over 350 academic institutions are partially catalogued by:

- Archives Hub
  https://archiveshub.jisc.ac.uk

London has many specialist institutions, a few of which are mentioned below. For a union catalogue of their archives, see:

- Aim 25: Archives in London and the M25 Area
  https://aim25.com

Despite their size, these union catalogues only partially record the holdings of the institutions covered. Most also have their own catalogues.

Both the union catalogues and the catalogues of specific institutions should be consulted. The information in them is not necessarily duplicated.

Record offices are listed by:

- Find an Archive in the UK and Beyond
  https://discovery.nationalarchives.gov.uk/find-an-archive

Local historians usually find the majority of their sources in local record offices, especially in the period *c.*1580–1830. County record offices were created to house Quarter Sessions archives, but now usually hold records from a wide diversity of sources. National institutions also hold many records. TNA is particularly important for the records of central government, which frequently relate to specific localities. Its holdings will be frequently mentioned in subsequent chapters. The three Palatinates – Durham, Chester and Lancaster – were separately administered.[1] Their records are therefore in their own separate TNA classes.

TNA's extensive website **www.nationalarchives.gov.uk** includes its Discovery catalogue, and numerous invaluable research guides. The publications of the List and Index Society **www.listandindexsociety. org.uk** sometimes provide additional information on TNA classes.[2] So do the volumes in the similarly named (but distinct) *Lists and indexes* series issued by the Public Record Office (the old name for TNA) between 1832 and 1936.[3] There is much of local historical interest in:

- Bevan, Amanda. *Tracing your Ancestors in the National Archives.*
  7th edition. National Archives, 2006.

Many local documents have strayed to the British Library. It holds numerous estate records, monastic cartularies, copies of the heralds'

Local record offices such as Wiltshire & Swindon History Centre hold many local archives.

The National Archives.

visitations, and a wide range of other records. See its manuscripts' catalogue:

- British Library: Catalogues and Collections
  www.bl.uk/catalogues-and-collections/catalogues

Similar but smaller collections are held by the Bodleian Library and Cambridge University Library, as well as other universities. A variety of national repositories deal with specialist topics. Lambeth Palace Library **www.lambethpalacelibrary.org**, with the Church of England Record Centre, holds the records of many ecclesiastical organisations. Sources for local history are listed, county-by-county, in its online Research Guide: 'Sources for British and Irish Local History'. The Society of Antiquaries **www.sal.org.uk** holds many papers of antiquarians. The Society of Genealogists **www.sog.org.uk** has extensive collections of genealogical transcriptions, and many online sources. Dr Williams's Library **https://dwl.ac.uk** holds a wide range of sources for the history of nonconformity (p.198). The Wellcome Library **https://wellcomelibrary.org** is devoted to medical history.

National institutions outside of London include, amongst others, the Museum of English Rural Life **https://merl.reading.ac.uk** and the Modern Records Centre **https://warwick.ac.uk/services/library/mrc**. In York, the

Borthwick Institute **www.york.ac.uk/borthwick** holds the archives of the Diocese of York, which covered much of northern England.

The many printed catalogues and listings of major institutions such as TNA, the British Library, and the old universities, or of overseas institutions, such as California's Huntington Library and Washington's Folger Shakespeare Library, have not been mentioned here. It may still be helpful to browse serendipitously through them, but they have now mostly been superseded by online catalogues.

C. *The Internet*
In recent years, the internet has revolutionised local history research. This book is full of references to useful websites. They can be divided into four categories. We have already discussed digitised books and online catalogues. Also important are guides to sources and digitised original sources.

Guides to sources can frequently be found on the internet. Be aware of the provenance of these guides. Those issued by major institutions such as TNA and the London Metropolitan Archives are generally excellent, although they are not always as up to date as they should be. Elsewhere on the web, the quality of advice offered can be very variable, and care should be taken.

A huge range of digitised documents are available online. Many are on the websites of commercial hosts. Some of these, such as Ancestry, **www.ancestry.co.uk**, Findmypast **www.findmypast.co.uk** and The Genealogist **www.thegenealogist.co.uk** cater primarily for the interests of genealogists, and include innumerable census schedules, parish registers, probate records, newspapers and other sources. FamilySearch **www.familysearch.org** is similar, but free. Usually, but not invariably, the local historian can search these sites by place name as well as by surname.

A number of commercial hosts serve the academic market. Proquest **www.proquest.com,** for example, has the Parliamentary papers. **Gale www.gale.com/intl/primary-sources/state-papers-online** has State Papers Online. Unfortunately, such websites can frequently only be accessed through institutional subscriptions, making it difficult for unaffiliated local historians to gain access.

Some record offices have digitised parts of their own collection and placed databases on their own websites. For TNA's free digital sources, see Free Online Records: Digital Microfilm **www.nationalarchives. gov.uk/help-with-your-research/research-guides/free-online-records-digital-microfilm.**

There are many important databases created by academics. Domesday Book Online **www.domesdaybook.co.uk**, the Clergy of the Church of England database **https://theclergydatabase.org.uk** and the Gazetteer of Markets and Fairs **https://archives.history.ac.uk/gazetteer/**

gazweb2.html are good examples. Many medieval and early modern TNA documents are digitised by the Anglo-American Legal Tradition **http://aalt.law.uh.edu**. Numerous digitised sources for London can be found at London Lives 1690 to 1800: Crime, Poverty and Social Policy in the Metropolis **www.londonlives.org**. Many other examples are mentioned in succeeding chapters.

Numerous transcripts and indexes are also available online, especially on the commercial hosts mentioned above, but also elsewhere. It is important to evaluate the accuracy of such material. Note too that websites which host the same sources, such as the census, do not necessarily use the same indexes. The index to the Apprenticeship Duty Registers hosted by Findmypast, and compiled by the Society of Genealogists many years ago, is quite different to Ancestry's index of the same source. It may be useful to search the same source on an alternative website if information cannot be found.

Numerous websites of interest to local historians are listed by:

- Fillmore, Jacqueline. *Internet Sites for Local Historians: A Directory*, ed. Alan G. Crosby. 4th edition. British Association for Local History, 2017. Updated editions regularly issued.

D. Reading Old Documents

Medieval and early modern handwriting may appear illegible to the novice, as it uses different letter forms from those in use today. It was, however, meant to be read. Reading it just requires practice. An excellent introduction is provided by TNA's tutorial:

- Palaeography: reading old handwriting, 1500 – 1800: A practical online tutorial
  www.nationalarchives.gov.uk/palaeography

Other online courses are listed at:

- Transcribing Medieval Manuscripts and Archival Material
  www.cerl.org/resources/links_to_other_resources/tools_decribing_ mss_and_archival_materials

Comprehensive printed introductions are provided by:

- Marshall, Hilary. *Palaeography for Family and Local Historians*. [Revised edition] Phillimore, 2010.
- Forrest, Mark. *Reading Early Handwriting 1500–1700*. 3rd edition. British Association for Local History, 2019.

Booklets describing the forms of early modern letters include:

- Buck, W.S.B. *Examples of Handwriting, 1550–1650*. Society of Genealogists, 1965 (reprinted 2008).
- Ison, Alf. *A Secretary Hand ABC Book*. The Author, 1982.

Latin poses greater problems. It remained the language of the law until 1733, although documents such as wills and apprenticeship indentures ceased to use it at earlier dates. Helpfully, some documents follow a common form. In parish registers, for example, words such as *baptizatus erat, nupti erat,* and *sepultus erat* are endlessly repeated, and their meaning is obvious. Latin is used in the first paragraph of every bond, but the wording is always identical, and you only need to pick out names, dates and amounts. Standard wording was used in some medieval deeds, and names can be easily read.

An excellent online introduction to medieval Latin and palaeography is available:

- Reading Old Documents
  www.nationalarchives.gov.uk/help-with-your-research/reading-old-documents

A detailed guide to Latin and palaeography in medieval manorial records is provided by:

- Stuart, Denis. *Manorial Records: An Introduction to their Transcription and Translation*. Phillimore, 1992.

See also:

- Newton, K.C. *Medieval Local Records: A Reading Aid*. Historical Association 1971.

Printed guides to medieval Latin include:

- Stuart, Denis. *Latin for Local and Family Historians*. Phillimore, 1995.
- Gooder, Eileen A. *Latin for Local History: An Introduction*. 2nd edition. Routledge, 1978.

For useful tips, see:

- Westcott, Brooke. *Making Sense of Latin Documents for Family and Local Historians*. Family History Partnership, 2014.

Medieval Latin is not the same as Classical Latin. Medieval scribes used numerous abbreviations, and Latinised many names of persons and places. A detailed guide to abbreviations, medieval words and Latinised names, is provided by the indispensable:

• Martin, Charles Trice. *The Record Interpreter: A Collection of Abbreviations, Latin Words and Names Used in English Historical Manuscripts and Records.* 2nd edition, with introduction by David Iredale. Phillimore, 1982.

For a more extensive dictionary of medieval Latin, see:

• Dictionary of Medieval Latin from British Sources
  www.dmlbs.ox.ac.uk/web/dmlbs.html

In the medieval period, documents were occasionally written in Anglo-Norman-French. Some help is provided by:

• The Anglo-Norman Online Hub
  www.anglo-norman.net

Pre-Conquest charters may be in either Latin or Old English. For an introduction to the latter, see:

• Old English Online
  https://lrc.la.utexas.edu/eieol/engol

In more recent centuries, many words have become obsolete. Probate records in particular are full of them. Their meanings are defined in:

• Raymond, Stuart A. *Words from Wills and other Probate Records: A glossary.* FFHS, 2004.

See also:

• Bristow, Joy. *The Local Historian's Glossary of Words and Terms.* 3rd edition. Countryside Books, 2001.

Detailed etymologies of archaic words are provided in:

• Oxford English Dictionary
  www.oed.com (available through subscribing libraries)

E. Dates and Calendars

A variety of dating methods were used in historical documents. These include, for example, regnal years, saints' days and the law terms. Quakers have their own calendar. Researchers need to be aware of the 1752 switch from the Julian to the Gregorian calendar. Eleven days were 'lost', and the beginning of the year switched from 25 March to 1 January. Useful guides include:

- Introduction to Dating Documents
  www.nottingham.ac.uk/manuscriptsandspecialcollections/ researchguidance/datingdocuments/introduction.aspx.
- Cheney, C.R. *Handbook of Dates for Student of British History*, rev. Michael Jones. New ed. Royal Historical Society Guides and Handbooks, 4. Cambridge University Press, 2000.
- Munby, Lionel M. *Dates and Times for Local Historians*. British Association for Local History, 1997.

F. Boundaries and Maps

Written sources are frequently dependent on boundaries. Manorial surveys relate to land within the boundaries of a manor. Tax lists are arranged by hundred and by parish, or sometimes by township. Electoral registers are arranged by ward. Churchwardens' accounts deal with specific parishes. It is therefore necessary to identify local administrative units, and to know where their boundaries were.[4] The boundaries of medieval manors and parishes are not necessarily identical, nor are the boundaries of modern secular and ecclesiastical parishes, which were separated in 1894.

Before the nineteenth century, administrative boundaries changed only infrequently. Many show remarkable continuity; indeed, some probably date from prehistoric times. County boundaries remained almost unchanged from their creation in the Anglo-Saxon and Norman periods until local government reorganisation in 1974. Diocesan boundaries were not quite as long-lasting; six new dioceses were created in the 1540s, and another twenty in 1836.[5]

The basic administrative unit of both church and state was the parish. Parishes were created between the eighth and the thirteenth centuries, earlier in the south than in the north. Northern parishes were sometimes much larger than those in the south, and townships were administratively important. Few changes took place between c.1300 and c.1800. Thereafter, many boundaries were adjusted to take account of changing needs.

A detailed listing of local administrative units, including boundary changes is provided by:

The post-Reformation Dioceses of England and Wales.

- Youngs, Frederic A. *Guide to the Local Administrative Units of England.* 2 vols. Royal Historical Society Guides and Handbooks, 10 & 17. 1980–91.

For maps of administrative jurisdictions in 1851, see:

- Family Search: Administrative Jurisdictions 1851 **www.familysearch.org/mapp**

For an indispensable map of English parishes and their boundaries, based on Ordnance Survey data, see:

- Cockin, T.C.H. *The Parish Atlas of England: Atlas of English Parish Boundaries.* Malthouse Press, 2017.

Boundary changes can also be identified by using successive editions of the 1-inch to the mile Ordnance Survey map. Ordnance Survey maps are also useful for other purposes. They identify landscape features such as rivers and hills, roads and other transport links, prehistoric and other monuments, the distribution of settlement, land use, and industrial development. They can, with skill, be made to reveal the landscape features of successive ages lying on top of each other. They are essential for the student of place names. The 6-inch and 25-inch are indispensable for more detailed study. Current Ordnance Survey Explorer and Landranger maps, at a scale of 1:25,000 and 1:50,000 respectively, are also likely to be useful.

Ordnance Survey maps are available on a number of websites. The Vision of Britain website has already been mentioned. The National Library of Scotland's map page is important for the whole UK:

- National Library of Scotland: Map Images
  maps.nls.uk

This can also be accessed through:

- The Charles Close Society for the Study of Ordnance Survey Maps
  https://charlesclosesociety.org

For a brief guide, see:

- The National Archives: How to Look for Records of Ordnance Survey
  www.nationalarchives.gov.uk/help-with-your-research/research-guides/ordnance-survey

Detailed guides include:

- Oliver, Richard. *Ordnance Survey Maps: A Concise Guide for Historians*. 3rd edition. Charles Close Society, 2013.
- Harley, J.B. *Ordnance Surveys Map: A Descriptive Manual*. Ordnance Survey, 1975.

Older printed county maps are listed by:

- Chubb, Thomas. *The Printed Maps in the Atlases of Great Britain and Ireland: A Bibliography, 1579–1870*. Ed. J. Burrow & Co., 1927. Reprinted Dawsons of Pall Mall, 1966.

Maps of parish boundaries are juxtaposed with nineteenth-century county maps in:

- Humphery-Smith, Cecil. *The Phillimore Atlas and Index of Parish Registers*. 3rd edition. Phillimore, 2003. Digitised at **https://www.ancestry.co.uk/search/collections/8830**

For town maps, see:

- Kain, Roger P., & Oliver, R. *British Town Maps: A History*. British Library, 2015. This is accompanied by an online catalogue at **https://townmaps.history.ac.uk**

Detailed information concerning buildings, land use, and urban design in major cities is provided by the Goad maps, drawn for fire insurance purposes between 1886 and 1930. These are digitised at:

- Fire Insurance Maps and Plans
  www.bl.uk/onlinegallery/onlineex/firemaps/fireinsurancemaps.html

See also:

- Aspinall, Peter J. 'The Use of Nineteenth-Century Fire Insurance Plans for the Urban Historian', *Local Historian* 11(6), 1975, p.343–9.
- Rowley, Gwyn. 'British Fire Insurance plans: the Goad productions, *c.*1885–1970', *Archives*, 17(74), 1985, p.67–78.

Plans, showing proposed canals, docks, turnpikes, tramways and other public utilities, had to be submitted when private acts of parliament were sought. For these, see p.143.

Manuscript maps may be important. Enclosure maps, tithe maps, estate maps, and their accompanying documentation, all provide much information on estate boundaries, place names, owners and tenants. They will be discussed in later chapters. A detailed guide to UK map collections is provided by:

- Wallis, Helen, ed. *Historians' Guide to Early British Maps*. Royal Historical Society Guides and Handbooks, 18. 1994.

On the uses of maps, see:

- Hindle, Paul. *Maps for Historians*. Phillimore, 1998.

G. Photographs and Prints

Photographs, film and prints are invaluable sources of topographical, social and economic information. Topographical postcards (often sold on eBay **www.ebay.co.uk**) are particularly useful. It is still possible for the local historian to make substantial collections covering their own patch by attending postcard fairs. The Post Office first permitted their use in 1894, and many topographical scenes on postcards are now of historic interest. So is the text written on their backs.

Local studies libraries and record offices hold substantial print and photographic collections (including postcards). For the millions of photographs held by TNA, see:

- Photographs
  www.nationalarchives.gov.uk/help-with-your-research/research-guides/photographs

Over 12 million photographs, drawings, reports and publications are available online at:

- The Historic England Archive
  https://historicengland.org.uk/images-books/archive

An important commercial photographic collection is searchable at:

- Francis Frith: the UK's Leading Publisher of Local Photographs since 1860
  http://www.francisfrith.com/uk

Millions of aerial photographs are held by:

- NCAP: National Collection of Aerial Photographs
  https://ncap.org.uk

See also:

- Cambridge Air Photos
  www.cambridgeairphotos.com

For film, much useful material is on:

- YouTube
  www.youtube.com

Other major UK collections include:

- BFI National Archive
  www.bfi.org.uk/archive-collections

See especially *Your Britain on Film* page.

- BBC Archive
  www.bbc.co.uk/archive

A number of regional film archives are listed under 'United Kingdom' at:

- List of Film Archives
  https://en.wikipedia.org/wiki/List_of_film_archives

H. Mass Observation
Much useful twentieth-century information is in the Mass Observation archives **www.massobs.org.uk** at Sussex University. The participants in this continuing social survey wrote 500 diaries, and regularly answered questionnaires on the daily life of ordinary people in Britain, mainly between 1937 and 1949. The project was revived in 1981. See:

- Mass Observation: Recording Everyday Life in Britain
  www.massobs.org.uk

I. Parliamentary Papers
The sessional papers of the House of Commons (frequently referred to as 'blue books') form one of the most extensive series of documents ever published. Many are cited below. They use a complicated numbering system to locate hard copies; these numbers have not been cited here, since it is usually easy to find papers online without them. They have been digitised by **https://parlipapers.proquest.com/parlipapers**. This is a subscription site available through some research libraries. Specific papers are frequently found on digitised book websites (p.12), and also in the Wellcome Library **https://wellcomelibrary.org**. Hard copies or microfiche versions are available in many libraries. For a select list, see:

- Powell, W.R. *Local History from Blue Books: A Select List of the Sessional Papers of the House of Commons*. Help for Students of History 64. Historical Association, 1969.

The term 'Parliamentary papers' also includes the *Journals* of both the House of Commons (from 1547) and the House of Lords (from 1510), Acts of Parliament, Bills and Hansard. The *Journals* (available on British History Online **www.british-history.ac.uk**) track the progress of bills through Parliament. Acts are either public or private. The public acts from 1485–1792 have been printed in *Statutes of the Realm*, and from 1702 as *Statutes at Large*. For Interregnum legislation, see:

- Firth, C.H., ed. *Acts and Ordinances of the Interregnum, 1642–1660.* 3 vols. HMSO, 1911.

Private acts (and bills which may have been amended) relating to matters such as enclosure, turnpikes, and personal estates can frequently be found in local record offices. A full collection of private acts is held by the Parliamentary Archives **www.parliament.uk/business/publications/parliamentary-archives**. They are indexed in:

- Chronological Table of Local Acts
  www.legislation.gov.uk/changes/chron-tables/local
  Covers from 1797, and printed (for 1797–1994) in *Chronological Table of Local Legislation.* 4 vols. HMSO, 1996.
- Chronological Table of Private and Personal Acts (1539–2006)
  www.legislation.gov.uk/changes/chron-tables/private
  Printed to 1997 in *Chronological Table of Private and Personal Acts 1539–1997.* HMSO, 1997.

For Parliamentary records, see:

- UK Parliament: Parliamentary Archives
  https://archives.parliament.uk
- Bond, Maurice. *The Records of Parliament: A Guide for Genealogists and Local Historians.* Phillimore & Co., 1964.
- Bond, Maurice. *Guide to the Records of Parliament.* HMSO, 1971.

J. Newspapers and Journals

Local newspapers reported on a huge range of matters. They printed advertisements, birth, marriage and death notices, situations vacant, property sales, and details of absconding apprentices, all of which are invaluable sources for local historians. Newspapers are particularly important from the 1850s onwards. For detailed guidance, see:

- Bates, Denise. *Historical Research Using British Newspapers.* Pen & Sword, 2016.

Newspapers used to be difficult to use, given their bulk and their lack of indexing. The British Library's huge collection is currently being digitised. More than 40,500,000 pages from many hundred titles could be easily read at the date of writing. See:

- British Newspaper Archive
  www.britishnewspaperarchive.co.uk

Many public libraries subscribe to:

- Times Digital Archive 1785–2014
  www.gale.com/intl/c/the-times-digital-archive

For Welsh newspapers, visit:

- Welsh Newspapers
  https://newspapers.library.wales

Local newspapers are listed by:

- Gibson, Jeremy, Langston, Brett, & Smith, Brenda W. *Local newspapers 1750–1920: England and Wales, Channel Islands, Isle of Man: A Select Location List*. 3rd edition. Family History Partnership, 2011.

Historic journals are also useful. Over 500 are available in the British Periodicals subscription database **www.proquest.com/products-services/british_periodicals.html**. Many are also available on the digitised books websites noted above (p.12). The *Gentleman's Magazine* (1731–1922)[6] and *Notes and Queries*, are particularly useful and fully indexed. The former included many notices of births, marriages and deaths, together with obituaries. The latter includes a wide variety of brief notes on miscellaneous subjects. For details of digitised volumes visit **https://onlinebooks.library.upenn.edu/search.html**.

Over 450 Welsh journals are digitised at:

- Welsh Journals
  https://journals.library.wales

Nineteenth-century periodicals are listed and indexed by the subscription-based:

- Waterloo Directory of English Newspapers and Periodicals 1800–1900
  www.victorianperiodicals.com/series3/index.asp

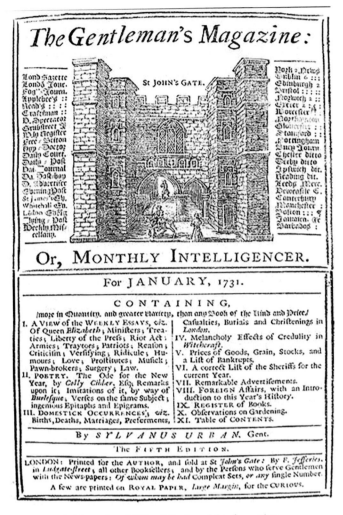

Gentleman's Magazine, 1731 – full of useful information.

Further sources of information are listed by:

- Victorian Periodicals. Aids to Research: A Selected Bibliography. Rosemary T. Van Arsdel
  http://victorianresearch.org/periodicals.html

Finally, the official notices in the *London Gazette* **www.thegazette.co.uk**, which cover topics ranging from official appointments to bankruptcy, from roads, railways and canals to aliens, should be searched. See:

- Thomas, James. 'The London Gazette and the Local Historian', *Local Historian*, 15(4), 1982, p.212–7.

K. Place Names

Place names frequently reveal how particular places were perceived by early inhabitants. They derive from a variety of languages: Celtic, Latin, Old English, Scandinavian, Norman-French, and others, and may refer to landscape, wildlife, vegetation, land use, administration, or particular people(s). They are a major source of information on early medieval England.

Speculation about place-name meanings is unwise, except by linguists. A good knowledge of several ancient languages, and of how they have changed over time, is needed. Onomastics, to give it its technical name, is dependent on assembling all variant early spellings of particular place names. Most of them have already been collected. However, many minor place names escaped medieval documentary notice. Their first mention may be in sixteenth- or seventeenth-century manorial court rolls and deeds, or even nineteenth-century tithe maps. Local historians using such sources may identify place names not hitherto noticed, and it may be possible for them to map the distribution of place-name elements such as leah (wood or clearing) and worth (settlement). See:

- Carroll, Jayne, & Kilby, Susan. 'Preparing the Ground: Finding Minor Landscape Names in Medieval Documents', *Local Historian*, 49(4), 2019, p.276–300.

For detailed introductions to place-name studies, see:

- Gelling, Margaret. *Signposts to the Past: Place-Names and the History of England*. 3rd edition. Phillimore, 2007.
- Gelling, Margaret. *Place-Names in the Landscape: The geographical roots of Britain's place-names*. J.M. Dent, 1984.

Several dictionaries of English place names are available. Recent works include:

- Watts, Victor, Insley, John, & Gelling, Margaret, eds. *The Cambridge Dictionary of English Place-Names, based on the collections of the English Place-Name Society*. Cambridge University Press, 2004.
- Mills, A.D. *A Dictionary of British Place-Names*. Oxford University Press, 2011. Available online via subscribing libraries at **www.oxfordreference.com**

See also:

- Key to English Place-Names
  http://kepn.nottingham.ac.uk

More detailed guides to the place names of specific counties are being published by the English Place-Name Society **www.nottingham.ac.uk/ research/groups/epns**. A few volumes are on the society's website. Volumes issued since the Second World War provide much more detailed analysis of minor place names than their earlier predecessors.

For field names, see:

- Cavill, Paul. *A New Dictionary of English Field-Names*. English Place-Name Society, 2018.

Published studies are listed by:

- Spittal, Jeffrey, & Field, John. *A Reader's Guide to the Place-Names of the United Kingdom: A Bibliography of Publications (1920–89) on the Place-Names of Great Britain and Northern Ireland, the Isle of Man and the Channel Islands*. Stamford: Paul Watkins, 1990.

L. Oral History

Oral history is important for historians of the recent past. Reminiscences may provide valuable information, and are frequently key components in community studies. Their accuracy should, however, be carefully evaluated. The Oral History Society's website **www.ohs.org.uk** offers much advice and includes a good bibliography. Good introductions are provided by:

- Thompson, Paul, & Bornat, Joanna. *The Voice of the Past; Oral History*. 4th edition. Oxford University Press, 2017.
- Howarth, Ken. *Oral History: A Handbook*. Sutton Publishing, 1998.
- Step by Step Guide to Oral History. **http://dohistory.org/on_your_own/toolkit/oralHistory.html**

Many institutions have created collections of oral recordings; these are listed in the British Library's Directory of Sound Recordings **www.bl.uk/ projects/uk-sound-directory**.

M. Mensuration

Measurements of quantities recorded in historical documents should be treated with care. It might be obvious that inflation has dramatically reduced the value of money, but it is perhaps not so obvious that units of land measurement such as the acre, and measures of volume such as the gallon, have varied considerably over the centuries, and between different regions. For land measurements, see:

- Jones, Andrew. 'Land Measurement in England, 1150–1350', *Agricultural History Review*, 27(1), 1979, p.10–18.

Mensuration in England was increasingly standardised from the sixteenth century. See:

- Introduction to Weights and Measures
  www.nottingham.ac.uk/manuscriptsandspecialcollections/ researchguidance/weightsandmeasures/introduction.aspx

For the value of money, see:

- Munby, Lionel. *How Much is That Worth?* 2nd edition. Phillimore, for the British Association for Local History, 1996.

N. Statistics and Quantitative Methods
Much of the data collected by local historians could be subjected to statistical analysis. Quantitative information can easily be obtained from the census, from parish registers, and from probate inventories. Some knowledge of statistical methods and sampling techniques is therefore desirable. For good introductions, see:

- Floud, Roderick. *An Introduction to Quantitative Methods for Historians.* Routledge, 2005.
- Hudson, Pat. *History by Numbers: An Introduction to Quantitative Approaches.* Hodder Arnold, 2000.

For sources of statistical information, see:

- Great Britain Historical Database Online Documentation
  http://hds.essex.ac.uk/gbhd/docs/db_index.asp
- Mitchell, B.R. *British Historical Statistics.* Cambridge University Press, 1988.

Many data sets of use to local historians are held by:

- History Data Service
  http://hds.essex.ac.uk

Chapter 3

PEOPLE AND POPULATION: THE SOURCES

How many people lived in your community? Who were they? Where did they come from? What were their relationships with each other? Demography and family history are important topics for investigation. They use the same sources, especially registers of baptisms (or births), marriages and burials (or deaths), and the nineteenth- and twentieth-century censuses. This chapter explores these and a wide range of other sources.

A. Births, Marriages and Deaths

The civil registration of births, marriages and deaths began in 1837. The annual reports of the Registrar General, digitised at Histpop (p.36), regularly report birth and mortality rates, fertility, migration, and other statistics based on these registers. Unfortunately, the actual birth and death registers are not accessible and, therefore, cannot be used by local historians directly to study topics such as migration, occupations and health. Only the certificates needed for genealogical research can, of course, be obtained from the Registrar General.

Some marriage registers are, however, available. Anglican, Jewish and Quaker marriages post-1837 were registered by their celebrants. Entries were made in duplicate printed books. One copy was returned to the District Registrar, the other retained by the church. The latter is likely to now be in a record office. Entries record places of marriage, dates, names of parties, ages, 'conditions' (i.e. marital status), ranks or professions, residences at the time of marriage, fathers' names and ranks or professions, whether by banns, licence, or registrar's certificate, and signatures of parties, ministers and witnesses. These registers excluded marriages conducted by registrars. Researchers must assess how significant that exclusion is in their area.

Although the civil registers began to be kept in 1837, parish registers did not cease. They provide alternative sources of information. That is just as well; full comprehensiveness of the civil registers was not achieved until after 1874, when failure to register births and deaths became punishable.

Parish registers recording baptisms, marriages and burials (rather than births and deaths) were mandated in 1538. Few sixteenth-century copies survive. Information entered in early registers was not standardised, and varies from parish to parish. Standardisation of entries began with Hardwicke's Marriage Act 1753, when printed forms for marriages were introduced and every marriage (except those of Jews and Quakers) had to be conducted by an Anglican priest. Printed forms for baptism and burial registers were mandated by Rose's Act, 1812. The details given in parish registers provide much scope for studies of demography and other topics.

Not all registers were comprehensive. Nonconformists and Roman Catholics frequently refused to have their babies baptised by Anglican priests. Their baptisms were only entered in parish registers during the years 1695–1705 and 1783–94, when tax was imposed on baptisms. Many clandestine and irregular marriages also escaped notice, especially in early eighteenth-century London. These were conducted without licence or banns but were recognised by the common law until 1754.[1]

Burial entries in parish registers are likely to be more comprehensive. Until the nineteenth century, nonconformists and Roman Catholics had little alternative to burial in parish churchyards.

The Parochial Registers and Records Measure 1978 required most registers (and other records) over 100 years old to be deposited in record offices. Since then, innumerable registers have been digitised by

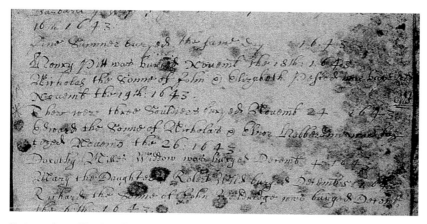

Extract from Harting (Sussex) parish register, showing burials of three un-named soldiers killed during the Civil War.

commercial web hosts and others. Many have been printed by family history, parish register, and record societies. Unprinted transcripts are widely available in local studies libraries, the Society of Genealogists, local family history societies, and elsewhere. There are numerous online indexes, such as the International Genealogical Index **www. familysearch.org/wiki** and Boyd's Marriage Index **www.findmypast. co.uk/articles/world-records/full-list-of-united-kingdom-records/life-events-bmds/boyds-marriage-index-1538–1840**.

For a detailed discussion, giving details of related sources such as licensing records and bishops' transcripts, see:

- Raymond, Stuart A. *Parish Registers: A History and Guide.* Family History Partnership, 2009.

On marriage licences, see:

- Elliott, Vivien. 'Marriage Licences and the Local Historian', *Local Historian*, 10(6), 1973, p.282–90.

For a detailed listing of bishops' transcripts and licensing records, see:

- Gibson, Jeremy. *Bishops' Transcripts and Marriage Licences, Bonds and Allegations: A Guide to Their Location and Indexes.* 6th edition. Family History Partnership, 2013.

Nonconformists and Roman Catholics also kept registers, mostly of baptisms, and mostly from the mid-eighteenth century (although Quaker registers are earlier). Registers deposited with the Registrar General in 1840 and 1857 are now in TNA's RG classes, as are the two central registries created by nonconformists. The Protestant Dissenters Registry recorded dissenters' births from 1742, with some earlier entries. The Wesleyan Metropolitan Registry recorded Wesleyan Methodist births and baptisms from 1818.

The registers in TNA's RG classes have been digitised:

- BMD Registers
  https://bmdregisters.co.uk

In the nineteenth century, interment in urban churchyards steadily diminished, and increasing numbers of cemeteries were opened. From 1853, they were required to keep burial registers. Many registers of cemeteries and crematoria are digitised at:

- Deceased Online
  www.deceasedonline.com

Cemeteries are worthy of study in their own right, see:

- Rugg, Julie. 'Researching Early Nineteenth-Century Cemeteries: Sources and Methods', *Local Historian*, 28(3), 1998, p.130–44.

Undertakers' records, such as accounts, also provide burial data. Registers of births and deaths in workhouses were kept by Guardians. Unions also kept vaccination registers, which should record all births in each Union from 1853.

Registers of vital events, and especially parish registers, have many uses for local historians. They are important for both genealogical and demographic purposes; indeed, proving descent was the original purpose of parish registers. They may be used to calculate average life expectancy, child mortality, age at marriage, and a range of other statistics. A number of methods of analysis have proved fruitful.

Aggregative analysis involves counting baptisms, marriages and burials to establish demographic trends. It should reveal, for instance, years of high mortality and low fertility, and may reveal outbreaks of plague and other diseases.[2] Seasonal variations may also be revealed, indicating, perhaps, sudden outbreaks of disease, or baby booms. Migration may be studied by counting spouses 'not of this parish', and by analysing the survival of surnames.

Aggregative analysis is only reliable if events were recorded comprehensively. But comprehensiveness was not always achieved, as has been seen. Account must be taken of the numbers missing from registers, and of the extent of migration into and out of the parish.

The technique of family reconstitution – that is, genealogy by another name – avoids such problems. If all families living in a parish at any one date can be reconstituted from surviving records – not just the parish registers – then parish population can be established. This technique requires much more work than simple aggregative analysis. It is not always easy to ensure correct identifications of the people being studied, particularly if many of them bear the same name, e.g. John Smith. For demographic studies based on these techniques, see:

- Wrigley, E.A., & Schofield, R.S. *The Population History of England, 1541–1871: A Reconstruction:* Edward Arnold, 1981.
- Wrigley, E.A. *English Population History from Family Reconstitution, 1580–1837.* Cambridge University Press, 1997.

B. Memorial Inscriptions

Memorial inscriptions complement parish and civil register evidence. Many transcriptions are deposited with local studies libraries, local family history societies, and the Society of Genealogists **www.sog.org.uk**. Some have been published; others are listed on internet sites, notably:

- Find a Grave
  www.findagrave.com
- Billion Graves
  www.billiongraves.com
- Interment.net: Cemetery Records Online
  www.interment.net

Memorial brasses commemorate prominent people, see:

- Monumental Brass Society
  www.mbs-brasses.co.uk

Twentieth-century war memorials and rolls of honour deserve study, see:

- Tiller, Kate. *Remembrance and Community: War Memorials and Local history*. British Association for Local History, 2013.
- Tall, Susan. *War Memorials: A Guide for Family Historians*. Family History Partnership, 2014.

C. The Census

'The numbering of the people at regular intervals is a duty which the people owe to themselves, and to the generations that are to follow them.' The editor of the *Illustrated London News* was absolutely right when he wrote these words in 1851. By then, five decennial censuses had already been taken. Reports on these and later censuses may be consulted at:

- Histpop: The Online Historical Population Reports Website
  www.histpop.org

These reports are fully listed by the *Guide to Census Reports, Great Britain, 1801–1966.* (HMSO, 1976) (partially digitised at **www.visionofbritain.org.uk/census/Cen_Guide**). They provide details of population totals, males and females, houses inhabited, uninhabited and building, acreages, and occupations. Population tables deriving from these reports are printed in *VCH* volumes.

Census reports can usefully be compared with the civil registration data provided by the Registrar General's reports (p.32), although care has to be taken in using the earliest reports, which were based on different administrative units. The earliest censuses were based on the historic parishes. From 1841, the newly formed registration districts, based on poor law union districts, were used (although the 1841 data was rearranged in the reports to facilitate comparison with earlier data). Districts were supposed to cover about 200 houses. However, demographic growth and reluctance to change boundaries resulted in twenty-three districts having populations exceeding 3,000 by 1901.

For details of registration districts, sub-districts and boundary changes, see:

• Registration Districts in England and Wales
  www.ukbmd.org.uk/reg

The census reports for 1801–51 are corrected in:

• Wrigley, E.A. *The Early English Censuses*. Records of Social and Economic History, new series, 46. 2011.

Between 1841 and 1921, manuscript census enumerators' schedules provide a huge amount of detailed information. They are digitised, with personal name indexes, on all the major web hosts listed above. The originals are held by TNA, but are not normally produced.

Between 1801 and 1831, data was collected by overseers and clergy. In 1801, overseers were asked for:

• The numbers of inhabited and uninhabited houses, and the number of families living in each house
• The total numbers of male and female inhabitants
• Details of occupations

Clergy were asked:

• The number of baptisms and burials in each decade of the eighteenth century
• The number of marriages in each decade since 1754
• Whether they had any other comments

In 1811, the question relating to uninhabited buildings asked for houses being built to be distinguished from existing uninhabited houses. Refinements were made in the question relating to occupations, and the clergy were asked for the numbers of baptisms, marriages and burials in the previous ten years. Further refinements followed in 1821 and 1831.

Most returns sent to London between 1801 and 1831 were destroyed after the data had been extracted for the various census reports. Only the 1831 clergymen's returns (TNA HO 71) survive. These record numbers of baptisms, burials and marriages in each parish between 1821 and 1830, together with the number of illegitimate children born in 1830, and clergy's remarks. See:

- Royle, Stephen A. 'Clergymen's Returns to the 1831 Census', *Local Historian*, 14(2), 1980, p.79–90.

Names were not required in these early censuses. However, some overseers compiled nominal listings, occasionally using printed household schedules to do so. These were useful, not only for compiling the census but also for poor law administration and for clergy purposes. About 800 survive in local record offices. See:

- Wall, Richard, Woollard, Matthew, & Moring, Beatrice. *Census Schedules and Listings 1801–1831: An Introduction and Guide.* Research tools 2. University of Essex Dept. of History, 2004 (2012). Available online at **www1.essex.ac.uk/history/documents/research/RT2_Wall_2012.pdf**

See also:

- Gibson, Jeremy & Medlycott, Mervyn. *Local Census Listings 1522–1930. Holdings in the British Isles.* 3rd edition. FFHS, 1997.

From 1841, parish overseers and clergy were replaced by local enumerators recruited by the Registrar General. The census was taken on a single night, rather than over a period. Questions asked changed over time; full lists of questions are given at Histpop **www.histpop.org**. Householders completed householders' schedules (those for 1841–1901 have been lost), and enumerators transferred that information to their enumerators' schedules. These schedules, when they reached the Census Office, were checked and corrected, and marked in various ways.

The schedules begin with preliminary pages (for 1841 only, there are also end pages). It is advisable to read these first. They describe the district covered (with boundaries), and include enumerators' instructions. Enumerators compiled statistical tables, not always accurately. With the Registrar, they also signed the schedules. Descriptions sometimes went beyond what was required, perhaps including details of local geology or a map. Descriptions of boundaries were essential where the enumeration district was not a historic parish. The statistical tables provided the basis for interim reports. They indicate how many people were temporarily present or absent. Unfortunately, most host systems have not digitised all of these preliminaries.

The 1841 enumerators' schedules provided columns for 'place', 'houses uninhabited or building', 'names of each person who abode therein the preceding night', 'age and sex', 'profession, trade, employment or of independent means', and 'where born'. Entries in the 'place' column frequently lack precision. For the 'houses' column see p.67–8. The 'names' column commences with the head of the household, but does not indicate relationships between residents. Individuals not present in their normal place of residence were recorded where they slept on census night. In the 'age' column, ages of everyone aged over 15 were rounded down to the nearest number divisible by five. Occupations stated were frequently subjective; see below, p.149–51. The 'where born' columns inquired whether respondents were born in the county where they were now living. Those born in 'Ireland Scotland or foreign parts' were also recorded.

The 1851 census included a number of refinements. Places were generally better recorded than in 1841. Enumerators numbered houses to ensure that none were missed, but the numbers given are not to be equated with modern house numbering. Uninhabited houses, and those in the process of being built, were noted. Most importantly, the relationship between the head of the household and other residents was now stated; wives, sons, daughters, other relatives, visitors and servants were all recorded. 'Boarder' was added as a possibility in 1861. A 'condition' column was added, indicating whether residents were married, unmarried, widows, or widowers. Ages ceased to be rounded down in the way that they had been in 1841. Parishes and counties of birth were stated.

Further refinements were added in later censuses. In 1861, a column for disabilities was added, indicating whether residents were blind, deaf, or dumb. In 1871, that column also records imbeciles and idiots. These terms were replaced in 1891 by 'lunatic, imbecile or idiot'.

The 1891 census asked how many rooms (if fewer than five) were occupied by one family, and whether workers were employers, employees, or neither of these. The latter category appears to have been used for the self-employed without employees. In 1901, the category became 'employer, worker, or own account'. This census also divided houses into four categories: those occupied, temporarily uninhabited, not usually occupied, and those being built.

Language featured in the 1881 census, when respondents in Scotland were asked if they spoke Gaelic. A similar question was asked in Wales in

1891, and in the Isle of Man in 1901. The effects of war caused orphaned children to be enumerated in 1921.

The 1911 and 1921 census documents differ from previous censuses. Householders' schedules have been preserved, as have enumerators' summary books. The householders' schedules give details of individuals; summary books record information on buildings and housing, but only name householders. Additional questions were asked; we learn how long couples had been married, how many children had been born to the marriage and how many had died. Greater precision was given to the questions relating to occupations, and to places of birth.

The household was the normal basis on which the census was compiled. However, special schedules were provided for institutions such as workhouses, prisons, hospitals and barracks. These did not record family relationships. In 1861, only the initials of those in institutions were recorded. There was also different treatment for Royal Navy ships, the merchant marine, and for boats in inland waterways. The 1851 and later schedules for the merchant marine required much useful preliminary information: the name and registration number of the ship, its home port, its tonnage, whether it was employed in trading, conveying passengers, or fishing, the name of the master, and the number of his master's certificate. From 1891, information was sought on whether vessels were powered by sail or steam. Soldiers stationed overseas were never fully enumerated.

Enumerators' schedules present a variety of problems; some have already been mentioned. Householders sometimes recorded their data incorrectly, whether due to error, lack of knowledge, or deliberate falsification. Not everyone knew their date of birth. Some wished to conceal their true ages, and even their names. Not everyone knew where they were born; a high percentage of places of birth recorded in the census are known to be incorrect. Terms used for disabilities, especially mental ones, were frequently pejorative, and parents were unwilling to admit that their children suffered from them. Statistics relating to disabilities are unreliable.

Enumerators also made mistakes. They missed some houses, and some individuals. It is impossible to know how many. Their arithmetic was frequently corrected by Census Office clerks, who also made other corrections. Handwriting is sometimes poor, especially when in pencil (as it was in 1841). Names are not necessarily spelt consistently. Comparison between successive censuses may reveal other discrepancies.

The censuses are static documents, revealing the situation as it was on a single day (from 1841 onwards) every ten years. They do not record changes in the intervening period. Householders may have moved house several times over a ten-year period. Some infants were born and died without mention in a census. Household composition frequently changed: servants and lodgers moved on, young adults married, aged relatives moved in during their last illness. Birthplace data only reveals where people were born; it does not reveal movements between their birth and census day.

Given that the census can only be consulted online (or on microfilm), researchers must rely on indexers. Indexers' mistakes may therefore make specific entries difficult to find.

The census was intended to be used for a variety of purposes, and that still applies. Most present-day researchers use it to trace family history. However, it can also be used to trace increases in population, and in numbers of houses (p.167–8), to analyse family size and the incidence of illegitimacy, to study migration, to determine occupational structures (see Chapter 7), or to examine the prevalence of disabilities such as blindness, deafness, and mental illness.

Further Reading:
Basic census introductions include:

- Raymond, Stuart A. *The Census 1801–1911: A Guide for the Internet Era*. Family History Partnership, 2009.
- Christian, Peter, & Annal, David. *Census: The Family Historian's Guide*. 2nd edition. Bloomsbury, 2014.
- Jolly, Emma. *Tracing your Family History Through the Census: A Guide for Family Historians*. 2nd edition. Pen & Sword, 2020.

For comprehensive interpretative guides, see:

- Higgs, Edward. *Making Sense of the Census Revisited: Census Records for England and Wales, 1801–1901: A Handbook for Historical Researchers*. Institute of Historical Research / National Archives, 2005.
- Lawton, Richard, ed. *The Census and Social Structure: An Interpretative Guide to 19th Century Censuses for England and Wales*. Frank Cass, 1978.

See also:

- Mills, Dennis, & Pearce, Carol. *People and Places in the Victorian Census: A Review and Bibliography of Publications Based Substantially on the Manuscript Census Enumerators' Books, 1841–1911*. Historical Geography Research series 23. 1989.

D. Domesday Book

Domesday Book, recording data from *c.*1066 and *c.*1086, is written in two volumes held by TNA (but closed to public access), and based on returns sent in from most counties (excluding those in the far north).[3] Returns for London and Winchester are missing. It provides the earliest written evidence for most of the *c.*15,000 place names it records. The original returns for most counties were heavily abridged by the Domesday scribes. More detailed returns are available for several counties in East Anglia and the south-west. Those for Suffolk, Norfolk and Essex may be the original unabridged returns. There are a number of related documents.

The origins of *Domesday Book* have been debated at length; it appears to be a register of land ownership, but its purpose is far from clear. The Domesday debate continues in the works listed below.

Domesday scribes listed manors by counties and tenants in chief. They apparently recorded the population of manors, giving numbers of villeins, bordars, slaves, and a variety of occupations. The figures given probably represent households (except in the case of slaves and clergy). However, it is probable that Domesday scribes did not intend to include everyone. Clergy, for example, are only mentioned intermittently, and monks are omitted entirely. It is probable too that some statistics are notional rather than actual. Domesday demographic statistics represent a bare minimum of inhabitants in 1086. Nevertheless, they may help us to estimate total population; see Moore (p.56).

Domesday scribes recorded manors, not settlements, which were not individually mentioned. Hoskins has argued that each villein mentioned was working a Domesday farm, and that in areas of dispersed settlement we should be able to identify those farms on the ground.[4] The number of plough teams in use and the number actually needed, were both noted. Pasture, meadow and woodland were also recorded. Cattle, sheep and horses were counted in the original returns, but frequently omitted in the abbreviated text of the Exchequer Domesday. Domesday statistics are mapped in Darby's *Domesday Geography* series of studies,[5] providing the context for more local studies.

Domesday Book records the names of manorial lords in both 1066 and 1086. For biographical notes on them, see:

- Keats-Rohan, K.S.B. *Domesday People: A Prosopography of Persons Occurring in English Documents 1066–1166. 1. Domesday Book.* Boydell, 1999.

Excellent editions of *Domesday Book* (for some counties) have been published in the *VCH*. The Alecto edition is a facsimile of the original volumes. Phillimore has published a series of translated county editions edited by John Morris. For a complete modern translation, see:

- Williams, Ann, & Martin, G.H., eds. *Domesday Book: A Complete Translation*. Penguin Classics, 2002.

Domesday is also available online, on a number of sites. For the Latin text, see:

- Open Domesday
  https://opendomesday.org

For translated extracts, see:

- Domesday Book Online
  www.domesdaybook.co.uk

For useful introductions to Domesday Book, see:

- Domesday Book
  www.nationalarchives.gov.uk/help-with-your-research/research-guides/domesday-book/#7-accessing-printed-editions-of-domesday
- Finn, R. Welldon. *Domesday Book: A Guide*. Phillimore & Co., 1973.
- Hull Domesday Project.
  www.domesdaybook.net/home

For a recent study, see:

- Roffe, David. *Domesday: The Inquest and the Book*. Oxford, 2000.

Many other works are listed by:

- Bates, David. *A Bibliography of Domesday Book*. Boydell Press, 1986.

E. The Hundred Rolls

The Hundred Rolls (p.97) for 1279–80 are particularly useful for demographic purposes. They record numbers of villeins, freemen and cottagers, enabling estimates of population to be made, bearing in mind that sub-tenants and landless labourers are not recorded.

F. Inquisitions Post-Mortem

Inquisitions post-mortem (p.100) state the ages of heirs, and thus enable us to calculate life expectancy amongst the upper classes. The 'manorial extents' (surveys) sometimes attached to them may enumerate the population in the same way that Domesday does.

G. Manorial Records
Manorial records (p.59–62) provide much genealogical information. Court rolls record the descent of tenancies. Surveys list tenants, and enable them to be counted. The value of manorial records for demographic purposes is demonstrated by:

- Razi, Zvi. *Life, Marriage and Death in a Medieval Parish: Economy, Society and Demography in Halesowen 1270–1400.* Cambridge University Press, 1980.

H. Deeds
Deeds (p.101–13) record the transfer of property from one owner to another, sometimes naming wives, children, and other relations. They may also identify past and present tenants, neighbouring landowners, friends acting as trustees, witnesses, scribes, and a range of other people. Strict settlements (p.109–10) are particularly useful; they may record the names of every member of the wider family. Deeds frequently reveal the network of connections between families, friends, business associates, and professional advisers which characterised particular communities, but which are otherwise difficult to identify and describe.

I. Tax Lists
Tax assessments usually list heads of households and may be used to track mobility, to study social structure, and for genealogical purposes. Their usefulness is variable, as evasion was rife, and the poor were frequently exempt. Consequently, many assessments are not comprehensive. Some assessments were communal and do not identify individuals. If, however, particular assessments were not subject to significant evasion or exemptions, then their raw data can be used to estimate total population. There has been much discussion of the multipliers which should be used.[6] Comparisons should always be made with all sources available.

Most records of national taxation pre-dating 1689 are in TNA, class E179, although occasionally returns are found in local record offices. These taxes included the subsidy, poll taxes, the military survey, and the hearth tax, amongst many others.

The earliest surviving assessments on individuals date from the 1225 subsidy. Between 1290 and 1330, and in the 1520s, subsidy assessments provide reasonably comprehensive lists of householders.

Later assessments have fewer names but may be useful for tracing individuals. Between 1334 and 1522, the subsidy was a communal tax and assessments did not mention names. For a basic introduction to subsidies, see:

• Beresford, Maurice W. 'Lay subsidies', *Amateur Historian*, 3(8), 1958, p.325–8; 4(3), 1959, p.101–9.

Poll tax assessments made in 1377, 1379 and 1381 also list names. The tax was levied on everyone aged over 16 (14 in 1377). Women were named with their husbands, servants with their masters' households. Taxpayers constituted between a third and a half of the population. Beggars were exempt. Returns are printed in:

• Fenwick, Carolyn C., ed. *The Poll Taxes of 1377, 1379 and 1381*. 3 vols. Records of Social and Economic History new series 27. Oxford University Press for the British Academy, 1998–2005.

For tax records of the Tudor period, see:

• Hoyle, Richard S. *Tudor Taxation Records: A Guide for Users*. Public Record Office readers guide 5. PRO Publications, 1994.

The fairly comprehensive, if few, name lists of the 1522 military survey, are discussed by:

• Cornwall, Julian. 'A Tudor Domesday: the Musters of 1522', *Journal of the Society of Archivists*, 3(1), 1965, p.19–24.

For the seventeenth century, a few levies are listed by Gibson and Dell's *Protestation Returns* (p.49). Poll taxes of 1641, 1660, 1667 and 1677 theoretically identify every householder. So do the hearth tax assessments of Charles II's reign, which also sometimes list the exempt poor. Many hearth tax returns have been transcribed in the British Record Society's Index Library **www.britishrecordsociety.org**. Some transcripts are digitised at:

• Hearth Tax Digital
  http://gams.uni-graz.at/context:htx

County record societies (p.10) have also printed numerous tax lists. Published countywide tax lists make it easy to trace surnames across wide areas.

An extensive listing of the E 179 class is provided by:

- E 179 Database
  www.nationalarchives.gov.uk/e179

For more information, see:

- Jurkowski, M., Smith, C.L., & Crook, D. *Lay Taxes in England and Wales, 1188–1688*. Public Record Office, Handbook 31. PRO Publications, 1998.

A number of later tax lists are also available. Land, window, and income taxes are discussed below (p.115, p.116–17 and p.167).

Between 1695 and 1705, a duty was imposed on baptisms, marriages and burials. It is frequently mentioned in parish registers. Few full returns survive (none in TNA). But see:

- Glass, D.V., ed. *London Inhabitants Within the Walls, 1695*. London Record Society, 2. 1966.
- Ralph, Elizabeth, & Williams, Mary E., eds. *The Inhabitants of Bristol in 1696*. Bristol Record Society Publications 25. 1968.

Rates (see p.117) were local property taxes. Early parish rate lists are useful for identifying individuals. The rate books of local authorities in the nineteenth and twentieth centuries are frequently substantial volumes arranged by street, with no indexes, and therefore difficult to search.

J. Briefs and St Paul's Cathedral Rebuilding Fund c.1678

Briefs were requests for charitable assistance issued under letters patent, and were widely distributed. Their appeals were frequently for victims of fire and flood, or for the ransom of Englishmen enslaved by Barbary corsairs. Collections are frequently recorded in churchwardens' accounts (p.64–6). Records of the authorised brief distributors are held by the William Salt Library, Stafford, and by the British Library. See:

- Harris, Mark. 'The Finding and Use of Brief Records', *Archives*, 21, 1994, p.129–44.

In 1678, briefs were issued appealing for funds to rebuild St Paul's Cathedral after the 1666 great fire of London. Lists of contributors from *c*.3,300 parishes are held by London Metropolitan Archives. Some effectively list heads of households; others give null returns. For brief details, search **https://search.lma.gov.uk**.

K. The Militia

During the sixteenth and seventeenth centuries, all able-bodied adult males were liable to military service, and required to attend musters. Muster rolls list attendees, giving details of armour, weapons, and sometimes occupations. Rolls are mostly amongst TNA's State Papers, and listed in the published calendars (p.91–2). The fullest are those from 1569, 1573, 1577 and 1580. Many have been published; see, for example:

- Beauchamp, Peter C., ed. *The Oxfordshire Muster Rolls, 1539, 1542, 1569.* Oxfordshire Record Society, 60. 1996.

For a full listing, see:

- Gibson, Jeremy, & Dell, Alan. *Tudor and Stuart Muster Rolls: A Directory of Holdings in the British Isles.* 2nd edition. FFHS, 1989.

The militia was moribund by the mid-eighteenth century but was reconstituted in 1757. Constables compiled lists of able-bodied men aged between 18 and 50 (45 from 1762). Ballots determined who should serve. Militia ballot lists (in local record offices) are effectively censuses of active adult males. Between 1758 and 1802, they record names, occupations, and infirmities. More details were required thereafter.

Enrolment lists (TNA WO 68) and militia muster and pay lists (TNA WO 13) record the names of those recruited by ballot. For militia officers, see the *List of … the officers of the Militia …,* regularly published by the War Office from 1794.

The 1798 *posse comitatus* lists, and the 1803–4 *Levée en masse* lists are similar to militia ballot lists but had a slightly different purpose. They listed men who could be called on if the French invaded. Early lists included names and occupations of all men aged between 15 and 60 not already serving. Millers, bakers, and the owners of waggons and barges were separately listed. Later *Levée en masse* lists were more detailed. Men were listed by age group, marital status, and numbers of children under 10; actual ages were sometimes given. Quakers and aliens were identified. Non-combatants needing evacuation were separately listed; that included women, children, the old and the infirm. There were separate lists for specific trades required in an emergency.

For a brief introduction to militia records, see:

- Militia
  www.nationalarchives.gov.uk/help-with-your-research/research-guides/militia

Records are listed by:

- Gibson, Jeremy, & Medlycott, Mervyn. *Militia Lists and Musters, 1757–1876.* 5th edition. Family History Partnership, 2013.

For useful guides, see:

- Spencer, William. *Records of the Militia & Volunteer Forces, 1757–1945.* Public Record Office Readers Guide 3. PRO Publications, 1997.
- Beckett, I.F.W. 'The Amateur Military Tradition: New Tasks for the Local Historian', *Local Historian* 13(8), 1979, p.475–81.

L. Chantry Certificates
The number of 'housling people', that is, communicants, is frequently stated in the chantry certificates of 1547 (p.191). It may be assumed that this is a count of all adults aged over 10, and therefore perhaps 75 per cent of the population.[7] The reliability of these figures is, however, debatable.

M. Ecclesiastical and Local Censuses
In 1563, the bishops were asked by the Privy Council to state the number of households in each parish. In 1603 they numbered communicants and recusants. For details, see:

- Dyer, Alan, & Palliser, David M., eds. *The Diocesan Population Returns for 1563 and 1603.* Records of Social and Economic History. New Series, 31. Oxford University Press, 2005.

A later count of Anglican communicants, nonconformists and Roman Catholics is printed in:

- Whiteman, Anne, ed. *The Compton Census of 1676: A Critical Edition.* Records of Social and Economic History, new series 10. Oxford University Press for the British Academy, 1986.

Replies to bishops' queries (p.71–3) from the seventeenth century onwards frequently include counts of communicants, nonconformists and Roman Catholics. Numerous listings of inhabitants have been compiled by local clergy and others. See:

- Gibson, J.S.W., & Medlycott, M., eds. *Local Census Listings 1522–1930: Holdings in Great Britain*. 3rd edition. FFHS, 2001.
- Chapman, Colin R. *Pre-1841 Censuses and Population Listings in the British Isles*. 5th edition. Lochin Publishing, 1998.

N. The Protestation

On the eve of Civil War, in 1641–2, Parliament required all adults aged over 16 (usually males only) to take an oath 'to live and die for the true protestant religion, the liberties and rights of subjects, and the privilege of Parliament'. This 'Protestation' was intended to winkle out Roman Catholics, who opposed Protestantism, and Royalists, for whom the oath challenged their loyalty to the Crown. It was taken in church before the incumbent. Oath-takers, absentees and refusers were all listed by churchwardens and constables. Occasionally, they collected signatures, which may be used to study literacy. Local gentry usually head the lists. Surviving returns cover approximately one-third of English parishes. The vast majority are in the Parliamentary Archives, and are digitised:

- Protestation Returns for Family History
  https://archives.parliament.uk/research-guides/family-history/ protestation-returns-for-family-history

For published returns, and those held locally, see:

- Gibson, Jeremy & Dell, Alan. *The Protestation Returns, 1641–42 and Other Contemporary Listings: Collection in Aid of Distressed Protestants in Ireland; Subsidies; Poll Tax; Assessment or Grant; Vow and Covenant; Solemn League and Covenant*. FFHS, 2004.

O. Probate Records

Wills are amongst the very few documents written which have a continuous history from Anglo-Saxon times to the present day. They are, perhaps, the most personal documents local historians are likely to encounter, and are of vital importance for family history. Their demographic value is much more limited. They can be used to determine the size of families, since they normally identify all living children. To a lesser extent, they can be used to study migration, as they frequently mention the birth parishes of testators.

For married men, the prime purpose of a will was to make provision for their wives and children, especially those who had not already been provided for. Bequests frequently provided younger children with apprenticeship premiums, or dowries for daughters. Eldest sons frequently received merely token bequests, as they automatically inherited their fathers' freehold estates. Younger sons, who stood to gain most from their fathers' wills, might be named as executors in preference to their older brothers.

Widows too aimed to support their children. They had, however, less need to consider them in their wills, and were more likely to mention other kin. Unmarried women had fewer family responsibilities, and frequently mentioned more distant relatives and friends in their wills. Until 1882, married women could only make wills with the permission of their husbands.

Before 1858, most wills were proved in ecclesiastical courts. There were hundreds of these courts. Most executors used archdeaconry courts. If, however, a testator had property in two archdeaconries, his executor took the will to the bishop's Consistory Court. If he had property in two dioceses, probate went to the Prerogative Court of either Canterbury or York. There were also many peculiar courts, where local bishops did not have jurisdiction (see p.58). In practice, the higher courts had the greater prestige and were frequently used for that reason.

Administration of intestate estates was granted to an administrator. Administrators and executors, together with two sureties, are named in the administration bonds submitted to obtain grant of probate. Between c.1500 and c.1750, bonds are frequently accompanied by probate inventories, listing personal effects (including leasehold property) but excluding freehold estates. Accounts were occasionally submitted when administration was complete.

Wills, inventories, accounts, administration bonds and other probate records are mostly held with diocesan records. For indexes, visit **https:// search.findmypast.co.uk/search-world-records/england-and-wales- published-wills-and-probate-indexes-1300–1858**. Many wills have been digitised. Over 1 million from the Prerogative Court of Canterbury (TNA, class PROB 11) are on Ancestry **www.ancestry.com**. TNA also holds many undigitised probate records. For Welsh wills, visit **www. library.wales/discover/library-resources/wills**. Many wills, sometimes draft or unproved, survive amongst estate records. Bishops' registers (see p.70) contain many pre-Reformation wills.

Numerous probate records have been printed. Original wills, digitised wills, transcripts, indexes and published editions, are all listed by:

- Gibson, Jeremy, & Raymond, Stuart A. *Probate Jurisdictions: Where to Look for Wills*. 6th edition. Family History Partnership, 2016.

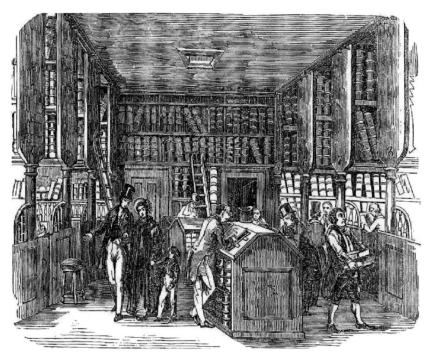

Searching for Prerogative Court of Canterbury wills in the nineteenth century.

For detailed guides, see:

- Raymond, Stuart A. *The Wills of our Ancestors: A Guide for Family & Local Historians.* Pen & Sword, 2012.
- Grannum, Karen, & Taylor, Nigel. *Wills & Probate Records: A Guide for Family Historians.* 2nd edition. National Archives, 2009.

Uses of probate records are discussed in:

- Arkell, Tom, Evans, Nesta, & Goose, Nigel, eds. *When Death do us Part: Understanding and Interpreting the Probate Records of Early Modern England.* Leopards Head Press, 2004.
- Riden, Philip, ed. *Probate Records and the Local Community.* Alan Sutton, 1985.

Post-1858 wills were proved before the Court of Probate and its successors. They are fully indexed online; see:

- Find a Will
  https://probatesearch.service.gov.uk/#wills

P. Depositions

Depositions in the church courts (p.71–3) provide much biographical detail on witnesses. That may include not just their ages, occupations and parishes, but also the length of time they have been resident there, and also any previous parishes.

Q. Freemen's Records

Borough freemen (p.82) had frequently been born elsewhere. Freemen's registers and other borough archives record their admissions, stating birthplaces, and thus providing a useful source for tracing migration.

R. Poll Books and Electoral Registers

The franchise was very limited before 1832. In county constituencies, it was limited to owners of freehold property worth more than 40s per annum. Between 1780 and 1832, land tax returns (p.115–16) were used to determine eligibility to vote. Borough franchises were diverse – ranging from the twelve landowners in the infamous 'rotten borough' of Old Sarum to the thousands of householders in Westminster. In the City of London, it was limited to members of the twelve major city livery companies (guilds).

Poll books, introduced in 1696, record the names of voters and the votes cast, sometimes noting addresses and occupations. Some were annotated by electoral agents intent on getting out the vote. There is no consistency in either the information given or in their arrangement, which may be alphabetical, by ward, or even in the order of the votes cast. Some are manuscript, others printed. They are useful for identifying the more substantial inhabitants, and for the study of politics.

Poll books continued to be published until the introduction of the secret ballot in 1872. They are listed by:

- Gibson, Jeremy, & Rogers, Colin. *Poll Books, 1696–1872: A Directory to Holdings in Great Britain*. 4th edition. Family History Partnership, 2008.
- Sims, J. A *Handlist of British Parliamentary Poll Books*. University of Leicester History Dept. Occasional Paper 4. 1984.

For much general information and a database of London voters' names, see:

- London Electoral History 1700–1850
  http://leh.ncl.ac.uk/

Electoral registers commenced in 1832. Since then, they have been printed annually, except in 1916–17 and 1940–44. Both poll books and electoral registers are available between 1832 and 1872.

Early registers state places of abode and the 'qualification' which gave entitlement to vote; later registers give streets and house numbers. Coverage steadily expanded as the franchise was extended, although only those who registered are listed. They are usually arranged by street. Survival is patchy. The holdings of local studies libraries and record offices (but not those of the British Library) are listed by:

- Gibson, Jeremy. *Electoral Registers 1832–1948; and Burgess Rolls: A Directory of Holdings in Great Britain.* 3rd edition. Family History Partnership, 2008.

For the British Library's holdings, and for links to other digitised registers, visit:

- British Library: UK Electoral Registers
  www.bl.uk/collection-guides/uk-electoral-registers

S. Heraldic Visitations

Coats of arms were important status symbols in early modern societies. Between 1530 and 1688, the heralds conducted county visitations to determine who had the right to bear them. Proof of descent from an ancestor who had been granted arms was required. Heralds therefore recorded pedigrees. Original visitation pedigrees are held by the College of Arms **www.college-of-arms.gov.uk**, but normally may only be consulted by heralds. Numerous copies (some of dubious provenance) are held by the British Library and elsewhere. Many have been published by the Harleian Society **https://harleian.org.uk.** Its recent publications are generally more reliable than earlier editions. For useful guidance, see:

- Squibb, G.D. *Visitation Pedigrees and the Genealogist.* 2nd edition. Pinhorn, 1978.
- Wagner, Anthony Richard. *The Records and Collections of the College of Arms.* Burke's Peerage, 1952.

For heraldry, consult:

- Friar, Stephen. *The Sutton Companion to Heraldry.* New ed. Sutton Publishing, 1994.
- Woodcock, Thomas, & Robinson, John Martin. *The Oxford Guide to Heraldry.* Oxford University Press, 1990.

T. Evacuation Records

At the beginning of the Second World War, the government evacuated *c.*2 million people from the major conurbations, where heavy bombing was expected. Local authorities organised billeting, kept registers of those billeted, and paid householders receiving evacuees. School registers give details of evacuee children. Records are in local record offices, although they are sometimes closed for privacy reasons. TNA has many relevant policy files, notably the records of the Advisory Committee on the Evacuation of Children, HLG 7/310–19, and details of evacuation trains, AN2.

U. Biographical Sources
Information on prominent people with local connections may be found in biographical dictionaries. See especially:

- Oxford Dictionary of National Biography
  www.oxforddnb.com (public libraries frequently subscribe)
- The History of Parliament: British Political, Social & Local History
  www.historyofparliamentonline.org

Numerous other biographical dictionaries are indexed by:

- *Biography and Genealogy Master Index: A Consolidated Index to more than 3,200,000 Biographical Sketches in over 350 Current and Retrospective Biographical Dictionaries.* 8 vols. Gale, 1980. Supplements, 1981–5, 1986–90, and annually from 1991. Also available online at **www.ancestry.com**.

Full-length biographies, or perhaps autobiographies, exist for many local worthies. For these, check library catalogues, and:

- McColvin, L.R., ed. *The Librarian Subject Guide to Books. Vol.2. Biography, Family History, Genealogy, etc.* James Clarke & Co., 1960.
- *Biography Index: A Cumulative Index to Biographical Material in Books and Magazines.* H.W.Wilson, 1946– . Annual. Also available online in major reference libraries.
- Burnett, J., Vincent, D., & Mayall, D., eds. *The Autobiography of the Working Class: An Annotated Critical Bibliography.* 3 vols. Harvester Press, 1984–9.
- Burnett Archive of Working Class Autobiographies **www.brunel. ac.uk/life/library/Special-Collections/Burnett-Archive-of-Working-Class-Autobiographies**

Local surnames, especially those of clergy, should be checked in registers of university students, which include useful biographical information:
- Emden, A.B. *A Biographical Register of the University of Oxford to 1500.* 3 vols. Clarendon Press, 1957–9. A further volume covers 1501–40.

- Foster, J. *Alumni Oxonienses 1500–1886*. 8 vols. Parker & Co., 1887–92. Reprinted in 4 vols., Kraus Reprint, 1980. Not as accurate as it should be.
- Emden, A.B. *A Biographical Register of the University of Cambridge to 1500*. Cambridge University Press, 1963.
- Venn, J., & Venn, J.A. *Alumni Cantabrigienses*. Pt. 1. [1500]–1751 (4 vols). Pt 2. 1751–1900. 6 vols. Cambridge University Press, 1922–54.

V. Surnames

The study of medieval surnames offers useful evidence to the local historian. Migration, for example, can be studied through locative surnames. Occupational surnames provide useful evidence for economic historians. Early forms of names can be traced in sources such as lay subsidy rolls and manorial records. For a useful introduction, see:

- Redmonds, George. *Surnames and Genealogy: A New Approach.* FFHS, 2002.

Monographs of the English Surnames Survey (University of Leicester) on specific counties demonstrate the potential. See, for example:

- Postles, David. *The Surnames of Devon.* Leopards Head Press, 1995.

For a comprehensive dictionary of surnames, see Hanks, Patrick; Coates, Richard & McClure, Peter, *The Oxford Dictionary of Family Names in Britain and Ireland*, Oxford University Press, 2016.

W. Further Reading on Demography and Genealogy

For an excellent introduction to English demography, see:

- Hinde, Andrew. *England's Population: A History since the Domesday Survey.* Hodder Arnold, 2003.

More recent demography is covered by:

- Populations Past: Atlas of Victorian and Edwardian Population **www.populationspast.org**

Two studies demonstrate how family history and local history are interlinked:

- Rogers, Colin D., & Smith, John H. *Local Family History in England. 1538–1914*. Manchester University Press, 1991.
- Hey, David. *Family History and Local History in England.* Longman, 1987.

A model local study is provided by:

- Munby, Lionel. *Hertfordshire Population Statistics, 1563–1801*, ed. Heather Falvey. 2nd edition. Hertfordshire Record Society, 2019.

For a practical guide to 'counting people', see:

- Moore, John S. *Counting People: A DIY Manual for Local and Family Historians*. Oxbow Books, 2013.

Four sources – the hearth tax, the Compton census, poll taxes, and marriage duty assessments – are reviewed in:

- Schurer, Kevin, & Arkell, Tom, eds. *Surveying the People: The Interpretation and Use of Document Sources for the Study of Population in the Later Seventeenth Century*. Leopards Head Press, 1992.

For current demographic research, see:

- Cambridge Group for the History of Population and Social Structure **www.campop.geog.cam.ac.uk**
- Local Population Studies Society **www.localpopulationstudies.org.uk** Publisher of the important journal *Local Population Studies*.

Mortality statistics are introduced in:

- Introduction to Mortality Statistics in England and Wales: 17th–20th century **https://wellcomecollection.org/works/mzud2qv4**

Chapter 4

LOCAL AND NATIONAL GOVERNMENT: THE SOURCES

Medieval government was conducted through a multitude of frequently overlapping authorities, with the Crown at the centre. Sheriffs governed the counties, which were occasionally visited by 'Justices in Eyre' – judges from the central courts. In the fourteenth century, Justices of the Peace (originally designated 'Keepers of the Peace') began to sit regularly in Quarter Sessions. They governed their counties for the succeeding 500 years, overseen by Assize judges. From the mid-sixteenth century, Lord Lieutenants took responsibility for defence and the militia (p.47–8), and appointed deputy lieutenants. Sheriffs became ceremonial figures, whose administrative duties were exercised by under-sheriffs.

Manorial courts exercised wide-ranging jurisdiction over tenurial matters, roads and petty crime, and (originally) appointed constables. Precise powers varied from manor to manor. Their activities gradually diminished over time.

The parish took over many manorial duties. Originally an ecclesiastical unit, it was a convenient autonomous unit, independent of aristocratic control, and amenable to the supervision of Quarter Sessions and bishops. Its role gradually expanded from the mid-sixteenth century. It became the basic local government unit until the nineteenth century, when it progressively lost responsibility for paupers, law and order, health, roads and education. For its history, see:

- Pounds, N.J.G. *A History of the English Parish: The Culture of Religion from Augustine to Victoria.* Cambridge University Press, 2000.

Secular authority was supported by diocesan bishops and their archdeacons, who also held courts. The issues they dealt with have been aptly summed up as 'sin, sex and probate'.[1] Many matters now considered secular came before ecclesiastical judges. From the thirteenth century, bishops and archdeacons increasingly conducted visitations to ensure that ecclesiastical affairs were being conducted properly. Ecclesiastical court and visitation records are further considered below (p.70–3).

Many areas were 'peculiars', outside of the jurisdiction of the local diocesan bishop. They were governed by a variety of institutions and individuals, such as cathedral chapters, monasteries, the Crown, and manorial lords. For example, Uffculme (in the Diocese of Exeter) was under the jurisdiction of a prebendary of Salisbury Cathedral. Consequently, Uffculme probate records are in Wiltshire, not in Devon. Local historians need to be aware of where jurisdiction lay in the parishes being studied.

There were a variety of other local administrative units and officers. Boroughs sometimes had their own Quarter Sessions, operating independently of county authorities. The Hundred, or, in northern counties, the Wapentake (the Rape in Sussex), was an administrative unit between the parish and the county. Escheators upheld the Crown's feudal rights in the localities. Commissioners for Sewers (the old name for waterways) attempted to control flooding, and were responsible for waterways and coastal defences. During the Civil War, Parliamentary county committees had responsibility for military administration.

The eighteenth and nineteenth centuries saw a proliferation of new bodies. Poor law unions, highway boards, school boards, turnpike trusts, improvement or paving commissioners, boards of health, county courts, and a variety of other local organisations were established. Many of their functions were taken over by county councils (created 1888), and by urban and rural district councils (created 1894). Since 1897, details of the principal officers and councillors of local authorities have been regularly recorded in the *Municipal Year Book*.

The classic guide to local government history is still:

• Webb, Sidney & Beatrice. *English Local Government from the Revolution to the Municipal Corporations Act: The Parish and the County.* Longmans, Green & Co., 1906.

Many questions can be answered by consulting the extensive records of local government. Who had the power to decide? Did government deal with social and economic problems effectively? Which matters were not dealt with by government? This chapter describes governmental records and the uses to which they can be put.

A. The Manor

The medieval manor was both a territorial and economic unit, and a legal entity, although its territory was not necessarily all in one place. Classically, it consisted of a demesne allocated for the lord's own use (although sometimes leased to a 'farmer'), plus holdings tenanted by the peasantry, who owed various dues and duties to the lord, but its form was fluid, and its characteristics varied. The lords themselves might hold by knight service direct from the Crown, or alternatively from a mesne lord who himself held from the Crown. The descents of manorial lordships are traced by thousands of parish histories in the *VCH*. The descents of peasant holdings within manors have rarely been traced.

Manors were managed by stewards appointed by lords. Bailiffs and reeves were responsible for day-to-day activities. There might also be haywards, who supervised haymaking, pinders, responsible for the manorial pound for stray beasts, and other minor officers. The manorial demesne was supposedly farmed by the lord himself (although frequently leased), using the 'boon work' of his tenants, and/or employing labourers. The rest of the land was either tenanted, or left as 'waste' (which nevertheless had value for fuel, hunting, timber, etc.).

Stewards administered manors through manorial courts, operating in accordance with manorial customs. Customs varied from manor to manor, covering such matters as entry fines (payable on admittance to a holding), merchet (due on the marriage of a tenant's daughter), heriots (due on the tenant's death), and chevage (paid by villeins who left the manor). Courts regulated agricultural activities, and dealt with the wider matters mentioned above.

Technically, the work of manorial courts was divided between court baron and court leet. The court baron dealt with transfers of copyhold land, determined the custom of the manor, and enforced payment of services due to the lord. The court leet exercised jurisdiction over communal agriculture, and over petty crime. In practice, these two functions were intermingled in the records.

Many lords acquired the right to hold 'views of frankpledge'. Frankpledge was a system of surety in which every man belonged to a 'tithing' of ten or twelve who held mutual responsibility for the behaviour of each other. Those who offended were liable to be presented at a 'view'. The 'view' and the court leet eventually came to be treated as alternative names for the same jurisdiction.

Manorial courts gradually declined in importance after the fifteenth century, increasingly becoming land registration and rent-collecting agencies. Other functions were gradually taken over by parish or by

Quarter Sessions, although some courts leet were still dealing with criminal matters in the seventeenth century, and a few were still recording tenancy changes in 1925, when copyhold tenure was abolished. Even today, the manorial court at Laxton (Nottinghamshire) continues to supervise its open fields, which have never been enclosed.

Manorial documents fall into two broad categories. Court rolls and account books record the day-to-day life of the manor. Surveys, extents, rentals, and similar documents provide snapshots of manorial resources at specific dates.

Court rolls (or books), beginning in the thirteenth century, name lords, stewards and the 'homage' or jury, note changes in tenancy, and record presentments of the homage. Presentments dealt with matters ranging from cropping arrangements in the open fields and the stocking of the commons, to the maintenance of roads, fences and buildings, from the rights and misdeeds of tenants, to the supervision of boundaries. Amercements (fines) were imposed on those who committed misdemeanours such as failing to attend court, or failing to repair property.

Many long runs of court rolls survive. A particularly notable collection, dating from the thirteenth to the twentieth century, is being published in the Wakefield Court Rolls series **www.yas.org.uk/Publications/ Wakefield-Court-Rolls-Series**.

Ministers' and receivers' accounts record income and expenditure. They may cover several manors and are primarily concerned with agricultural matters, including prices and wages. The estreats they record list dues such as entry fines, heriots, and amercements imposed by the manorial court.

Custumals (the earliest form of survey) list tenants and revenues due to the lord, and outline manorial customs. Extents are detailed valuations, recording the demesne, the names of tenants, the size of holdings, and the forms of tenures. Less information is recorded in fifteenth-century rentals, which list tenants and their dues. Surveys of the sixteenth century and later may be more detailed. They record boundaries, manorial customs, tenants, lands held, types of tenure and rents paid. In more recent centuries, briefer rentals listing tenants and rents due were compiled annually. Later surveys are sometimes accompanied by maps, which may reveal much about the organisation of open fields. Surveys tended to be compiled when property changed hands, and may therefore be many years apart. Tenure is discussed in more detail in Chapter 5; agriculture in Chapter 6.

Manorial records are not always held locally. Many are in TNA, especially in SC 2 (court rolls), SC 6 (ministers' accounts), and SC 11–12 (rentals and surveys). See also the Crown estate records (CRES 5), and Duchy of Lancaster records (DL 29–30). More recent rentals of Crown lands are in LRRO 12 and 65. A register of Crown property, *c.*1716–1999 is provided by WORK 50 (recent files are not open for public consultation). Many other manorial records can be found in institutions such as the British Library, and in university and college archives. Invaluable assistance in locating court rolls is provided by:

- Manorial Documents and Lordships and how to use the Manorial Documents Register
  www.nationalarchives.gov.uk/help-with-your-research/research-guides/manorial-documents-lordships-how-to-use-manorial-document-register

For brief introductions to manorial records, see:

- Johnson, W. Branch. 'Notes before reading Court Rolls', *Amateur Historian* 4, 1958–60, p.98–100.
- Winchester, Angus J.L., & Straughton, Eleanor A. 'Sources in Local History: Finding and Using Manorial Records', *Local Historian*, 37(2), 2007, p.120–26.
- Latham, R.E. 'Hints on interpreting the public records: (4) ministers' accounts', *Amateur Historian*, 1(4), 1953, p.112–116.
- Kerridge, Eric. 'The manorial survey as an historical source', *Amateur Historian*, 7(1), 1966, p.2–7.

More detailed discussions are provided by:

- Ellis, Mary. *Using Manorial Records*. PRO Publications, 1997.
- Harvey, P.D.A. *Manorial Records* [Revised edition]. Archives and the User 5. British Records Association, 1999.

Valuable introductions to court rolls are included in:

- Bailey, Mark, ed. *The English Manor, c.1200–1500: Selected Sources.* Manchester University Press, 2002.
- Hone, Nathaniel J. *The Manor and Manorial Records.* 3rd edition. Methuen, 1925.
- Maitland, F.W., ed. *Select Pleas in Manorial and other Seignorial Courts*, vol.1. Selden Society 2. 1888.
- Hearnshaw, F.J.C. *Leet Jurisdiction in England: Especially as Illustrated by the Records of the Court Leet of Southampton.* Southampton Record Society, 3. 1908.

For an outstanding example of edited manorial records, see:

- Harvey, P.D.A. *Manorial Records of Cuxham, Oxfordshire, circa 1200–1359.* Oxfordshire Record Society, 50. 1976.

For a detailed bibliography, see:

- The Manor Court: a Short Bibliography / C.J.Harrison
  www.mtholyoke.edu/courses/hgarrett/bibliographies/manorcourt.html

B. The Parish

The English parish was originally the area under the care of a single priest. Parishes were established between *c*.900 and *c*.1300, perhaps later in Wales and northern England. There were just over 8,000 parishes in 1291, and 11,297 in 1801 (including some chapelries). Priests in charge were called rectors; they were supported by tithes and other offerings, and by glebe lands. During the medieval period, many rectories were appropriated by monasteries, which became institutional rectors. They appointed vicars to undertake rectorial duties. Appropriations are frequently mentioned in monastic cartularies (p. 207).

Originally, priests were expected to maintain their parish church. However, appropriations frequently meant they could not afford to do so. Consequently, in the thirteenth century, responsibility for maintaining church buildings was placed on the laity. Priests retained responsibility for chancels. Churchwardens – usually two in each parish – were appointed to maintain church buildings.

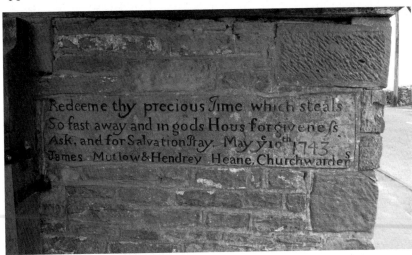

Churchwardens' names are frequently recorded in inscriptions such as this one at Ruardean (Gloucestershire).

Parishes had constables before churchwardens were appointed. Constables were responsible for the maintenance of law and order. They dealt with vagrants, collected taxes, removed paupers, escorted prisoners to gaol, and raised the militia. They maintained the parish armour, the beacon, the stocks, the village lockup, the pillory, and/or the cucking stool. Originally, they were manorial appointees. When manorial courts ceased to meet, appointments were made by Justices of the Peace.

Two more parish officers were created under the Tudors. Highway surveyors (waywardens) responsible for road maintenance were

Lockups like this one at Hilperton (Wiltshire) could be used to punish minor offences.

Unusual stocks for punishing errant parishioners at Painswick (Gloucestershire).

appointed under the Highways Act 1555. Poor law overseers were created in 1572 to relieve the poor. Their activities were greatly extended under acts of 1598 and 1601. Churchwardens became ex officio overseers.

Legally, parish officers worked independently of each other. In practice, their activities were coordinated through the Vestry, which took the leading role in parish affairs from the sixteenth century onwards. Parish officers created many (although not all) of the documents stored in parish chests. Some parish records are discussed here. For pauper apprenticeship records, school records, service registers and charity documentation, see the index.

Accounts

Parish officers raised money independently, and spent their income in different ways. Their accounts reveal a great deal about their activities. Most date from *c.*1700–1900, but a few survive from much earlier periods.

Before the Reformation, churchwardens frequently relied on income from 'church ales' and other communal fund-raising events. Puritan disapproval caused these to cease, but similar events were revived in the eighteenth and nineteenth centuries, and can be traced in accounts.

Medieval churchwardens also frequently made 'gatherings', although the regular taking of a collection during services is a Victorian innovation. Sometimes, accounts recording collections give the names of donors.

In some parishes, especially in towns and cities, churchwardens relied on income from property gifted to the church. Accounts in these parishes may identify the tenants of church property.

Fees for burials, for the ringing of the knells, or for the hire of the church bier, were frequently levied. If decedents' names were recorded, accounts may provide a useful substitute for burial registers.

All parish officers could levy rates. Rate lists effectively provide censuses of heads of households. As has already been seen (p.46), these may prove useful for demographic and genealogical purposes.

The primary focus of churchwardens' expenses was the repair and maintenance of the church. Carpenters, masons, plumbers, painters and other tradesmen had to be paid, and are likely to be named in accounts. Tradesmen did not, of course, confine their attentions to one parish, and it is sometimes possible to trace generations of craftsmen by consulting churchwardens' accounts of neighbouring parishes. Tradesmen who travelled much greater distances may also be identified. Bell founders, for example, were usually located in cities such as London or Gloucester.

Expenditure on worship was also the churchwardens' responsibility, and is discussed below (p.188). An important role in worship was played by the parish clerk, who led the responses and the singing, and could be called on to write up the parish register, ring the bells, clean the church and wind the clock. His wages were recorded in accounts. So were the

The Coleford (Gloucestershire) funeral bier. Fees for using it may have been recorded in churchwardens' accounts.

wages of other parish servants, such as the organist, the sexton, dog-whippers, and the Vestry clerk.

Accounts were also kept by other parish officers. Overseers' accounts record expenditure on doles, food, clothing, fuel, shelter, premiums for pauper apprentices (p.153–5), and workhouse costs. Overseers were supposed to provide work as well as relief. The Workhouse Act 1722 gave parishes authority to erect workhouses; Gilbert's Act 1782 enabled parishes to unite for the purpose. For an early directory of workhouses, see *An Account of Several Work-Houses for Employing and Managing the Poor* (2nd edition. 1732).

Overseers' accounts are occasionally accompanied by inventories of paupers' goods.[2] Goods could be seized when paupers claimed relief, or when they died. Inventories reveal details of the material life of the poorest members of society.

Overseers' accounts were not always kept separately; sometimes they are incorporated in churchwardens' accounts. Separate accounts for highway surveyors and constables are found much less frequently. See, however:

- Tupling, G.H. 'Highway Surveyors' Accounts', *Amateur Historian* 1(10), 1954, p.301–4, and ditto, 'Constables Accounts', 1(11), 1954, p.335–8

Vestry Minutes

Most major decisions came before the Vestry, which appointed or nominated parish officers and servants, approved rates and accounts, and decided on matters as diverse as erecting church buildings, appointing school masters, establishing policy on pauper apprenticeship, and promoting enclosure. Sometimes Vestry decisions were controversial. Opposition to church rates (abolished in 1868) was frequently vociferous. Vestry minutes tell us how decisions were made, and describe relationships between Vestry members, officers, and incumbents. Minutes should be compared with officers' accounts, which record how Vestry policy was put into action.

Seating Plans

Pews became common in the fifteenth century, although not universal until much later. The right to a seat in church was important, especially in a status conscious society, where everyone was required to attend. The gentry sat at the front, the middling sort in the middle, and the poor at the back. Many took a proprietorial attitude towards their pews, which were frequently rented (income from them was recorded in churchwardens' accounts) or even owned. The possession of a pew was a mark of status, and disputes were common. Churchwardens had oversight of seating arrangements, and frequently drew up seating plans. These plans should list all the families in each parish, and can be used as parish censuses. They also tell us where particular individuals stood in the social pecking order.

Inventories of Church Goods
Most parishes compiled inventories of church goods. These were sometimes written into parish registers, churchwardens' accounts, or other books. They describe the wide range of vessels, cloth, furniture, and other items used in worship. For Reformation inventories, see p.190.

Glebe Terriers
The glebe was the property set aside for the support of the incumbent. Glebe terriers (from the Latin *terra* – earth, land) are detailed descriptions of glebe lands and houses. They may include information on tithing customs, parish boundaries, charities, church goods and other topics. Terriers date from 1571, although not many survive from the sixteenth century. They were occasionally updated. For most parishes, several terriers can usually be found. They were compiled by incumbents and churchwardens at the behest of bishops, and are generally preserved amongst diocesan archives, although copies were occasionally kept in parish chests. For a brief introduction, see *Short Guides 1*. Many are in print; see below, p.69.

Easter Books
Easter books list communicants, mostly householders, who paid dues to incumbents at Easter. See:

- Wright, S.J. 'A Guide to Easter Books and Related Parish Listings', *Local Population Studies* 42, 1988, p.18–31; 43, 1989, p.13–27.

Settlement Papers
'Settlement' was a key poor law concept. Paupers could only obtain relief from the parish in which they were 'settled'. The Act of Settlement, 1662, defined the 'settled' as those who had been born in the parish, ratepayers, serving or former apprentices and parish officers, servants who had served for more than a year, and anyone who had been in the parish (with notice) for more than forty days. Subsequent acts modified these conditions. Constables 'removed' those paupers who were not 'settled' in their parish of residence.

Settlement produced documents. Justices of the Peace examined paupers and wrote 'settlement examinations'. These mini-biographies may indicate ages, places of birth, family information, migrations, work experience and apprenticeship details.

Once settlement had been determined, removal to the parish of settlement followed. Parish constables executed removal orders, escorting paupers to their parishes of settlement. Orders (sometimes attached to settlement examinations) travelled with the pauper, and were signed by constables as the pauper was passed from one parish to the next.

Many poor migrants obtained settlement certificates from the overseers of their parishes of settlement in order to work elsewhere. These certified their acceptance of liability to pay poor relief if claimed.

Settlement papers provide evidence for the life cycles of the poor, their migration patterns, occupations, and a range of other topics. They are filed amongst parish and Quarter Sessions records.

Bastardy Records

The cost of maintaining bastard children frequently fell on the parish. Overseers sought to recoup costs from bastards' fathers. Bastardy examinations and bonds were written by Justices of the Peace; they name parents and children. For these and other records, see:

• Paley, Ruth. *My Ancestor was a Bastard: A Family Historian's Guide to Sources for Illegitimacy in England and Wales.* [Revised edition]. Society of Genealogists Enterprises, 2011.

The Nineteenth and Twentieth Centuries

The power of parish vestries gradually diminished in the nineteenth century, as other authorities acquired their powers. In 1894, secular and ecclesiastical powers were separated entirely, and churchwardens ceased to have secular powers. Elected parish councils took over remaining secular parish functions, such as planning, street lighting and allotments. Local ecclesiastical governance devolved on parish church councils, established in 1919. The minutes of both secular and ecclesiastical councils may provide useful information, although not all are in record offices.

Further Reading:

Parish records are discussed at much greater length in:

• Raymond, Stuart A. *Tracing your Ancestors' Parish Records: A Guide for Family and Local Historians.* Pen & Sword, 2015.

See also:

• Tate, W.E. *The Parish Chest: A Study of the Records of Parochial Administration in England.* 3rd edition. (reprint). Phillimore, 1983.

Useful brief guides to some parish officers' accounts are included in *Short Guides 2*. For churchwardens' accounts, see:

- Cox, J. Charles. *Churchwardens' Accounts from the Fourteenth Century to the Close of the Seventeenth Century.* Methuen & Co., 1913.
- Hitchman, Valerie, & Foster, Andrew, eds. *Views from the Parish: Churchwardens' Accounts c.1500–c.1800.* Cambridge Scholars, 2015.

Surviving churchwardens' accounts are listed by:

- The Churchwardens' Accounts of England and Wales
  https://warwick.ac.uk/fac/cross_fac/myparish/projects/cwa/

Many London parish records are digitised at:

- London Lives 1690 to 1800
  www.londonlives.org

Many churchwardens' accounts are in print. See, for example:

- Craven, Alex, ed. *The Churchwardens' Accounts of St Mary's, Devizes, 1633–1689.* Wiltshire Record Society, 69. 2016.

Few accounts of other parish officers have been published. See, however:

- Norman, Philip, ed. *The Accounts of the Overseers of the Poor of Paris Gardens, Southwark, 17 May 1608 to 30 September 1671.* Roworth & Co., 1901.
- Bennett, Martyn, ed. *A Nottinghamshire Village in War and Peace: The Accounts of the Constables of Upton, 1640–1666.* Thoroton Society Record Series, 39. 1995.

Many glebe terriers are in print. See, for example:

- Potts, Richard, ed. *A Calendar of Cornish Glebe Terriers, 1673–1735.* Devon & Cornwall Record Society, new series 19. 1974.
- Hobbs, Steve, ed. *Wiltshire Glebe Terriers 1588–1827.* Wiltshire Record Society 56. 2003.

For settlement and bastardy examinations, see:

- Hitchcock, Tim, & Black, John, eds. *Chelsea Settlement and Bastardy Examinations, 1733–1766.* London Record Society, 33. 1999.

C. The Diocese

The jurisdiction of bishops and archdeacons over the parishes in their dioceses and archdeaconries was exercised through consistory, archdeaconry, and other courts, through visitations, and through the bishops' right to institute clergy to benefices.

Before the Reformation, episcopal administrative acts were recorded in bishops' registers, dating from the early thirteenth century. Early registers recorded the whole range of episcopal business: ordinations and institutions of clergy, judicial business, visitations, letters, indulgences, commissions, licences, dispensations, appropriations of benefices, estate and financial records, probate, and much more. Topics covered included, for example: morality, heresy, witchcraft, the consecration of churches, prayers, the clergy.

By the fifteenth century, separate files or registers were being created for some of these topics. After 1660, bishops' registers only included ordinations and institutions, and other records began to be kept. Act books recorded proceedings in ecclesiastical courts. Grants of probate, and records of licences granted to curates, midwives, schoolmasters and surgeons, were sometimes included in them, sometimes recorded separately. Clerical oaths of loyalty were recorded in subscription books. Consecration papers record the consecration of new churches (especially in the nineteenth century). Other diocesan archives include documents discussed elsewhere: bishops' transcripts; marriage licensing records, probate documents.

Episcopal visitations took place every three or four years from the mid-fifteenth century. Elizabethan bishops began the practice of

The Consistory Court at Chester.

issuing queries before visitation. Replies to bishops' queries provide increasingly detailed surveys of the state of the church, covering topics such as services, pluralism, charities, education, and terriers, as well as more spiritual matters.

Archdeacons conducted visitations every six months, except when bishops were conducting their visitations. Clergy books or *libri cleri* were prepared in advance of visitation, listing the names of clergy and churchwardens expected to be present, and leaving room for recording names of new churchwardens. These books are prime sources for identifying churchwardens. They may also list surgeons, midwives, schoolmasters and curates, who were expected to exhibit their licences.

At visitations, churchwardens (and sometimes clergy) made presentments covering matters such as bastardy, adultery, fornication, brawling, defects in church buildings and goods, regularity of services, the work of priests and churchwardens, nonconformity, and a wide range of other matters. Sometimes presentments led to cases in episcopal and archdeaconry courts. Such cases were office causes, that is, they were commenced by the court's officers. They were sometimes referred to as correction business, since it was the bishop's duty to correct his flock. Some presentments were dealt with summarily, without proceeding to court. Prior to the Civil War, details were sometimes entered in *libri comperta*, or books of detection. Office causes could also be commenced by registrars citing defendants to appear. Citations may provide names, parishes, and brief summaries of accusations being made. If the accused appeared and was tried, the verdict was entered in the act book. The guilty were sentenced to do penance, supervised by their parish priest. He certified its performance. Non-performance might mean excommunication. That meant exclusion from the church and, theoretically, ostracisation by the whole community. Most excommunicants eventually sought absolution, which was recorded in the act books. Those who did not could be imprisoned by secular authorities. A *significavit* could be directed to the Court of Chancery, to ask for their arrest. *Significavits* are in TNA, class C 85 (for the period 1220–1611) and C 207/1–12 & 23 (for 1727–1843).

Office procedure was also used to obtain faculties approving alterations in church buildings, such as altering seating arrangements, erecting galleries, or replacing entire church buildings. Petitioners for faculties had to present a citation 'with intimation', against the rector and churchwardens, so that objections could be made. Citations detail the alterations required, and may name those affected.

Instance causes concerned matters disputed between litigants. Topics dealt with involved defamation, matrimony, probate and (until *c.*1700) tithes. The plaintiff presented a written libel outlining his case, to be answered by the defendant. Witnesses made written depositions, providing invaluable eye-witness accounts of a multitude of events that took place hundreds of years ago.

Appeal from the decisions of diocesan courts lay to the Court of Arches, or, in the Northern Province, to the Archbishop's Court of Chancery. Arches records have been microfiched:

- *Records of the Court of Arches, 1554–1911, at Lambeth Palace Library.* Microfilm. Chadwyck-Healey, *c.*1983. There is a published index edited by Jane Houston, incorporated, with additions, in the catalogue of Lambeth Palace Library **https://archives. lambethpalacelibrary.org.uk/CalmView**.

Bishops and archdeacons ceased to operate during the Interregnum. During that period, a Commission of Inquiry undertook a survey of church livings. Returns provide information concerning the living, the incumbent, and his maintenance. The commissioners also considered reconfiguring parish boundaries. Returns are in TNA, class C94, and in Lambeth Palace Library.

Eighteenth-century parishes were occasionally united or sub-divided. Many alterations to parish boundaries were initiated in the nineteenth century by the Ecclesiastical Commission. They were announced in the *London Gazette* **www.thegazette.co.uk**.

Further Reading:
For brief introductions to bishops' and archdeacons' records, see *Short Guides 2*. The authoritative guide to diocesan records is:

- Owen, Dorothy M. *Records of the Established Church in England, Excluding Parochial Records.* Archives and the user series, 1. British Records Association, 1970.

For surviving bishops' registers, see:

- Smith, D.M., ed. *Guide to Bishops' Registers of England and Wales: A Survey from the Middle Ages to the Abolition of Episcopacy in 1646.* Royal Historical Society, 1981. Supplement, Canterbury and York Society, 2004.

Many have been published by:

- The Canterbury and York Society **www-users.york.ac.uk/~cf13/index.htm**

For Archdeaconry records, see:

- Brinkworth, E.R.C. 'The Study and Use of Archdeacons' Court Records, illustrated from the Oxford Records (1566–1759)', *Transactions of the Royal Historical Society* 4th series, 25, 1943, p.93–119.

For some printed churchwardens' presentments, see:

- Peyton, Sidney A., ed. *The Churchwardens' Presentments in the Oxfordshire Peculiars of Dorchester, Thame and Banbury*. Oxfordshire Record Society 10. 1928.

Many replies to bishops' queries have been published. See, for example:

- Episcopal Visitation Returns, 1744 and 1779 [for Devon] **www.foda.org.uk/visitations/intro/introduction1.htm**
- Broad, John, ed. *Bishop Wake's Summary of Visitation Returns from the Diocese of Lincoln, 1706–1715*. 2 vols. Records of Social and Economic History new series 49–50. Oxford University Press for the British Academy, 2012.

For the church courts, see:

- Tarver, Anne. *Church Court Records: An Introduction for Family and Local Historians*. Phillimore & Co., 1995.
- Tarver, Anne. 'English Church Courts and their Records', *Local Historian*, 38(1), 2008, p.4–22.
- Dils, Joan. 'Deposition Books and the Urban Historian', *Local Historian*, 17(5), 1987, p.269–76.

Some documents from the Northern Province are digitised:

- York's Archbishops Registers Revealed **https://archbishopsregisters.york.ac.uk**
- Cause Papers in the Diocesan Courts of the Archbishopric of York 1300–1858 **www.dhi.ac.uk/causepapers**

D. Quarter Sessions
Justices of the Peace first met at Quarter Sessions in 1361. At various times, they heard criminal suits, supervised the poor law and apprenticeship, regulated fairs and markets, helped organise local defence, maintained highways, gaols and 'houses of correction', levied rates, licensed various

THE

Justice of the Peace,

AND

PARISH OFFICER.

By RICHARD BURN, LL.D.

LATE CHANCELLOR OF THE DIOCESE OF CARLISLE.

THE TWENTY-THIRD EDITION:

With CORRECTIONS, ADDITIONS, and IMPROVEMENTS.
The CASES brought down to the End of Easter Term,
1 GEO. IV. 1820.
And the STATUTES to the 1 GEO. IV. 1820.

By GEORGE CHETWYND, ESQ. M.P.

BARRISTER AT LAW,
AND CHAIRMAN OF THE GENERAL QUARTER SESSIONS OF THE PEACE
FOR THE COUNTY OF STAFFORD.

Dr. Burn has great merit: He has done great service, and deserves great commendation. *Per* Lord MANSFIELD C. J.   Burr. S. C. 548.

IN FIVE VOLUMES.

VOL. I.

LONDON:

Printed by A. STRAHAN, Law-Printer to the King's Most Excellent Majesty:
For T. CADELL and W. DAVIES, in the Strand;
F. C. & J. RIVINGTON, St. Paul's Church-Yard, & Waterloo-Place;
JOSEPH BUTTERWORTH and Son, Fleet-Street;
and LONGMAN, HURST, REES, ORME, and BROWN,
Paternoster-Row.
1820.

Burn's Justice of the Peace was the leading handbook for eighteenth- and nineteenth-century Justices.

trades, set wage and land carriage rates, took oaths, tried to root out Roman Catholicism and nonconformity, licensed nonconformist meeting houses, maintained county bridges, and undertook a multitude of other tasks. Procedure, even in administrative matters such as bad roads, was judicial; presentments had to be made before action could be taken. Quarter Sessions administered county affairs until county councils were established in 1888. They survived as criminal courts until 1971. Petty Sessions increasingly administered less important aspect of the jurisdiction.

Some fourteenth-century Quarter Sessions rolls were sent to the central courts, and are now in TNA, class JUST 1. Locally, records only begin in the late sixteenth century. Order/minute books record formal proceedings. Sessions rolls bundle the documents used in each session. These include precepts, informations, presentments, recognizances, indictments, examinations, reports, jury lists and calendars of prisoners, amongst others. As time progressed, specific types of documents were removed from the rolls and placed in their own files. When proceedings ended, the clerk prepared process or indictment books, listing indictments and presentments for the sheriff to take action. He also prepared estreats listing fines to be collected (p.88). Space precludes a full discussion of Quarter Sessions records. Particularly useful documents are described below.

A Quarter Sessions roll.

Exeter Castle. Quarter Sessions and the Assizes were held here.

Presentments

Presentments were regularly made by Hundred jurors and constables, by the Grand Jury, and by individual Justices. Presentments of offences such as larceny and assault might initiate criminal prosecutions. Administrative matters, such as the state of roads and bridges, could also be presented. Presentments (and the indictments discussed below) were labelled *billa vera* (a true bill) if the Grand Jury thought they warranted further action, *ignoramus* if not. *Billa vera* then proceeded to trial. From *c*.1700, constables and jurors increasingly presented *omnia bene* – all well.

Recognizances

Recognizances (bonds) required those bound to perform a specified action or to pay a penalty. Justices used them for a wide range of purposes. They could, for example, require criminal suspects to attend court, victims to undertake prosecutions, witnesses to appear in court, barrators (those who stirred up quarrels) to keep the peace, bastards' fathers to pay maintenance, alehouse keepers and pedlars to obey the conditions of their licences, and constables to perform their duties.

Recognizances name the persons bound, their abodes and occupations. They name two sureties, and may explain their purpose. Frequently they led to no further action, but may be endorsed with a discharge. Clerks of the Peace kept registers of recognizances, especially in more recent centuries.

Calendars of Prisoners

Gaol calendars record the names of prisoners remanded for trial. They name the accused, the offence, and the committing magistrate. From *c.*1750, they began to be printed. They provide increasing amounts of information in the nineteenth and twentieth centuries, giving brief life histories, and perhaps listing previous offences.

Until *c.*1800, gaols only held prisoners on remand and debtors (who were not listed on the calendars). Before then, convicted felons were hanged, transported, or pardoned, but rarely gaoled. Houses of correction, sometimes known as Bridewells, were used to incarcerate the work-shy, the mothers of illegitimate children, and disobedient servants.

Detailed information about conditions in individual gaols were reported at length in John Howard's *State of the Prisons in England and Wales*. There were four editions of this work, between 1777 and 1792, with many changes between editions. In the nineteenth century, responsibility for prisons was gradually transferred to the Home Office. By 1877, Quarter Sessions had ceased its involvement. For Home Office records, see:

- Prisons
  www.nationalarchives.gov.uk/help-with-your-research/research-guides/prisons/

Criminal registers (TNA HO 26 & 27), are digitised at:

- England & Wales, Criminal Registers, 1791–1892
  www.ancestry.co.uk/search/collections/1590

Indictments

These were usually written on parchment, and in Latin, until 1733. Based on gaol calendars and on Justices' preliminary examinations, indictments give names, parishes and occupations of the accused, dates and places of offences, names of any victims, the value of goods stolen, and the supposed intentions of the accused. If they were 'true bills', pleas might be noted on them: *cogn (cognovit)* for guilty, or *po se (ponit se)* if the accused elected for trial by jury. If the accused refused to plea, *stat mute* or *nichil dicit* – nothing to say – might be noted. Verdicts were also noted – *cul (culpabilis)* if found guilty, or *non cul* if not. The goods of felons could be seized, so juries were asked if there were any. The answer was usually no, so *nec retraxit* was written.

Jury Lists

The statutory qualification for jury service at Quarter Sessions, from 1592, was ownership of land valued at 80s per annum. This was increased to £10 in 1692. Listings of those qualified to serve in each parish were compiled annually; from 1696 they were copied into special 'Freeholders' books'. These listings are likely to identify the leading landowners.

Justicing Books

Justices were encouraged to keep records of cases which came before them out of sessions. Many of their 'justicing books' can be found. These usually cover relatively small areas, so are particularly useful at the local level.

Petitions

Many people petitioned Quarter Sessions. Paupers complained about inadequate relief from overseers; maimed soldiers petitioned for pensions; victims of accidents and fires sought assistance; prisoners sought release; the homeless sought permission to erect cottages; parishes complained

The fifteenth-century bridge at Lostwithiel (Cornwall).

about local nuisances; travellers demanded the repair of roads and bridges; householders complained about local parish officers. Petitions cover all aspects of life, and can be found on Quarter Sessions rolls.

Further Reading:
For a detailed guide, see:

• Raymond, Stuart A. *Tracing your Ancestors in County Records: A Guide for Family & Local Historians.* Pen & Sword, 2016.

Records are summarily listed by:

• Gibson, Jeremy. *Quarter Sessions Records for Family Historians: A Select List.* 5th edition. Family History Partnership, 2007.

There are numerous published editions of order books and sessions rolls. For a full listing, see Raymond (above). For particularly useful introductions, see:

• Peyton, S.A., ed. *Minutes of Proceedings in Quarter Sessions Held for the Parts of Kesteven and the Parts of Holland 1674–1695.* Part 1. Lincoln Record Society, 25. 1931.
• Powell, Dorothy L., & Jenkinson, Hilary, eds. *Surrey Quarter Sessions Records: Order Book and Sessions Rolls, 1659–1661.* Surrey Record Society, 13.1934.

Typical 'justicing books' are printed in:

• Crittall, Elizabeth, ed. *The Justicing Notebook of William Hunt, 1744–1749.* Wiltshire Record Society, 37. 1981.
• Morgan, Gwenda, & Rushton, Peter, eds. *The Justicing Notebook (1750–1764) of Edmund Tew, Rector of Boldon.* Surtees Society, 205. 2000.

E. Clerks of the Peace
Clerks of the Peace maintained Quarter Sessions records, kept a variety of registers, and received various documents under acts of parliament. These included: lists of freemasons (1799–1967); registers of friendly societies (1793–1846); gamekeepers' deputations (1710–1900); game duty registers (1784–1807); savings bank rules (1817–63); bargains and sales (1535–1845); lists of printing press owners (1799–1869); land tax returns (mostly before 1832); registers of Papists' estates (1715–88); various oath rolls; and a variety of other records. Some of these are discussed elsewhere in this book.

F. Associations for Prosecuting Offenders

In the late eighteenth and early nineteenth century, in the absence of public prosecutors, many private associations were formed for the prosecution of offenders. See:

- Hastings, R.P. 'Private Law-Enforcement Associations', *Local Historian*, 14(4), 1980, p.226–31.

G. The Borough

Boroughs were urban centres with their own governments, independent of county Quarter Sessions. Some were counties in their own right. After 1696, a few boroughs obtained acts of parliament creating 'corporations of the poor' to administer the poor law within their boundaries. The Municipal Corporations Act 1835 reformed 178 existing boroughs, giving them councils elected under a uniform franchise. Most unreformed boroughs were abolished in 1883. Further drastic reform followed in 1974 when urban and rural areas ceased to be differentiated for local government purposes.

Many boroughs are mentioned in *Domesday Book*. During the medieval period, leading inhabitants of urban centres sought charters. Charters gave boroughs legal status, defined their areas, and determined how they were to be governed. They provided trading rights, such as freedom from tolls and the right to hold markets and fairs. Most boroughs received several charters over the centuries, frequently culminating with grants from Charles II or James II.

Early charters were sometimes granted by manorial lords, but most were royal grants. Many were entered on the Charter Rolls (until 1516), or the Patent Rolls (see p.104–105). A few are in C 248. Original charters were preserved by boroughs themselves, and are now in local record offices. Borough charters are listed by:

- Ballard, Adolphus. *British Borough Charters 1042–1216*. Cambridge University Press, 1913.
- Ballard, Adolphus, & Tait, James. *British Borough Charters, 1216–1307*. Cambridge University Press, 1923.
- Weinbaum, Martin. *British Borough Charters, 1307–1660*. Cambridge University Press, 1943.

For an older collection, which includes borough charters, see:

- Hardy, D.T., ed. *Syllabus (in English) of the Documents Relating to England and Other Kingdoms Contained in the Collection known as 'Rymer's Fœdera.'* 3 vols. Longmans Green & Co., 1869–85. For other editions, see **https://en.wikipedia.org/wiki/Thomas_Rymer**

Medieval boroughs are listed by:

- Beresford, Maurice W. & Finberg, H.P.R. *English Medieval Boroughs: A Handlist.* David & Charles, 1973. Updated in *Urban History Yearbook* 8, 1981, p.59–65.

Grants of incorporation were also made to urban organisations such as trade guilds and schools. Guilds merchant were formed by the mercantile establishment of boroughs, and were sometimes indistinguishable from borough authorities. Membership was frequently confined to borough freemen, and gave exclusive trading rights. Guilds for specific trades emerged in the fourteenth century. Religious guilds provided prayers for the dead, and social welfare for the living.

Many guild charters were enrolled on the Patent and Close Rolls (p.104–105). See also the State Papers (p.91–2). For some fourteenth-century guild ordinances, see:

- Smith, J. Toulmin. *English Gilds: The Original Ordinances of More Than One Hundred Early English Gilds.* Early English Text Society, 40. 1870.

See also:

- Gross, Charles. *The Guild Merchant.* 2 vols. Oxford University Press, 1890.

Borough records are full of references to guilds. Guild records themselves are likely to include minutes, accounts, ordinances, records of apprenticeship, and a variety of other documents.

The constitutional arrangements of boroughs on the eve of local government reform are set out in the appendix to the *First report of the Royal Commission appointed to inquire into the Municipal Corporations of England and Wales.* (1835). It lists charters and private acts of parliament then still operative, and provides detailed discussion of administrative procedures and powers.

The process of borough administration generated many records. Minutes of the governing body (sometimes referred to as act, hall or assembly books), are generally substantial. After 1835 they were printed, becoming more formal, and perhaps less detailed. However, newspaper reports provide increasing detail. Minutes record the involvement of councillors and aldermen, and deal with all the topics that concerned local government: staffing, finance, buildings, roads, health, social care, fire precautions, markets, charities, and, in the nineteenth century, municipal undertakings such as gas, electric and water utilities. Much business was delegated to committees, whose minutes and reports provide useful information.

Before 1835, freemen played important roles in the borough. They might sit on its governing bodies, and were entitled to trade within it. Some were entitled to vote. Eligibility for admittance to the freedom varied between boroughs, but it was usually open to former apprentices (p.151–4), and to freemen's sons (patrimony). Freedom could also be purchased, or granted as an honour. Admittances were recorded in the minutes, and sometimes in freemen's registers. Poll books (p.52–3) may also identify freemen. Exeter freemen, identified in a variety of sources, are listed with their trades, former masters, and admittance qualifications, in:

• Rowe, Margery M., & Jackson, Andrew M., eds. *Exeter Freemen 1266–1967*. Extra series 1. Devon & Cornwall Record Society, 1973.

Financially, boroughs operated in various different ways. Most had chamberlains (treasurers). Responsibility for specific matters might be assigned to separate officers. Before the nineteenth century, officers were part-time, not necessarily paid, and not necessarily competent, although accounts were likely to be audited annually.

Civic finance expanded greatly in the nineteenth and twentieth centuries, as boroughs took on responsibility for health, police, housing, welfare, education and other matters. That required the employment of professional staff and much improved accounting procedures. That in turn meant greater formality, and perhaps less detail.

Civic income came from a wide range of sources. Rates were ubiquitous. Boroughs frequently owned property, or had other investments which yielded an income. They imposed tolls on markets and fairs, and on bridges. Ports levied quay dues on shipping. Fees were normally paid for admittance to the freedom. New members of common councils, and new aldermen, might be charged fees. So might those who refused to take up office. Borough courts imposed fines on offenders. Information relating to these and other sources of income was sometimes recorded in detail. Rate lists, for example, identify all householders. Quay accounts record the names of ships. Rentals identify tenants. Market toll records provide information about traders and goods sold.

Records of expenditure may also be informative, especially if accounts can be matched with invoices and other vouchers. Council officers and others received various fees and allowances. Uniforms and staves of office had to be provided. Expenditure on dinners and other entertainment for council officers and official guests had to be met. Wages were paid to workmen who maintained council property, cleaned streets, and kept watch. Boroughs erected town halls, gaols and bridges. New streets were laid out. Disputes with neighbouring authorities, landowners, and others required the payment of legal costs. Accounts provide much information on all this activity, and record the implementation of council decisions

Boroughs had their own courts, frequently staffed by mayors, aldermen and/or councillors. Some had their own Quarter Sessions and Justices of the Peace. Others had courts leet to deal with petty law and order, pie powder courts, which regulated markets and fairs, and courts of record (or requests) to adjudicate debt. Liverpool had a Court of Passage to deal with disputes over imports and exports.

Useful guides to borough records include:

- West, John. *Town Records.* Phillimore & Co. 1983.
- Porter, Stephen. *Exploring Urban History: Sources for Local Historians.* B.T. Batsford, 1990.

H. Coroners

Between the twelfth century and 1888, coroners were elected by county freeholders, or appointed by boroughs. They are now appointed by local authorities. They were, and are, responsible for holding inquests on unnatural, sudden, and suspicious deaths, and on deaths in prison. Until 1927, inquests were usually heard with a jury. Medieval inquests, 1128–1426, are in TNA, class JUST 2. Coroners' inquests in cases of homicide were used as indictments in King's Bench; see TNA, classes KB 9, KB 11–14 and KB 140. From 1752, inquests were filed with Clerks of the Peace, and are now in local record offices, perhaps accompanied by precepts to hold an inquest, and depositions of witnesses. Inquests name the deceased (if known), identify finders of bodies, value deodands (the objects which caused the death, which were forfeited to the Crown), and report the circumstances and causes of deaths.

From 1752, coroners could claim travelling expenses. Bills list inquests held, note the nature of each death, record the distance travelled and the expenses claimed. For Wiltshire bills, see:

- Hunnisett, R.F., ed. *Wiltshire Coroners' Bills, 1752–1796.* Wiltshire Record Society, 36. 1981.

Coroners' records provide useful sources for studying topics such as road accidents, disease and homicide, as well as family history. In recent centuries, inquests are frequently reported in newspapers. Surviving records and related publications, are listed by:

- Gibson, Jeremy, & Rogers, Colin. *Coroners' Records in England and Wales.* 3rd edition. Family History Partnership, 2009.

I. Poor Law Unions

Poor Law Unions were created in 1834 to administer the New Poor Law. Guardians were elected, and instructed to build workhouses to house paupers. Poor relief henceforth was to be given in accordance with the 'less eligibility' principle: paupers should never be better off than the poorest labourer earning his own livelihood. Not all poor law functions were immediately transferred to the Guardians in 1834; overseers continued to collect rates until 1862, and parishes continued to exercise responsibility for settlement matters until 1865.

Unions created mountains of paper. Admittance and discharge registers, creed registers (recording denominational allegiances from 1869), punishment books, relieving officers' reports, indoor and outdoor relief lists, medical officers' returns, workhouse school registers, and workhouse birth/baptism and death registers, all provide much biographical information on paupers. From 1862, rate books record the names of rate payers. From 1865, Union settlement examinations and removal orders were similar to those formerly kept in parish chests, except that notices of chargeability were attached to them. Records of disbursements, such as relieving officers' order books, reports of district

Oliver Twist and Mr Bumble in the Workhouse.

medical officers, and personnel records provide detail. Policy can be studied in Guardians' minutes (see *Short Guides 1*), in letter books and in newspaper reports. For a detailed listing of surviving Union records, see:

- Gibson, Jeremy, et al. *Poor Law Union Records*. 2nd/3rd edition. 4 Vols. FFHS/ Family History Partnership, 1997–2014.

Union records are complemented by the correspondence of the Poor Law Commission and its successors, 1834–1900, in TNA MH 12. For the period 1900–1929, much has been lost, but some correspondence is in MH 68. These papers include not only letters, but also inspectors' reports, returns of pauper lunatics and vaccinated children, staff appointment forms, and lists of pauper emigrants. See *Short Guides 2*, and:

- Carter, Paul, & Whistance, Natalie. *Living the Poor Life: A Guide to the Poor Law Union Correspondence, c 1834–1871 held at the National Archives*. British Association for Local History, 2011.

Other central records include registers of Union staff, 1837–1921 in MH 9, building plans in MH 14, and authorisations of capital expenditure in MH 34. Schemes drawn up to discharge Union functions when they were abolished in 1929 are in MH 54. For a detailed guide to TNA records, with links to some digitised MH 12 documents, see:

- Poverty and the Poor Laws
  www.nationalarchives.gov.uk/help-with-your-research/research-guides/poverty-poor-laws

For extensive guides to workhouses, see:

- Higginbotham, Peter. *The Workhouse Encyclopedia*. History Press, 2012.
- The Workhouse
  www.workhouses.org.uk

The records of both old and new poor laws are described by:

- Raymond, Stuart A. *Tracing your Poor Ancestors: A Guide for Family Historians*. Pen & Sword, 2020.

See also:

- A Guide to Records Created under the New Poor Law / Paul Carter
  www.balh.org.uk/education-resources (click title)

J. Police Forces

Municipal corporations were permitted to introduce paid police forces by the Municipal Corporations Act 1835. The County Police Act 1839 gave permission for counties to do the same. In 1856, paid police forces became compulsory. Force records provide much information on both the police and crime, although survival is patchy. Police or watch committees kept minutes, reports, letters, accounts and papers relating to police stations. Individual policemen kept beat notebooks. Every station had an 'occurrence book'. Charge books record persons charged, with details of offences. Attestation papers, constables' registers, discipline books, pension books, personal files, and other personnel records, yield biographical information on individual policemen. From 1859, chief constables sent annual reports on the state of crime to the Home Office; these are in TNA, HO 63, but copies may be held locally. Records may be in local record offices, police museums, or perhaps still held by police forces themselves.

For policing in the nineteenth century, see:

- Haliday, Gaynor. *Victorian Policing*. Pen & Sword, 2017.

See also:

- Foster, David. *The Rural Constabulary Act 1839: National Legislation and the Problem of Enforcement*. Bedford Square Press for the Standing Conference for Local History, 1982.

For policemen themselves, see:

- Wade, Stephen. *Tracing your Police Ancestors: A Guide for Family Historians*. Pen & Sword, 2009.

K. Other Local Government Bodies and County Councils

A variety of other institutions have been involved in local government down through the centuries. The Norman kings established separate courts to administer the royal forests, which were areas set aside for royal hunting (not necessarily woodland), covering a substantial part of England. Forest law forbade hunting without licence, prohibited assarting (converting forest to arable use), and restricted agricultural activities. Forest records are available in both TNA and local record offices. For one local court, see:

- Crowley, Douglas, ed. *Braydon Forest and the Forest Laws*. Wiltshire Record Society, 72. 2019.

During the Civil War, Parliamentary County Committees directed the local war effort. Most (not all) of their minutes are in TNA, class SP 28. See:

- Pennington, D.H., & Roots, I.A., eds. *The Committee at Stafford, 1643–1645*. Collections for a History of Staffordshire 4th series, 1. 1956.

In the late eighteenth and nineteenth centuries, improvement commissioners performed various functions of local government,[3] supplementing the work of boroughs. Other bodies – turnpike trusts (p.142–3), commissioners of sewers (p.132), highway boards, school boards (p.180–1), boards of health (p.172–4), county courts (p.124–5) – were created to perform specific local functions. Their records are mostly in local record offices.

County councils, established in 1888, took over the administrative roles of Quarter Sessions, and acquired responsibility for major roads, welfare, health, housing, and education. Urban and rural district councils were second-tier authorities, established in 1894. They took responsibility for minor roads, and became sanitary authorities. The history of these councils can be followed in their minutes and reports, in the letter books kept by their clerks, in their accounts and in newspapers. These records are major sources for slum clearance, air-raid precautions, public health, roads, public toilets, and a wide range of other aspects of twentieth-century society. See below for their role as planning authorities (p.168–9), and in education (p.181).

L. Central Government and the Localities

Interaction between central government and the localities produced a huge range of documents of interest to local historians, covering topics ranging from the Great Revolt of 1381 to the early nineteenth-century Chartist campaign, from nonconformist activity to pauper apprenticeship. *Domesday Book* has already been considered. For the medieval period, the pipe rolls (TNA class E 372) are another important source. They record the Crown's income and expenditure in the counties between the twelfth century and 1832. They record feudal dues, debts paid, fines imposed, income from, and expenditure, on Crown property, wages and alms paid by the Crown, and many other matters. Numerous names are mentioned. Many medieval rolls have been published by the Pipe Roll Society **www.piperollsociety.co.uk**. See:

- Medieval Financial Records: Pipe Rolls 1130-*c*.1300 **www.nationalarchives.gov.uk/help-with-your-research/research-guides/medieval-financial-records-pipe-rolls-1130–1300**
- *Introduction to the Study of the Pipe Rolls*. Pipe Roll Society 3. 1884.

From *c*.1200, the government began to keep regular records. By the mid-fourteenth century, over 100,000 letters were being sent out annually in the king's name. Many concerned local matters. The rolls in which these letters were recorded are discussed in Chapter 5.

Fines imposed by Quarter Sessions and Assize judges were collected by the sheriff and recorded on the pipe rolls. Clerks of the Peace sent estreats to the Exchequer listing the amounts due; these are now in TNA classes E 137, E 362 and (a few) E 389. Estreats from Clerks of Assize are in E 362 and various ASSI classes. On receipt, the Exchequer sent sheriffs 'summonses of the green wax', instructing collection.

The pipe rolls may be supplemented by the memoranda rolls in E 159, E 368 and E 370, some of which have been digitised at **aalt.law.uh.edu**. The Pipe Roll Society has published a few, covering 1199–1200, 1207–8 and 1230–31.

From 1323, escheators' accounts were enrolled separately. Escheators administered lands which fell into the Crown's hands by death or forfeiture. Accounts, perhaps revealing information on the landholdings of local families, are in TNA class E 136 and E 357. In the late sixteenth century, recusancy fines were similarly removed from the pipe rolls (p.195)

The Westminster law courts also played important roles, exercising appellate jurisdiction over most of the courts described above, and providing the Eyre and Assize judges who supervised sheriffs and local courts. General eyres only operated intermittently; they were suspended in 1294, although revived very briefly in the early fourteenth century. See:

- General Eyres 1194–1348
  www.nationalarchives.gov.uk/help-with-your-research/research-guides/general-eyres-1194–1348

From the fourteenth century until 1972, Assizes were the principal criminal courts, and heard serious cases referred to them by Quarter Sessions. Until the nineteenth century, their guilty verdicts resulted in capital sentences, frequently followed by commutation or pardon. Assizes also exercised civil jurisdiction over matters such as trespass, breach of contract, assault, or libel. For useful guides, see:

- Criminal trials in the Assize Courts 1559–1971
  www.nationalarchives.gov.uk/help-with-your-research/research-guides/criminal-trials-assize-courts-1559–1971
- Civil trials in the English Assize Courts 1656–1971 – key to records
  www.nationalarchives.gov.uk/help-with-your-research/research-guides/civil-trials-english-assize-courts-1656–1971-key-to-records

In London and Middlesex, Assizes did not sit. Instead, the court at the Old Bailey was presided over by the lord mayor and other judges. Its quasi-official printed proceedings, which include the names of many non-Londoners, are digitised:

- Proceedings at the Old Bailey, 1674–1913
  www.oldbaileyonline.org

In Wales, the Court of Great Sessions exercised Assize jurisdiction. Its records are in the National Library of Wales **www.library.wales**. See:

- Parry, Glyn. *A Guide to the Records of the Court of Great Sessions.* National Library of Wales, 1995.

For digitised Great Sessions gaol files, 1730–1830, see:

- Crime and Punishment
  https://crimeandpunishment.library.wales/index_s.htm

The extensive archives of the Westminster courts cannot be described here in any detail. Before 1875, when the Supreme Court of Judicature was created, courts were divided between those which adjudicated the common law and those which applied equity. The medieval common law courts – Common Pleas, the Exchequer of Pleas, the King's Bench – were more concerned with fact than justice. They did not recognise copyhold or mortgages, nor could they provide justice where deeds had been lost. Their judgements could be rigid, harsh and inequitable. Increasingly, medieval litigants petitioned the Crown rather than relying on the common law. That led to the growth of the equity courts, primarily the Courts of Chancery and Exchequer, but also Star Chamber, the Court of Requests, and the Court of Wards. The latter three were abolished during the Civil War. The equity jurisdictions of Chancery and Exchequer merged in 1841. The rise of the equity courts is discussed in:

- Elton, G.R. 'The records of the conciliar courts in the sixteenth century', *Amateur Historian*, 4(3), 1959, p.89–94.

Equity court procedure began with written bills of complaint from plaintiffs and answers from defendants. Plaintiffs could then make a replication requiring another answer, which might be followed by another replication. Interrogatories were prepared by both parties, posing questions to be answered by witnesses. Affidavits – sworn voluntary statements – might also be submitted. The court's orders and decrees were entered in act books. Many cases were settled before judgement was reached.

These documents contain eye-witness accounts of local events for probably every English parish. Many disputes concerned land, but others were about probate, trade and industry, or tithe. Some classes can be searched by place name in TNA's Discovery catalogue **discovery. nationalarchives.gov.uk**. Others are only indexed by surname, so local surnames should also be searched.

Before delving into court archives, it is important to understand their complexity; otherwise, much may be missed. See:

- Moore, Susan T. *Tracing your Ancestors Through the Equity Courts*. Pen & Sword, 2017.
- Horwitz, Henry. *Chancery Equity Records and Proceedings, 1600–1800*. Public Record Office, Handbook 27. PRO Publications, 1995.
- Horwitz, Henry. *Exchequer Equity Records and Proceedings, 1649–1841*. Public Record Office, Handbook 35. PRO Publications, 1998.

Common law procedure was initiated by writ, and heard orally before a jury. Consequently, the archives of common law courts are not as rich as those of the equity courts. Procedure was recorded in plea rolls. Many early plea rolls are in print; see:

- *Curia Regis* Rolls & Assize Rolls for the reigns of Richard I and John: a handlist and finding aid
  www.medievalgenealogy.org.uk/guide/curiaregis.shtml
  A further three volumes covering subsequent periods have recently been published.

For a brief guide, see:

- Latham, R.E. 'Hints on interpreting the public records: (5) plea rolls', *Amateur Historian*, 1(5), 1953, p.155–8.

For Kings Bench archives, see:

- Court of King's Bench records 1200–1702
  www.nationalarchives.gov.uk/help-with-your-research/research-guides/court-kings-bench-records-1200–1600
- Court of King's Bench (Plea Side) and King's/Queen's Bench Division cases 1702–1998
  www.nationalarchives.gov.uk/help-with-your-research/research-guides/court-of-kings-bench-plea-side-and-kings-queens-bench-division-cases-1702–1998

A court sitting in Doctors Commons.

- Court of King's Bench (Crown Side) and King's/Queen's Bench Division cases 1675–1988
  www.nationalarchives.gov.uk/help-with-your-research/research-guides/court-kings-bench-crown-side-1675–1875

For Supreme Court of Judicature records, see:

- Appeal cases after 1875
  www.nationalarchives.gov.uk/help-with-your-research/research-guides/appeal-cases-after-1875
- Chancery cases after 1875
  www.nationalarchives.gov.uk/help-with-your-research/research-guides/chancery-cases-supreme-court-after-1875

Between 1547 and 1782, most government business went through the secretaries of state. Their activities are recorded in the State Papers (TNA SP classes). These include letters, reports, petitions, muster rolls, commissions, warrants, proclamations, draft Parliamentary bills, and other documentation. State Papers cover virtually every topic of interest to government. Every parish in England and Wales is probably mentioned in them. They are abstracted in extensive published calendars, digitised at **www.british-history.ac.uk**. See TNA's research guides:

- Letters and Papers of Henry VIII
  www.nationalarchives.gov.uk/help-with-your-research/research-guides/letters-papers-henry-viii

- State Papers Domestic 1547–1649: Tudor and Stuart government papers
  www.nationalarchives.gov.uk/help-with-your-research/research-guides/state-papers-domestic-1547–1649
  Further guides cover 1642–60, 1660–1714, and 1714–82.

Original State Papers have been both microfilmed and digitised:

- *The Complete State Papers Domestic.* Many microfilm reels. Harvester Press, 1977.
- *Unpublished State Papers of the English Civil War and Interregnum.* Comprises 114 microfilm reels. Harvester Press, 1975–8.
- State Papers Online
  www.gale.com/intl/primary-sources/state-papers-online
  Available in selected research libraries only.

Many matters of local interest, e.g. enclosure riots, public health, harvest failures, came before the Privy Council. See:

- Privy Council since 1386
  www.nationalarchives.gov.uk/help-with-your-research/research-guides/privy-council-since-1386

Privy Council registers (TNA class PC 2) have been calendared:

- Nicolas, Nicholas Harris, Sir, ed. *Privy Council of England, Proceedings and Ordinances, 10. Richard II–33. Henry VII (1386–1542).* 7 vols. Record Commission, 1834–1837.
- Dasent, J.R., et al., eds. *Acts of the Privy Council of England, 1542–1631.* 45 vols. HMSO, 1890–1964.
- *Privy Council Registers Preserved in the Public Record Office Reproduced in Facsimile: 1 June, 1637–[August, 1645].* 12 vols. HMSO, 1967–8.

In 1782, the Home Office and the Foreign Office were formed. TNA's HO classes are as diverse in character as the older SP classes. The four main series of correspondence files in HO 44 (1773–1861), HO 42 (1782–1820), HO 45 (1839–1979) and HO 144 (1868–1959) are particularly important. See:

- Home Office Correspondence from 1782
  www.nationalarchives.gov.uk/help-with-your-research/research-guides/home-office-correspondence-1782–1979

TNA also holds the records of three Palatine jurisdictions: the Duchy of Lancaster (class DL); the Palatinate of Chester (class CHES); and the Palatinate of Durham (class DURH). Their jurisdiction extended beyond their respective counties. There was, for example, Duchy of Lancaster property in Devon. Palatinate records parallel those of the central government, including material such as court records, inquisitions post-mortem, manorial records and enclosure awards. TNA does not, however, hold the records of the Duchy of Cornwall, which are not publicly accessible.

Government in the nineteenth and twentieth century was dominated by electoral politics. Early pressure for greater democracy came from the mid-nineteenth-century Chartist movement. For 14,000 names of Chartists, see:

- Chartist Ancestors
  www.chartistancestors.co.uk

Sources for political history are discussed by:

- Ottewill, Roger. 'The Changing Character of Municipal Elections, 1835–1974', *Local Historian*, 34(3), 2004, p.159–78.
- Ottewill, Roger. 'Virgin Territory? Researching the Local Political History of Interwar Britain', *Local Historian*, 37(1), 2007, p.45–50.
- Ottewill, Roger. 'Local Electoral History: a Suitable Case for Treatment?', *Local Historian*, 46(3), 2016, p.209–19.

M. War Books

When Britain faced invasion in 1941, local defence committees (later known as invasion committees), were established in every parish. Their war books listed local resources such as water, food supplies, first aid posts, stretchers and phones. They named Home Guard members, ARP wardens, National Fire Service officers, first aiders, WVS volunteers, and others.[4] Some even compiled censuses of the entire population, indicating the roles individuals were to play in case of invasion. See:

- Cohen, Colin. 'The 1942 Burford Census and "War Books": a Unique Record', *Local Historian* 36(2), 2006, p.121–7. See also 36(4), 2006, p.237.

N. Bomb Damage Census, 1940–45

The history of the Blitz can be partially traced in TNA records. Bomb census reports (HO 198), give details of bombing, air-raid warnings, damage inflicted, and casualties. Bomb census maps (predominantly covering the London region) are in HO 193. More detailed investigations are reported in air-raid damage files in HO 192. See:

• Bomb Census Survey Records 1940–1945
  www.nationalarchives.gov.uk/help-with-your-research/research-guides/bomb-census-survey-records-1940–1945

For London, see:

• Bombsight: Mapping the WW2 Bomb Census
  http://bombsight.org/about

The Imperial War Museum **www.iwm.org.uk** holds many photographs of bomb damage. Much information may also be found in the archives of local councils, and in newspapers.

London bombed in the Second World War.

Chapter 5

LANDED PROPERTY, WEALTH AND POVERTY: THE SOURCES

L and ownership and occupation played a major role in determining where power lay in local society. Ownership of an entire parish gave the landlord power to do more or less what he liked: enclose the land; expel the tenants; refuse to allow the poor to settle; create a deer park; divert roads away from his house; demolish (or rebuild) the church; appoint the rector and churchwardens; build a model village. Where there were many landowners, their individual power was much less. Housing would not be limited, fewer restrictions were placed on the poor, nonconformity could flourish, co-operation (or conflict) could flourish. Open and closed parishes had a symbiotic relationship with each other. The lord of the closed parish could reduce poor rates by refusing to allow house building. His labourers could live in neighbouring parishes, where building was not restricted. Poor rates would be higher in open parishes. These are just a few of the reasons why who owned and occupied land is important. This chapter describes the sources needed to trace the pattern of landownership.

There were three major national discontinuities in English landownership, occasioned by the Battle of Hastings, the Reformation, and sales of landed estates in the early years of the twentieth century. After 1066, the Anglo-Saxon nobility was destroyed and Norman barons seized most of their lands. In the ensuing centuries, they gave much of the land to ecclesiastical institutions. By the fifteenth century, about a quarter of England was owned by either the Church or the Crown, with a further fifth owned by peers with incomes in excess of £100 per annum. In 1535, the Crown surveyed and valued all ecclesiastical land. Returns are now in TNA, class E 344, and were published as:

- Caley, John, ed. *Valor ecclesiasticus temp. Henr. VIII.* 6 vols. Record Commission 1810–1833.

Avebury Manor (Wiltshire), rebuilt by a purchaser of monastic estates.

Monastic and chantry lands were subsequently seized by the Crown, which sold most of it to raise money. The larger purchasers formed a new gentry class, but there were also many smaller purchasers. By the end of the seventeenth century, perhaps a quarter or a third of the land was owned by small proprietors. For the following two centuries, the trend was towards the establishment of large estates. This was reversed in the late nineteenth and early twentieth centuries, when landowners were badly hit by agricultural depression, changes in the law relating to ownership, death duties, and deaths of many heirs during the First World War. Many estates were sold, frequently to tenants. Owner occupying farmers occupied 11 per cent of the land in 1914, and 36 per cent in 1927.[1] The twentieth century saw a dramatic expansion in owner-occupied housing.

The descent of property depended on diverse inheritance customs. Every manor had its own. Primogeniture dominated much of the country: estates descended automatically to the eldest sons. In parts of East Anglia and Kent, partible inheritance was the custom, especially for unfree estates. Borough English, whereby the youngest son inherited, was also common. Free bench gave widows occupancy of their husbands' copyhold. Different customs meant variations in tenurial patterns.

There are many sources for tracing landowners and tenants. *VCH* parish histories have drawn heavily on deeds to trace manorial descents from the eleventh to the twentieth centuries. Numerous surveys and rentals list tenants. Manorial court rolls record the descent of copyhold property. Enclosure awards, tithe surveys (or apportionments), and the Inland Revenue valuation survey, with their associated maps, provide lists of landowners and, in some cases, tenants.

A. Domesday Book

The tracing of descents normally begins with *Domesday Book* (p.42–3). It provides the earliest record of most English manors and their lords. Keats-

Rohan's prosopography, listing the names of Domesday lords, has already been mentioned (p.42). She has also listed their immediate successors:

- Keats-Rohan, K.S.B. *Domesday Descendants: A Prosopography of Persons Occurring in English Document: 1066–1166, Vol. II: Pipe Rolls to Cartae Baronum.* Boydell Press, 2002.

This is complemented by:

- The Continental Origins of English Landowners, 1066–1166
  https://prosopography.history.ox.ac.uk/coel.htm

B. The Hundred Rolls
The Hundred Rolls (TNA class SC 5) record a series of four inquisitions into royal rights conducted between 1255 and 1280. The rolls, which are much more extensive than *Domesday Book*, name lords, freeholders, villeins and serfs, stating their obligations and the size of their holdings. Sadly, however, they only survive for a few counties. Many were published as:

- *Rotuli Hundredorum, temp Hen. III & Edw. I.* 2 vols. Record Commission, 1812–18.

The *quo warranto* proceedings are closely related:

- Illingworth, William, ed. *Placita de Quo Warranto, temporibus Edward I, II,& III.* Record Commission, 1818.

Since these books were published, other rolls have come to light. See:

- The Sheffield Hundred Rolls Project
  www.roffe.co.uk/shrp.htm

An introduction is provided by:

- Harley, J.B. 'The Hundred Rolls of 1279', *Amateur Historian* 5(1), 1961, p.9–16.

For detailed discussions, see:

- Raban, Sandra. *A Second Domesday? The Hundred Rolls of 1279–80.* Oxford University Press, 2004.
- Cam, Helen M. *The Hundred and the Hundred Rolls: An Outline of Local Government in Medieval England.* Methuen, c.1930.

C. The Return of Owners of Land 1873

This survey was conducted to disprove the allegation that landed property was held in very few hands, but in fact demonstrated that fewer than 7,000 landowners owned four-fifths of landed property. It lists by county and alphabetically everyone in possession of more than one acre of land, with their addresses, acreages and rental value, but does not state where their lands lay. It was based on rate books. Returns are now most easily available in digitised form at **www.ancestry.co.uk** and on other websites. They were very inaccurate, and the figures were reworked for the larger landowners in:

- Bateman, John. *The Great Landowners of Great Britain and Ireland.* 4th edition. Harrison, 1883. Reprinted with introduction by David Spring, Leicester University Press, 1971.

D. The Valuation Office Survey

The Finance Act 1909 imposed a duty on land values, and was followed by this detailed survey. It was based on poor law union rate lists, which gave the names of occupiers and owners, descriptions of properties, locations and areas, and rateable values. These details were copied into valuation books (now mostly in local record offices),[2] together with information from landowners. Field books (in TNA, class IR 58), used by surveyors in the field, were compiled from them. Surveyors annotated them with their valuations, sometimes added rough plans, and occasionally commented on the condition of buildings, building materials, trees, recent sales, and similar matters. Two sets of marked up Ordnance Survey maps were prepared. Each property was a 'hereditament', and every entry in the books was given a 'hereditament number'. These numbers are recorded on the maps, which therefore act as indexes to the books. The master maps are in TNA, IR 121 & 124–35. Working maps (sometimes with later amendments) are in local record offices.

This survey provides detailed descriptions of houses, farms, factories, docks, chapels, schools and other property, and may be used to study topics such as living conditions, agriculture and industrial history. It is, however, complex to use. *Short Guides* 2 includes a useful introduction, as does Beech (p.134). The authoritative guide is:

- Short, Brian. *Land and Society in Edwardian Britain.* Cambridge University Press, 1997.

For TNA documents, see:

- Land use, value and ownership: Valuation Office Survey 1910–1915
  www.nationalarchives.gov.uk/help-with-your-research/research-guides/valuation-office-survey-land-value-ownership-1910–1915

Two online databases are in preparation:

- Lloyd George Survey of Land Values: Gloucestershire
  www.glos1909survey.org.uk/index.html
- The Genealogist: The Lloyd George Domesday Survey [for London]
  www.thegenealogist.co.uk/lloyd-george-domesday

E. Feudal and Later Tenure

In feudal law, all land was ultimately held of the Crown. It granted property to tenants in chief, who in turn granted it to their followers (mesne tenants), who in turn let it to those who actually occupied the land. There were two basic categories of tenure: free and unfree. For the unfree, see p.118. Free tenants held by knight service, that is, by contributing to their lords' military forces (scutage), or by socage, that is, by performing labour services. These 'feudal incidents' were increasingly commuted to monetary payments known as quit rents. Burgage tenure occasionally involved service, although more usually rent was paid. Religious institutions frequently held by frankalmoign, or free alms, free of both service and rent.

Feudal tenants might face other demands for money, for example, when the lord needed to be ransomed, when his daughter needed a dowry, or when he was knighted. Lords also had the right to wardship – that is, control of tenants' lands and marriages during their minorities. Tenure by knight service was abolished in 1660.

Freehold property could be held in fee simple, fee tail, or for life. Fee simple meant that land automatically descended to heirs; fee tail was entailed, that is, it descended in accordance with a strict settlement (p.109–10). Land could also be leased for a fixed term of years (p.111).

In the twelfth and thirteenth centuries, a variety of inquiries into feudal tenure (in addition to the slightly later Hundred Rolls) were conducted. Some returns (mostly in TNA E 198) have been published:

- Hall, Hubert, ed. *The Red Book of the Exchequer.* Rolls Series, 99. HMSO, 1896. Covers 1166.
- Walmsley, John, ed. *Widows, Heirs, and Heiresses in the Late Twelfth Century: The Rotuli de Dominabus et Pueris et Puellis.* Arizona Center

for Medieval and Renaissance Studies, 2006. Inquiry into lands held by widows and minors, 1185.

- Maxwell-Lyte, H.C., ed. *Liber Feodorum: The Book of Fees, Commonly Called the Testa de Nevill.* 3 vols. HMSO, 1920–31. Covers 1198–1293.
- *Inquisitions and Assessments Relating to Feudal Aids, with other analogous documents preserved in the Public Record Office, A. D. 1284–1431.* 6 vols. HMSO, 1899–1920.

F. Inquisitions Post-Mortem

When a tenant in chief died, his heir paid a 'relief' to the Crown. If a minor, the Crown had the right of wardship, that is, the right to the income of the estate, together with the right to determine the marriage of the heir(s) or heiress(es). That right was a valuable asset and was usually sold. The Crown's escheator, with a local jury, conducted an inquisition to determine the rightful heir, his age, and details of the lands held. Inquisitions post-mortem provide both genealogical information and details of lands possessed by tenants in chief (including understated valuations). Perhaps a third of inquisitions are accompanied by extents (not printed in the older published calendars), providing fuller descriptions of particular manors. Proofs of age provide interesting insights into social and religious customs and practices.

Tenants in chief were not necessarily the wealthiest landowners; the smallest landowners sometimes held lands 'in chief'. Inquisitions are invaluable for tracing the estates of the minor gentry. They reveal much incidental information concerning, for example, the extent of royal forests, lay ownership of ecclesiastical patronage (advowsons), the development of place names and surnames, and the occupations of tenants.

Original inquisitions initiated by Chancery are in TNA C 132–42. Exchequer duplicates in TNA E 149–50 provided a check on escheators' accounts in TNA E 136. Inquisitions initiated by escheators themselves were sent directly into the Exchequer. Between 1540 and 1660, duplicate inquisitions were sent to the Court of Wards (TNA WARD 7). Inquisitions were also conducted in the Palatine counties of Cheshire, Durham and Lancashire, and in the Duchy of Lancaster; their records are in CHES 3, DURH 3, PL 4 and DL 7.

Feudal tenure was abolished in 1660. For more details, see:

- Inquisitions post-mortem: land ownership and inheritance in the medieval and early modern periods
  www.nationalarchives.gov.uk/help-with-your-research/research-guides/inquisitions-post-mortem
- Latham, R.E. 'Hints on interpreting the public records: (3) inquisitions post-mortem', *Amateur Historian*, 1(3), 1953, p.77–81.

For detailed discussions, see:

- Hicks, Michael, ed. *The Fifteenth-Century Inquisitions Post-Mortem: A Companion.* Boydell Press, 2012.

A database covering 1399 to 1447, including a useful introduction, is available at:

- Mapping the Medieval Countryside: Places, People and Property in the Medieval Inquisitions Post-Mortem **www.inquisitionspostmortem.ac.uk**

Some inquisitions have been published by local record societies, sometimes in more detail than the official calendars. For the latter, see:

- *Calendar of inquisitions post-mortem and other analogous documents preserved in the Public Record Office.* HMSO/Boydell & Brewer, 1904–To be continued. 1st series (26 vols. to date) covers 1235–1447. 2nd series (3 vols.) covers 1485–1509. All available at **www.british-history.ac.uk/search/series/inquis-post-mortem**

Between the early sixteenth century and 1660, wardship was administered by the Court of Wards, whose records are in WARD 1–16. In addition to inquisitions and grants of wardship, its records include many deeds, leases, surveys, accounts and other estate records, together with judicial records such as bills, answers, replications and rejoinders.

G. Parliamentary Surveys
Between 1649 and 1651, the Interregnum regime prepared to sell royal and bishops' lands. Its surveys (see *Short Guides 1*) record names of tenants, the extent of demesne lands, annual values, level of rents, revenue from feudal dues, profits of timber, and much topographical detail. They are mostly in TNA, classes E 317 and LR 2. See also DL 32, SC 12/39 and LRRO 37/4–5. For an example in print, see:

- Pounds, Norman J.G., ed. *The Parliamentary Survey of the Duchy of Cornwall.* 2 vols. Devon & Cornwall Record Society. New Series 25 & 27. 1982–4.

H. Deeds and Charters
Deeds of title record the transfer of land from one owner to another. Generally they only relate to land held by free tenure. Many are indentures, that is, written in duplicate or triplicate on one sheet, and then separated by

cutting along an indented line. Proof of authenticity could be provided by rejoining the copies. However, the term 'indentures' in the post-medieval period was also applied to many deeds which were not actually indented.

Medieval deeds are frequently described as charters, although that term also includes various grants of rights and privileges to boroughs and other institutions, and appointments to office. Deeds exist in abundance from Anglo-Saxon times until the twentieth century, and can be found amongst estate records in almost every record office in the country.

Major collections are listed in:

- Historical Manuscripts Commission. *Principal Family and Estate Collections.* 2 vols. Guides to sources for British History, 10–11. HMSO, 1996–9.
- Sayers, Jane. *Estate Documents at Lambeth Palace Library.* Leicester University Press, 1965.

Monastic estates were sometimes extensive. See:

- English Monastic Archives Database
  www.ucl.ac.uk/library/digital-collections/collections/monastic
- Religious Houses and their Lands *c.*1000–1530
  www.nationalarchives.gov.uk/help-with-your-research/research-guides/religious-houses-lands-1000–1530

The seizure of monastic lands at the Dissolution was administered by the Courts of Surveyors and Augmentations. Their records are in TNA classes E 298–330, in LR 1–16, and elsewhere. See:

- Dissolution of the Monasteries, 1536–1540
  www.nationalarchives.gov.uk/help-with-your-research/research-guides/dissolution-monasteries-1536–1540

For detailed listings of monastic lands, see:

- *List of the Lands of Dissolved Religious Houses.*7 vols. Supplementary Lists and Indexes Supplementary Series 3. Reprinted Kraus Reprint, 1964.
- Jurkowski, Maureen, & Ramsay, Nigel. *English Monastic Estates 1066–1540: A List of Manors, Churches and Chapels.* List & Index Society supplementary series 40–42. 2007.

The Crown is still a major landowner. Nineteenth- and twentieth-century deeds for its estates are in TNA's LRRO classes, with registers in LRRO 64 and 66.

Furness Abbey (Lancashire) was a typical monastic landlord.

Deeds and charters reflect land law. Using them requires some awareness of the complexity of that law. Deeds are not always what they purport to be. Land law cannot be considered in detail here, but a number of useful guides are listed at the end of this chapter.

The Law of Property Act 1925 limited the need to prove title to fifty years, thus eliminating the need for property owners to retain their deeds, and eliminating many deeds themselves. Many others are in local record offices.

Anglo-Saxon Charters
Anglo-Saxon charters are amongst the earliest sources available to local historians. They are especially useful for estate ownership and boundaries. Some record services and rents due from peasants to their lords. The earliest date from the 670s, and were grants to the church. From the eighth century, lay people increasingly benefited from them. They include long witness lists, providing names of kings, bishops, and others. Many record the earliest known forms of place names.

The term 'Anglo-Saxon charters' refers to three types of documents: diplomas, writs and wills. The diploma was (usually) a royal charter granting rights over land or other privileges. It was written mainly in Latin, but frequently described the boundaries of estates in Old English.

Writs were royal instructions, authenticated with a seal. They may include details of rights and privileges, and gradually replaced the diploma as evidence of land tenure.

Anglo-Saxon wills instructed executors how to dispose of testators' estates. They enable us to locate those estates, and provide information on a variety of other topics. Unlike wills of later centuries, they did not go through a probate process. For a detailed study of Anglo-Saxon wills and a full listing of the sixty-eight currently known to exist, see:

- Tollerton, Linda. *Wills and Will-making in Anglo-Saxon England*. Boydell & Brewer, 2011.

Over 1,000 Anglo-Saxon charters are extant, but only *c*.200 exist in their original form. The full corpus of Anglo-Saxon charters is in course of publication in the *Anglo-Saxon charters* series, published under the auspices of the British Academy. For a full list of surviving charters, see:

- The Electronic Sawyer: Online Catalogue of Anglo-Saxon Charters **https://esawyer.lib.cam.ac.uk/about/index.html**

Medieval Charters and Enrolments
After the Norman Conquest, charters were used by the Crown to make grants of lands, liberties, and privileges, to both individuals and institutions. Most Norman charters are calendared, or transcribed in full (with many facsimiles), by:

- Davis, H.W.C., et al., eds. *Regesta Regum Anglo-Normannorum 1066–1154*. 4 vols. Clarendon Press, 1913–69. The portion of this work dealing with William I's reign has been replaced by:
- Bates, David, ed. *Regesta Regum Anglo-Normannorum: The Acta of William I (1066–1087)*. Clarendon Press, 1998.

The great series of Chancery rolls in TNA, begun in the reign of King John (1199–1215), contain numerous enrolments of royal charters and private deeds, as well as much other potentially useful material. They include the close rolls (C 54), the charter rolls (C 53), the patent rolls (C 66), the fine rolls (C 60), and the confirmation rolls (C 56).[3] Calendars to these and similar sources are listed below; many are available online at British History Online **www.history.ac.uk/research/digital-history/british-history-online**.

Many rolls from Henry VIII's reign are calendared in:

- *Letters and Papers, Foreign and Domestic, Henry VIII*. 21 vols + addenda. HMSO, 1864–1932.

For a useful discussion of royal grants (including much more than just land grants), see:

- Royal Grants in Letters Patent and Charters from 1199
  www.nationalarchives.gov.uk/help-with-your-research/research-guides/royal-grants-letters-patent-charters-from-1199
- Latham, R.E. 'Hints on Interpreting the Public Records II: Letters patent', *Amateur Historian*, 1(2), 1952, p.47–50.

For royal charters in the Charter Rolls (C 53), see:

- Hardy, T.D., ed. *Rotuli Chartarum in Turri Londinensi Asservati, 1199–1216*. Record Commission, 1837.
- *Calendar of the Charter Rolls* … 6 vols. HMSO, 1903–1927. Cover 1226–1516.

The confirmation rolls (C 56) include enrolled confirmations of former royal grants. They have not been calendared, except as noted above.

Letters patent, sent 'open' with the great seal, include many grants and leases of land, as well as grants of office, denizations of aliens, presentations to ecclesiastical benefices, etc. They may sometimes be found amongst estate records, but were enrolled on the Patent Rolls (C 66). See:

- Hardy, T.D., ed. *Rotuli Litterarum Patentium in Turri Londinensi Asservati, 1201–1216*. Record Commission, 1835.
- *Patent Rolls of the Reign of Henry III*. 2 vols. HMSO, 1901–3. Similar volumes are available for most reigns up to Elizabeth I (1582). For 1509–48, see above.

The List and Index Society **www.listandindexsociety.org.uk** has published calendars of the patent rolls for the reigns of Elizabeth I and James I. See:

- Wilkinson, Louise. 'Completing the Calendar of Patent Rolls for the Reign of Elizabeth', *Local Historian* 35(1), 2005, p.31–43.

The close rolls (C 54) originally contained royal orders addressed to individuals under the great seal, and covering a wide range of topics, for example, the levying of subsidies, the repair of buildings, the payment of salaries, the delivery of lands to heirs, and the assignment of dower. They were folded, hence 'closed'. In the fourteenth century, the practice of endorsing private deeds on their backs developed. From *c*.1532, such deeds form the entire content of the rolls. They cease in 1903. Medieval rolls have been published:

- Hardy, T.D., ed. *Rotuli Litterarum Clausarum in Turri Londinensi Asservati, 1200–1227*. 2 vols. Record Commission, 1833–44.
- *Close Rolls of the Reign of Henry III*. 14 vols. HMSO, 1902–38.
- *Calendar of the Close Rolls*. 47 vols, HMSO, 1900–63. Covers 1272 to 1509.

For sixteenth-century rolls, see:

- Gray, Madeleine. 'The Close Rolls as a Source for Sixteenth-Century History', *Archives*, 17(75), 1986, p.131–7.

The fine rolls (TNA, C 60) relate to matters in which the Crown had some financial interest, for example, wardship, debts and land. Published rolls include:

- Hardy, T.D., ed. *Rotuli de Oblatis et Finibus in Turri Londinensi Asservati, tempore Regis Johannis*. Record Commission, 1835.
- Henry III Fine Rolls Project **https://finerollshenry3.org.uk**
- *Calendar of the Fine Rolls*. 22 vols. HMSO, 1911–62. Covers 1272–1509.

The 'liberate rolls' (TNA, C 62) record writs ordering payment of Crown expenses such as pensions and salaries, 1200–1436. Some are printed:

- Hardy, Thomas Duffus, ed. *Rotuli de Liberate ac de Misis et Praestitis, Regnante Johanne*. Record Commission, 1844.
- *Calendar of the Liberate Rolls Preserved in the Public Record Office: Henry III*. 6 vols. HMSO, 1916–64.

The *Cartae Antiquae* rolls (TNA, C 52) are medieval transcripts of charters mainly dating from *c*.1189 to *c*.1327, but including a few pre-dating the Conquest. Twenty of the thirty-nine rolls have been published:

- Landon, Lionel, ed. *The Cartae Antiquae Rolls 1–10*. Pipe Roll Society, new series, 17. 1939.
- Davies, J.Conway, ed. *The Cartae Antiquae Rolls 11–20*. Pipe Roll Society, new series, 33. 1957.

Numerous 'ancient deeds' from various TNA classes[4] are calendared in:
- Maxwell-Lyte, H.C., ed. *A Descriptive Catalogue of Ancient Deeds in the Public Record Office*. 6 vols. HMSO, 1890–1915.

Over 40,000 charters from various sources, dating from 1066 to 1315, are recorded by:

- Deeds: Documents of Early England Data Set
  https://deeds.library.utoronto.ca

Many collections of medieval charters have been published by local record societies and others. See, for example:

- Farrer, William, ed. *Early Yorkshire Charters, being a collection of documents anterior to the thirteenth century made from the public records, monastic chartularies, Roger Dodsworth's manuscripts, and other available sources*. 3 vols. Ballantyne Hanson & Co., 1914. This collection was completed by Sir Charles Clay in a further twelve volumes published by the Yorkshire Archaeological Society.

Charters recording lands gifted to monasteries and other ecclesiastical institutions were frequently copied into cartularies. About 2,000 cartularies survive. For a full listing, see:

- Davis, G.R.C. *Medieval Cartularies of Great Britain and Ireland*. 2nd edition. Revised by Claire Breay, Julian Harrison, and David M. Smith. British Library, 2010.

Private Deeds

Many of the documents so far discussed emanated from the Royal Chancery. There are also millions of private deeds deposited in both local and national record offices. Title deeds record the conveyance of land. They identify vendors, purchasers, trustees, lessees, and others concerned in conveyancing particular pieces of land. Neighbouring landowners may be named. Family relationships may be stated. Property may be described, perhaps giving acreages, field names, locations, and details of buildings. Deeds may provide information on agricultural practices such as 'floating' water meadows, keeping the land fertile, preserving timber, and folding sheep on the arable. Descriptions of properties tend to be fuller in more recent centuries.

A bundle of deeds enables you to trace the descent of a particular property over a century or two. Some, helpfully, recite previous deeds. Each bundle is likely to be accompanied by an abstract, which should be read first. It probably lists all the deeds in the bundle, explaining their purpose. Individual deeds may be endorsed on their backs with brief descriptions.

Some deeds (not all) are cumbersome. Archaic handwriting and Latin may be used. Legal language is technical, long, and repetitive. Nevertheless, deeds are actually easier to consult than may at first appear. They follow a basic structure. By familiarising yourself with that structure, you will know where to find the information required, avoiding the unnecessary verbiage. You are likely to encounter a variety of different types of deeds. The following notes may enable you to recognise each type.

The Feoffment

Feoffments recorded 'livery of seizin', in which the vendor performed the act of sale by handing the purchaser a clod of earth. They were not agreements between two parties, but, rather, stated what vendors had done. They may be in Latin or English and begin with the words *Sciant presentes et futuri* – 'Know for the present and future'. Feoffments record the names of parties and witnesses (probably neighbouring landowners) to the act of seizin. They include details of the property conveyed, and of the consideration, and are sometimes termed deeds of gift.

The Bargain and Sale

The Statute of Enrolments, 1535, provided landowners with an alternative to the feoffment. Bargains and sales were similar in form, although they did not require livery of seizin. Instead, they had to be enrolled either on the Close Rolls (TNA C 54), or by the Clerk of the Peace. Local enrolments are with Quarter Sessions records. For Somerset enrolments, see:

- Bates Harbin, Sophia W., ed. *Somerset Enrolled Deeds.* Somerset Record Society 51. 1936.

The Quitclaim

Quitclaims were used to release rights in a property. It was usually used when people such as heirs, creditors and annuitants had some claim against a property. Quitclaims are frequently in Latin and commence with the words *Omnibus Christi fidelibus* – 'to all the faithful in Christ'.

Fines, or Final Concords

The final concord is a record of a collusive legal case, giving conveyances greater security. The querent (the purchaser) sued the deforciant (the vendor) for possession of the property in the Court of Common Pleas. The deforciant did not defend himself, but agreed to warrant the claim.

Fines open with the words *Hec est finalis concordia* ... – 'this is the final agreement ...' They name the parties, but property details are not necessarily accurate, prices recorded are notional, and their purposes are not necessarily clear. Fines usually accompany other deeds, which may include a 'deed to lead the uses of a fine', explaining their purpose.

Fines were prepared in triplicate, in Latin, and in a very archaic style of handwriting. English was used between 1650 and 1660, and after 1733. Copies were given to each party. The third copy – the foot – was retained in court, and is now in TNA, class CP 25. Associated documents are in CP24, 26–8 and 30. There are indexes in various IND 1 classes. See:

- Land and Property Ownership: Conveyances by Feet of Fines, 1182–1833
  www.nationalarchives.gov.uk/help-with-your-research/research-guides/land-conveyance-feet-of-fines-1182–1833

For a detailed discussion, listing many published editions, see:

- Kissock, Jonathan. 'Medieval Feet of Fines: a Study of their Uses, with a Catalogue of Published Sources', *Local Historian* 24(2), 1994, p.66–82.

See also:

- Emmison F.G. 'Final Concords', *Local Historian*, 14(7), 1981, p.411–18.

The Lease and Release

These two documents, usually found together, developed in the seventeenth century, becoming the standard method of conveyancing until the 1840s. They avoided the necessity of enrolment, which was not welcomed by most landowners. The purchaser was granted a twelve-month lease of the property, and took possession. On the following day, the vendor released his interest in the property to the purchaser. Although neither deed formally transferred freehold, the two deeds together effectively did so.

The Strict Settlement

The gentry wished to preserve their family estates in perpetuity for their heirs. From the mid-seventeenth century until 1925, strict settlements provided a device by which this could be done. The marriage settlement, which made provision for newly married wives, was a variant. By the nineteenth century, perhaps half of English land was subject to strict settlement, and held in fee tail.

Settlements settled estates on trustees, making heads of families merely life tenants, not owners. Heirs became 'tenants in tail'. Jointures were provided for wives; portions for dependent children. Life tenants could only sell property if tenants in tail agreed. Adult heirs needed annuities to live on until they inherited; life tenants needed money for daughters' dowries, or to pay off debts. So did executors. When such needs coincided, settlements were broken by common recoveries (below) and remade. That frequently happened on the heir's coming of age, on his marriage, or on the life tenant's death.

Settlements provide detailed information on family relationships and may enable families to be traced through several generations. Occasionally, they were made by will. For a useful guide, see:

- English, Barbara, & Saville, John. *Strict Settlement: A Guide for Historians*. University of Hull Press, 1983.

The Common Recovery

This device, developed in the fifteenth century, broke entailments. Like the fine, common recoveries were the outcome of collusive legal cases, which restored full ownership to life tenants. They were originally enrolled on the plea rolls of the Court of Common Pleas, TNA CP 40. From 1583, a separate series of recovery rolls, CP 43, was begun. Indexes to CP 43 are in IND 1/17183–216. There are separate series for Palatinate jurisdictions: CHES 29–32, DURH 13, and PL 15.

Exemplifications of common recoveries are frequently found amongst estate records. They are not very informative. Their important point is that an entail had been broken. The property concerned was probably resettled, sold, or mortgaged soon after the recovery took place. See:

- University of Nottingham: Manuscripts and Special Collections: Common Recoveries
  www.nottingham.ac.uk/manuscriptsandspecialcollections/ researchguidance/deedsindepth/freehold/commonrecovery.aspx

Letters Patent

Former monastic properties were frequently granted by letters patent (see p.105). Entire manors might be granted to be held by feudal tenure. Many small pieces of ex-ecclesiastical land were granted to be held in free socage, as of the manor of East Greenwich. Letters patent provide full descriptions of properties and names of former owners. They are based on particulars for grants in TNA class E 318, which in turn are based on surveys of monastic property found in SC 12.

The Mortgage

Mortgages frequently took the form of leases by the mortgagor for long periods – frequently 500 or 1,000 years – at a 'peppercorn' rent, granted for a specific sum of money. If the capital was repaid with interest by a fixed date, the lease would be cancelled. If not, it became 'absolute', and the mortgagee became the owner of the property. In practice that rarely happened; the intention was that the mortgage would be perpetual. The lessor retained possession of the property, although that is not stated in the deed. Mortgages could also be effected by other types of deed.

Deeds of assignment were used to transfer mortgages between lenders. Before c.1800, mortgagees were usually local people, except in the case of large estates. Thereafter, the financial markets fell increasingly into the hands of bankers and attorneys. Building societies also entered the market, originally with the intention of enabling their members to build their own houses.

Leases

Many landlords leased their property for a term of years, frequently taking both an entry fine and payment of rent. Leases provide full descriptions of property. Terms varied, but the lease for three lives or 99 years was popular between the sixteenth and eighteenth centuries. The lives were usually family members. The lease ended when the three lives died, but was frequently surrendered and renewed earlier. Leases could be sold unless they specifically forbade sale. Reversionary leases were sometimes granted to take effect from the death of the last life.

For landlords, leasehold tenure was preferable to copyhold (p.117–18). It gave them greater control over their tenants, their rents, and methods of cultivation. Manorial courts and the customs of the manor could be ignored. See:

- Roebuck, Peter. 'Leases and Tenancy Agreements', *Local Historian* 10(1), 1972, p.7–12.

Bonds

Bonds were frequently used to strengthen transactions effected by other deeds. We have already seen the use of administration bonds in probate, of marriage bonds in securing licences, and of recognizances in keeping the peace. In property transactions, bonds promised to pay a fixed penalty if some aspect of the transaction failed. They name sureties and explain their purpose. They were also used to guarantee payments of debts, and are frequently valued in probate inventories and accounts (p.122–3).

Deeds Registries

Some deeds, as has been seen, were enrolled by the Westminster courts, and by Clerks of the Peace. Others were enrolled in medieval borough courts.[5] However, national registration of deeds did not commence until the Land Registry **www.landregistry-titledeeds.co.uk** opened in 1862, and was not compulsory until the twentieth century.

Registration made it easier to prove title to land. In the eighteenth century, deeds registries were established in the three Ridings of Yorkshire, in Middlesex, and in the Bedford Levels. They registered millions of deeds. Local historians in these counties must begin their research into title in the relevant registry, bearing in mind that the registers frequently contain abstracts, not necessarily full transcripts of deeds. See:

- Sheppard, F., & Belcher, V. 'The Deeds Registries of Yorkshire and Middlesex', *Journal of the Society of Archivists* 6(5), 1980, p.274–86.

Forfeited Estates Commission

This Commission was established to seize the lands of rebels after the 1715 Jacobite Rebellion.[6] Its archives (TNA FEC 1 & 2) include many deeds, surveys, rentals and other estate records, principally from the north of England, but also from other counties. The minutes, letters and registers of the Commission also provide much useful information. See:

- Barlow, D. *The Records of the Forfeited Estates Commission.* Public Record Office, Handbook 12. HMSO, 1968.

Ecclesiastical Commissioners

The Ecclesiastical Commissioners were established in 1833 and merged with Queen Anne's Bounty (p.160) to become the Church Commissioners in 1946. They took over the administration of church lands formerly in the possession of bishops, deans and chapters, and other ecclesiastical bodies. Their surveys and maps, with related property records, are now in the Church of England Record Centre's benefice files, and include details of an 1887 survey of church property and revenue. See:

- Lambeth Palace Library: Church Commissioners **www.lambethpalacelibrary.org/content/churchproperty**
- Robinson, E.J. 'Records of the Church Commissioners', *Local Historian* 9(5), 1971, p.215–21.

Further Reading:

For a basic introduction to title deeds, see:

- Wormleighton, Tim. *Title Deeds for Family Historians*. Family History Partnership, 2012.

More detail is provided by:

- Alcock, N.W. *Tracing History Through Title Deeds: A Guide for Family and Local Historians*. Pen & Sword, 2017.

Royal grants, and deeds registered in the central courts, are discussed by:

- Land and property ownership: enrolment and registration of title 1227–c.1930

   www.nationalarchives.gov.uk/help-with-your-research/research-guides/enrolment-of-deeds-registration-of-titles-land

For medieval conveyancing, see:

- Kaye, J.M. *Medieval English Conveyances*. Cambridge Studies in English Legal History. Cambridge University Press, 2009.

Seals used to authenticate signatures are discussed by:

- New, Elizabeth. *Seals and Sealing Practices*. Archives and the User series, 11. British Records Association, 2010.

I. Taxation

Some of the tax documents discussed above (p.44–6) as demographic sources also provide rough guides to the distribution of wealth. Many recorded taxes on land, and these may enable us to identify property occupiers. Assessments of individuals' wealth are generally notional, based on reputed rather than actual wealth, but are useful for comparative purposes.

The lay subsidy returns for the period 1290 to 1330, and for the 1520s, provide useful sources for assessing at least the distribution of wealth. Returns for other periods are less comprehensive. Subsidies were levied on the annual value of lands, the capital value of goods, or on wages. Assessments on wages are indicative of a landless labouring class, although those so assessed may include the adolescent sons of yeomen and husbandmen.

The 1334 subsidy assessment was communal, and did not record names. It does, however, provide a reasonable basis on which to assess the distribution of wealth across the country. Subsequent subsidies were rarely reassessed, except in case of flood or other disaster, so returns became fossilised, and are unusable as guides to wealth distribution. For the 1334 and 1524/5 subsidies, see:

- Glasscock, R.E., ed. *The Lay Subsidy of 1334.* 3 vols. Records of Social and Economic History, new series 2, 29, & 37. Oxford University Press for the British Academy, 1975–2005.
- Hoyle, R.W., ed. *The Regional Distribution of Wealth in England as Indicated in the 1524/5 Lay Subsidy Returns.* List & Index Society special series 28. 2 vols. 1998.

The 1524/5 subsidy may be compared with returns from the military survey of 1522.[7] Hoyle describes this as 'the most ambitious attempt' made in the sixteenth century to collect wealth statistics. Returns were used as the basis for forced loans; assessments were generally higher than those for the subsequent subsidy.

The inquisition of the ninths, levied in 1341, covers most of twenty-seven counties. It too was a communal assessment on the laity, so does not record names, but it may be used to assess the distribution of wealth across regions. It was imposed on corn, wool and lambs. The assessors compared their assessments with, and explained the differences from, the tax imposed on the clergy by Pope Nicholas in 1291. The names of those parishioners who swore to the correctness of the assessment are given. The Latin text of the returns is printed in:

- Vanderzee, George, ed. *Nonarum Inquisitiones in Curia Scaccarii, temp Regis Edwardi III.* Record Commissioners, 1807.

Poll taxes levied in 1377, 1379 and 1381, have already been mentioned (p.45). The two later levies were graduated. So too were their seventeenth-century successors. In 1667, for instance, servants paid a shilling for every pound of their wages, whereas baronets had to pay an additional flat rate of £15. These graduated poll taxes enable us to study wealth distribution in both the late fourteenth and the seventeenth centuries.

Hearth tax returns from the late seventeenth century (p.45) are particularly useful for assessing wealth levels. Returns in TNA (class E 179) date from the periods 1662–5 and 1670–3, when collection was not farmed out. Occasionally, returns may be found locally. They list all householders, and count hearths. The exempt poor were included in separate lists. Counting hearths is a useful way of assessing wealth levels; the more you had, the wealthier you probably were. Those with only one or two hearths lived in much humbler circumstances than those with more than six or seven. See:

- Arkell, Tom. 'Identifying Regional Variations from the Hearth Tax', *Local Historian*, 33(3), 2003, p.148–74.
- Barnwell, P.S., & Airs, Malcolm, eds. *Houses and the Hearth Tax: The Later Stuart House and Society*. Research Report 150. Council for British Archaeology, 2006.

In the sixteenth and seventeenth centuries, for most taxes, landowners possessed of property in more than one place were assessed only once. The commissioners receiving payment certified receipt; these certificates of residence (mostly in TNA, class E 115) were sent into the Exchequer, where appropriate adjustments were made to assessments made in other places.

Land tax assessments record the names of proprietors and occupiers, and the amount of tax paid. The tax was levied from 1692 until 1963 on land, and also on tithe. Annual or quarterly assessments (it is not always stated which) record the names of proprietors and occupiers (occupiers from 1786), and state the tax paid. From 1826, brief descriptions of property are given. Assessments are, however, full of pitfalls for the unwary. Before 1826, they rarely identify the land on which the tax was levied, and cannot be used to determine acreages. Tax paid by clergy may be based on tithes rather than on land. 'Proprietors' are sometimes actually copyholders or leaseholders. 'Occupiers' may be tenants or sub-tenants. From 1798, it became possible to purchase exemption from future levies. Redemption resulted in entries in assessments steadily diminishing. Occasionally, old exonerations are shown on post-1798 assessments. Assessments were made by parish, or perhaps by tithing, and only record ownership in that area, ignoring the fact that a small tenant in one parish may be a substantial landowner in neighbouring parishes. The liability of small proprietors whose land was valued at under £1 ceased in 1798; returns thereafter are therefore not full lists of landowners and occupiers.[8] The amount levied on each parish was fixed, so assessments did not vary from year to year, and bear little relationship to land values. From 1949, redemption was made compulsory on changes of ownership, and the tax was abolished in 1963.

These problems should not deter researchers from using land tax assessments. Researchers familiar with a parish should be able to identify landowners and occupiers, to trace changes in landownership, and to spot gaps in the record. Comparison with other sources, such as enclosure and tithe records, could be illuminating.

Returns survive in considerable quantities between 1780 and 1832, when they were used to identify those eligible to vote, and were kept with Quarter Sessions records. Otherwise, survival is patchy. An almost complete set of assessments for 1798 is in TNA, class IR 23. Assessments can occasionally be found amongst private estate records. Redemption records are in TNA, classes IR 20–25. Accounts of arrears are in E 181. Certificates relating to Roman Catholics liable to double taxation are in E 174. A full listing of assessments is provided by:

- Gibson, J.S.W., Medlycott, M., & Mills, D. *Land and Window Tax Assessments.* Federation of Family History Societies, 2003.

For brief guides, see *Short Guides 1* and:

- Grigg, David. 'A Source on Land Ownership: the Land Tax Returns', *Amateur Historian*, 6(5), 1964, p.152–6.

Land tax returns as a source are critiqued in detail by:

- Ginter, D.E. *A Measure of Wealth: The English Land Tax in Historical Analysis.* Hambledon Press, 1992.

A few returns have been published. See, for example:

- Davey, Roger, ed. *East Sussex Land Tax, 1785.* Sussex Record Society, 77. 1991.

The value of land tax and rate assessments for determining wealth is discussed by:

- Baigent, Elizabeth. 'Assessed taxes as sources for the study of urban wealth: Bristol in the later eighteenth century', *Urban History Yearbook*, 15, 1988, p.31–48.

Income and Property Tax was levied intermittently from 1799 until 1816. Some documentation is in TNA, class E 182. For a detailed list, see:

- Income tax payments 1799–1802
  http://doc.ukdataservice.ac.uk/doc/3785/mrdoc/pdf/guide.pdf

See also:

- Jackson, Thomas. *Income Tax, 1799–1802,* in Bristol Historical Resource
  http://humanities.uwe.ac.uk/bhr/Main

Income tax was reintroduced in 1842, but few records survive. Parish comparison lists for Income Tax Schedule A (on property) survive in IR 14 for 1842–3 and 1888–9, but do not record names. Some Parliamentary papers (p.25) published tax assessments. Schedule D assessment books, 1876–1975 (TNA IR 88, but closed for seventy-five years) record business income tax, giving the names of individuals, partnerships and companies, and the nature of their business. These have been heavily weeded. Most record offices hold ephemeral but potentially useful records amongst solicitors' collections and estate records. More substantial documentation is rare, but see:

- Colley, Robert, ed. *Devizes Division Income Tax Assessments, 1842– 1860*. Wiltshire Record Society, 55. 2002.

Rates were local taxes. They funded the church, poor relief, and other causes. Various county rates imposed by Quarter Sessions were collected separately, until unified into a single rate in 1739. In the late eighteenth and nineteenth centuries, sewer commissioners and poor law unions levied rates and compiled rate books. Responsibility for rates gradually passed to all-purpose local authorities during the nineteenth century. Rate lists/books record the names of occupiers and, sometimes, owners, together with property details and valuations. Before the nineteenth century, assessments tended to be customary and unchanging, frequently ignoring changes in land values. Documentation survives from the seventeenth century onwards, although much has been lost. See *Short Guides 1* and also:

- Beckett, J.V. *Local Taxation: National Legislation and the Problems of Enforcement*. Bedford Square Press, 1980.
- Beckett, John V. 'Local Taxation in England from the Sixteenth Century to the Nineteenth', *Local Historian*, 12(1), 1976, p.7–12.

J. Markets and Fairs
Deeds and charters were not only concerned with land. They also made grants of fairs. These are discussed below, p.146.

K. Manorial Court Rolls
Manorial court rolls (p.60) record names of the homage (the principal tenants), surrenders and admittances of copyhold tenants, entry fines payable on admittance to a holding, alienations, merchet payable on a daughter's marriage, heriots payable on the death of a tenant, and leyrwite payable on the birth of an illegitimate child. If rolls have survived, it should be possible to trace property descents over centuries.

Tenants varied in status, depending on forms of tenure. The villeins of *Domesday Book* were bound to their manors, and liable not only for rent but also for labour services, and renders in kind. Over several centuries, they morphed into copyholders (the first use of the word was recorded in 1483) and freeholders. There were also cottars or bordars, and leaseholders. Cottages and other small properties were frequently held 'at will', without formal documentation, but may occasionally be mentioned in estate records.

Copies of the court roll were given to customary tenants, who were said to hold by copy of court roll; hence the term copyhold. Copies occasionally survive. Most copyholders held either by inheritance, (where the property automatically descended in accordance with manorial custom), or for lives (where the property was held in succession by three named lives). Both forms of tenure could usually be bought and sold, although sales were not necessarily recorded in the rolls. Some tenants sub-let their land. Numbers of sub-tenants could be high, but they frequently escaped notice in manorial records.[9] The labour services and renders copyholders owed were gradually commuted to quitrents (monetary payments).

Freeholders paid a rent fixed in the medieval period, which eventually became insignificant. They might also be liable to pay a relief (frequently a year's rent) on taking possession, and a heriot on death. They were expected to attend manorial courts and serve as homagers.

Leaseholders stood outside of the manorial system. Originally, they leased (or 'farmed') the lord's demesne, which was not subject to manorial custom. Leasehold terms have already been discussed (p.111). Leases increased the power of landlords to negotiate with their tenants. Consequently, the long-term trend was to convert (enfranchise) copyhold land to leasehold.

Cottars had no land, except perhaps a cottage, and worked as labourers for the lord, or perhaps for freeholders. They received minimal notice in manorial records.

The importance of manorial court rolls gradually declined between the thirteenth and the twentieth centuries, as the trend to convert copyhold to freehold continued. An act of 1841 provided for compulsory enfranchisement at the request of either lord or tenant. Records of enfranchisement, 1841–1925 are in TNA, MAF 9 and 20. Copyhold was finally abolished in 1925.

L. Parliamentary Loans and Royalist Delinquents, 1642–56
At the beginning of the Civil War, Parliament raised loans to fund its army through the Committee for Advance of Money. Everyone with an estate valued at over £100 was expected to contribute, although

after 1646 only Royalists were liable. Proceedings are in TNA, SP 19. Royalists were also liable to suffer sequestration, although they were able to compound for their 'delinquency' through the Committee for Compounding with Royalist Delinquents. Royalist composition papers are in TNA SP 23. The two committees merged by 1650. Their records provide much information on the gentry and their lands, and are calendared in:

- Green, Mary Anne Everett, ed. *Calendar of the Proceedings of the Committee for Advance of Money, 1642–1656.* 3 vols. HMSO, 1888
- Green, Mary Anne Everett, ed. *Calendar of the Proceedings of the Committee for Compounding, &c., 1643–1660.* HMSO, 1889–92.

After the Restoration, many Royalists reclaimed lands. Records of commissions of enquiry, with witnesses' depositions, are in E 134 and E 178. Those who purchased land from Parliamentary commissioners were able to claim restitution of their purchase money. Records are in E CRES 6/1–8. Cases related to these lands were also heard in the equity courts (p.89–90).

M. Registers of Papists' Estates
After the 1715 Jacobite Rebellion, Roman Catholics had to register their estates with Clerks of the Peace, who sent copies to the Forfeited Estates Commissioners. Commissioners' registers are in TNA, class FEC 1/1113–1314. Registrations made after a subsequent act in 1722 are in E 174/1. Estates are described in some detail, and tenants are named. TNA registrations are briefly abstracted in:

- Estcourt, Edgar E., & Payne, John Orlebar. *The English Catholic Nonjurors of 1715, being a summary of the Register of their Estates.* Burns & Oates, [1885].

N. Enclosure Awards and Maps
Open field farming was common in medieval England, but it had almost completely disappeared by the nineteenth century. Most enclosures took place in the eighteenth century. Farming ceased to be a communal endeavour and became an individualistic enterprise. Common rights were extinguished. Farmers were freed from collective decision making. Incumbents exchanged controversial tithes for valuable land. The poor lost their common rights, and were forced into wage dependency and pauperisation.

Enclosure probably began in the medieval period, and at first was illegal. Many cases of illegal enclosure are recorded in TNA classes

C 43/2, 3, & 28, C 47/7/2, C 205 and elsewhere. For some Midland cases, see:

- Leadam, I.S., ed. *Domesday of Inclosures, 1517–1518*. 2 vols. Longmans Green & Co., 1897.

From the sixteenth century, landowners brought collusive cases in Chancery and other central courts in order to obtain decrees authorising enclosures. These are not necessarily easy to find; many of the records in TNA are indexed by surname only. A search of its Discovery catalogue for known landowners may identify relevant documents. Other evidence is found in Chancery decree rolls (classes C 78 and C 79). See:

- Beresford, M.W. 'The Decree Rolls of Chancery as a Source for Economic History, 1547–c. 1700', *Economic History Review*, New Series, 32(1), 1979, p.1–10.

The enclosure process in the eighteenth century is documented primarily by private acts of parliament, by enclosure maps, and by awards. Enclosure bills passing through the House of Commons can be traced in the *House of Commons Journal* (**www.british-history.ac.uk/ search/series/commons-jrnl**). Commissioners' records, including draft enclosure plans, are sometimes found in local record offices. Records relating to Crown lands are in TNA CRES 2 and 6. From the late eighteenth century, much information may be found in local newspapers (p.26–7).

The area enclosed might be the whole parish, but it could equally be merely one of the manors within that parish, or even just the waste. Enclosure awards list landowners, recording lands held before enclosure, and its redivision between proprietors. Some was allocated for public purposes, such as poor relief, or the use of the highway surveyor. Maps show the areas allocated to each proprietor. Awards and maps also indicate field names, land use, roads and footpaths, glebe lands, and the endowments of charities and schools.

Two copies of enclosure awards and maps were usually made. One set was deposited in the parish chest, the other with the Clerk of the Peace, or enrolled in deeds registries where these existed. Occasionally, local landowners had extra copies made for their own personal use. All copies are likely to be in local record offices. After 1845, when separate acts of parliament ceased to be necessary, further copies were made for the Board of Agriculture. These are now in TNA MAF 1.

Sources are briefly described by:

- Enclosure Awards and Maps
  www.nationalarchives.gov.uk/help-with-your-research/research-guides/enclosure-awards

For detailed guides, see:

- Hollowell, Steven. *Enclosure Records for Historians*. Phillimore, 2000.
- Chapman, J. *A Guide to Parliamentary Enclosures in Wales*. University of Wales Press, 1992.

Useful articles include:

- Wittering, Shirley. 'This Enclosure Business: Enclosure Commissioners' Papers as an Historical Source', *Local Historian*, 34(2), 2004, p.104–12.
- Turner, M., & Wray, T. 'A survey of sources for Parliamentary Enclosure: the *House of Commons Journal* and Commissioners' working papers', *Archives*, 19(85), 1991, p.257–88.

Enclosure acts and awards are listed by:

- Tate, W.E. *Domesday of English Enclosure Acts and Awards,* ed. M.E. Turner. University of Reading Library, 1978.

For enclosure maps see:

- Kain, Roger J.P., Chapman, John, & Oliver, Richard. *The Enclosure Maps of England and Wales, 1595–1918*. Cambridge University Press, 2004. This includes an online database at **http://enclosuremaps.data-archive.ac.uk**

A number of collections of digitised enclosure maps are available online. See, for example:

- New Landscapes: Enclosure in Berkshire
  www.berkshireenclosure.org.uk/research_reading_map.asp

O. Tithe Records

Tithing in England perverted the Biblical principle of giving one-tenth of one's income to God. The principle was widely accepted in the medieval period but became increasingly controversial after the Reformation, especially when tithing rights were sold to laymen, and especially amongst nonconformists.

The great majority of tithe payers were landowners and occupiers. They are frequently listed amongst parish records. Clergy occasionally kept tithing books recording details of tithes received. There were many tithe disputes, originally heard in the ecclesiastical courts, but, by the eighteenth century, mostly in the Westminster courts.

Disputes signalled increasing dissatisfaction with the system, leading ultimately to the Tithe Commutation Act 1836. It replaced tithes in kind with a rent charge based on the price of corn. It did not apply to parishes already enclosed, where tithes had already been commuted. Elsewhere, tithe surveys, maps and files were compiled. Surveys and maps list all landowners and tenants in the area covered, giving details of the lands they owned and occupied. The tithe files include associated letters and papers.

For more detail of the post-1836 documentation, see p.133–5. A brief introduction to earlier records is provided by:

- Evans, Nesta. 'Tithe Books as a Source for the Local Historian', *Local Historian*, 14(1), 1980, p.24–7.

P. Records of the Central Courts
The records of the central courts include much information on land ownership. They not only dealt with much litigation but also enrolled innumerable deeds. Some enrolments have already been mentioned. Others were made by the King's Remembrancer (E 159 and E 368), and on the *Coram Regis* rolls 1656–1805 (listed in KB 173/1–2). Enrolments can also be found amongst the archives of the Palatine jurisdictions of Chester, Lancaster and Durham.

Q. Probate Records
Probate records (p.49–51) are important, not only for family history and demography but also for the study of wealth and land ownership. Inventories and accounts are particularly important in this context. Inventories listed the goods of the deceased, with valuations. Accounts showed how assets had been distributed. Appraisers' valuations are also sometimes recorded in probate court act books.

Between *c.*1500 and *c.*1750, probate inventories provide much more reliable information on the wealth of individuals than tax lists, although the two sources should be compared. Inventories can also be used to trace increasing wealth over time.

Generally, inventories do not record freehold land, since that was outside of ecclesiastical jurisdiction. Very occasionally, such land is mentioned in wills, but generally it descended directly to the eldest son. Leases, however, are recorded. So is all other personalia, such as furniture, clothes, livestock and crops.

Inventories are also important sources for the study of lending and borrowing, since they record debts owing to the deceased. Debts owed by the deceased, and paid by their administrators, are recorded in probate accounts.

The legal background is important in studying inventories. It determined which goods were included and which excluded. Perishable foods, for example, were usually excluded, unless kept for sale. Grass in the field was also excluded, but hay was included. Inclusions and exclusions are noted by:

- Cox, Nancy & Jeff. 'Probate Inventories: The Legal Background', *Local Historian* 16(3 & 4), 1984, p.133–45 & 217–28.

For valuations, see:

- Cox, Nancy & Jeff. 'Valuations in Probate Inventories', *Local Historian*, 16(8), 1985 p.467–77; 17(2), 1986, p.85–100.

For probate accounts, an extensive introduction is included in:

- Spufford, Peter, et al. *Index to the Probate Accounts of England and Wales.* 2 vols. Index Library 112–13. British Record Society, 1999.

See also *Short Guides 2* and:

- Gittings, Clare. 'Probate Accounts: A Neglected Source', *Local Historian*, 21(2), 1991, p.51–9.

Inventories have been extensively studied. See:

- Overton, Mark. *A Bibliography of British Probate Inventories.* University of Newcastle upon Tyne, Dept. of Geography, 1983.

After 1858, estate valuations are printed in the probate calendars at **www.ancestry.co.uk/search/collections/1904**. Nineteenth-century death duty registers (TNA IR 26; indexes in IR 27), which provide abstracts of wills, also record valuations. These registers reveal what actually happened to estates, rather than what wills specified should happen, and provide information about legatees and next of kin. Annotations in them could be made several decades after initial entries. See:

- Owens, Alastair, & Green, David R. 'The Final Reckoning: Using Death Duty Records to research Wealth Holding in Nineteenth-Century England and Wales', *Archives*, 38(126), 2013, p.1–21.

For details of digitised registers, see:

- Death Duties, 1796–1903
  www.nationalarchives.gov.uk/help-with-your-research/research-guides/death-duties-1796–1903

R. Fire Insurance Records
Fire insurance began in the late seventeenth century. From the early eighteenth century, registers record names and occupations of policy holders, with details of the properties insured, including valuations (and sometimes tenants' names). For the records of many national companies, see:

- London Metropolitan Archives Research Guide: Fire Insurance Records **https://search.lma.gov.uk** (click 'Research Guides' and scroll down to 'Insurance policies')

Local record offices sometimes hold records of local agents and provincial companies. Policies are frequently found amongst estate and parish records. See:

- Wulcko, Laurance. 'Fire Insurance Policies as a Source of Local History', *Local Historian*, 9(1), 1970, p.3–8.

For more detailed guides, see:

- Hawkings, David T. *Fire Insurance Records for Family and Local Historians.* Francis Boutle Publishers, 2003.
- Cockerell, H.A.L., & Green, Edwin. *The British Insurance Business, 1547–1970: An Introduction and Guide to Historical Records in the United Kingdom.* Heinemann Educational, 1976.

Examples of policies from Devon are printed in:

- Chapman, Stanley D., ed. *The Devon Cloth Industry in the Eighteenth Century: Sun Fire Office Inventories of Merchants' and Manufacturers' Property, 1726–1770.* Devon & Cornwall Record Society new series 23. 1978.

S. Debtors and Bankruptcy
Debtors could be imprisoned at the instance of their creditors. Cases were originally heard in the sheriff's county court. These had become moribund by the eighteenth century, and some towns acquired new Courts of Request. For one of these, see:

- Finn, Margot. 'Debt and Credit in Bath's Court of Requests, 1829–39', *Urban History*, 21(2), 1994, p.211–23.

Debtors who were traders could escape the threat of imprisonment by applying to be made bankrupt. Bankruptcy proceedings are recorded in the *London Gazette* (p.28), and reported by newspapers (p.26–7). See:

- Bankrupts and Insolvent Debtors
  www.nationalarchives.gov.uk/help-with-your-research/research-guides/bankrupts-insolvent-debtors

In 1846, a new structure of county courts for the recovery of debts was created.[10] The few surviving records are in local record offices. Judgements were recorded in the central Registry of County Court Judgements, now TNA, class LCO 28. They were also frequently reported in newspapers. Imprisonment for debt ended in 1869.

A detailed guide to insolvents is provided by:

- Blake, Paul. *Tracing your Insolvent Ancestors: A Guide for Family & Local Historians.* Pen & Sword, 2019.

T. Local Authority Smallholdings
The Small Holdings Act 1892 endeavoured to encourage peasant proprietorship of smallholdings. An act of 1907 required county councils to establish smallholdings and allotments committees, and to purchase land which could be let. Their minutes and other papers are amongst county council archives in local record offices.

U. The Poor
Much of this chapter has been devoted to records relating to the relatively well-off. However, the poor were equally important; in fact, there were many more of them. Their poverty deserves attention.

The poor became a serious problem to government in the late sixteenth century. The population, and poverty, was growing. The monasteries, which had provided poor relief, had been dissolved. The Elizabethan poor law acts of 1598 and 1601 provided a legal framework for the parish to provide relief, but it is a mistake to assume that every parish immediately took on the responsibility. That probably did not happen in England until the late seventeenth century, and later in Wales.

Most records relating to the poor were created by the administration of the poor law, discussed in Chapter 4. Pauper apprentices will be discussed later, p.153–5. Other sources include medieval manorial records (p.59–62), hearth tax exemption certificates (p.45), and the records of both local and central courts. For London in the late nineteenth century, see:

- Charles Booth's London: Poverty Maps and Police Notebooks
  https://booth.lse.ac.uk

Here, attention will focus on the Parliamentary papers, which include a huge amount of relevant information. Many are listed by Powell (p.25). Only a few can be mentioned here. *The Abstracts of the returns made by the Overseers of the Poor,* published in 1777, provides information on the poor, poor rates and workhouses. Similar publications followed in subsequent years. The *Abridgement of the Abstract of ... Returns Relative to ... maintenance of Poor,* published in 1818, provides much information on workhouses, charities and friendly societies. Expenditure on the poor is reported, parish by parish, in the *Report from the Select Committee on Poor Rate Returns* published in 1821, but covering the previous eight years. A number of subsequent reports take the series up to 1835. See:

- Wittering, Shirley. 'How Reliable are the Government Poor Law Returns?', *Local Historian* 30(3), 2000, p.160–65.

The many volumes of the 1834 Poor Law Commissioners' report contain reports on numerous specific places. For an overall guide to poor law sources see:

- Poverty and the Poor Laws
  www.nationalarchives.gov.uk/help-with-your-research/research-guides/poverty-poor-laws

Charities were also important to the poor. Many provided almshouses, schools, apprenticeship premiums, health care, and similar benefactions. The Edwardian chantry certificates (p.191) list mid-sixteenth-century charities. Inquisitions conducted by the Commission for Charitable Uses under acts of 1597 and 1601 are in TNA C 93, depositions in C 91, and confirmations and exonerations of decrees in C 90. Incumbents gave details of parochial charities in their replies to bishops' queries (p.71 and p.73). Parish and borough officers frequently served as trustees of local charities, kept their records in parish chests, and memorialised them by erecting charity boards in their churches. Other charity records can be found amongst solicitors' archives.

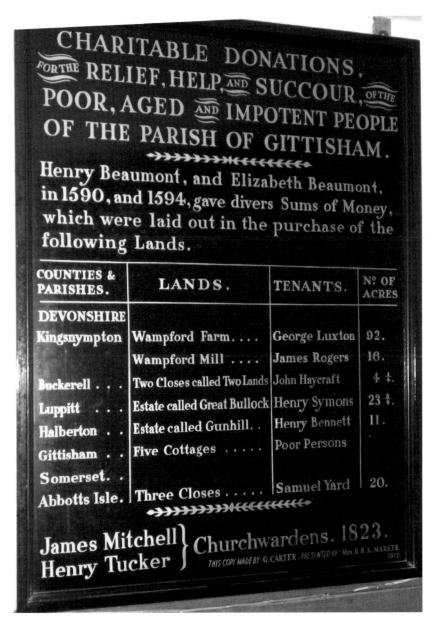

CHARITABLE DONATIONS, FORTHE RELIEF, HELP AND SUCCOUR, OFTHE POOR, AGED AND IMPOTENT PEOPLE OF THE PARISH OF GITTISHAM.

Henry Beaumont, and Elizabeth Beaumont, in 1590, and 1594, gave divers Sums of Money, which were laid out in the purchase of the following Lands.

COUNTIES & PARISHES.	LANDS.	TENANTS.	N° OF ACRES
DEVONSHIRE			
Kingsnympton	Wampford Farm. . . .	George Luxton	92.
	Wampford Mill	James Rogers	16.
Buckerell . . .	Two Closes called Two Lands	John Haycraft	4 ¼.
Luppitt . . .	Estate called Great Bullock	Henry Symons	23 ¼.
Halberton . .	Estate called Gunhill. .	Henry Bennett	11.
Gittisham . .	Five Cottages	Poor Persons	
Somerset. .			
Abbotts Isle.	Three Closes	Samuel Yard	20.

James Mitchell } Churchwardens. 1823.
Henry Tucker }   THIS COPY MADE BY :G.CARTER . PRESENTED BY : Mrs.R.R.A.MARKER 1972

Many churches have boards like this one at Gittisham (Devon), recording charitable donations.

Early nineteenth-century Parliamentary papers include many reports by the Charity Commission, drawn on heavily by the *VCH*. The papers forming the basis for these reports are in TNA CHAR 2. In 1853, the permanent Charity Commission **www.gov.uk/government/organisations/charity-commission** was established and began its register of charities. A *Digest of Endowed Charities* was published in the Parliamentary papers irregularly between 1867 and 1913. Charity Commission records are discussed by:

- Grady, Kevin. 'The records of the Charity Commissions: a source for urban history', *Urban History Yearbook*, 9, 1982, p.31–7.

Friendly societies provided mutual help to the poor. They were closely connected with trade unions (see p.156–7), and offered the poor insurance against sickness, old age, widowhood, unemployment, funerals and other eventualities. Most were local, although a few had a wider remit. They were given statutory protection in 1793. In 1846, the Registrar of Friendly Societies was established. His collection of rules made under the 1793 act are now in TNA FS classes, which also include correspondence with societies and lists of the members of dissolved societies. Quarter Sessions also retained some records. Society membership peaked in the mid-nineteenth century, but rapidly declined after the inauguration of the welfare state in 1911. Local societies' records rarely survive, but their activities were sometimes mentioned in newspapers.

For the history of friendly societies, see:

- Cordery, Simon. *British Friendly Societies, 1750–1914*. Palgrave Macmillan, 2003.

Their records are described by:

- Neave, David. 'The Local Records of Affiliated Friendly Societies', *Local Historian*, 16(3), 1984, p.161–7.
- Fisk, Audrey. 'Friendly Societies and Local History', *Local Historian*, 29(2), 1999, p.91–101.
- Logan, Roger. *An Introduction to … Friendly Society Records*. Federation of Family History Societies, 2000.

A wider remit is taken by:

- Weinbren, Daniel. *Tracing your Freemason, Friendly Society & Trade Union Ancestors: A Guide for Family Historians*. Pen & Sword, 2019.

Records from 755 societies are edited in:

- Morley, Shaun, ed. *Oxfordshire Friendly Societies 1750–1918*. Oxfordshire Record Society 68. 2011.

Chapter 6

AGRICULTURAL HISTORY:
THE SOURCES

Who farmed the land? How many farms were there? What was their area? Was land held in common or in severalty? What was the size of the agricultural labour force? Were labourers the children of farmers, or were they paid servants? What happened at enclosure? What arable

Medieval ploughing with oxen.

crops were grown? How many animals were kept? What implements were used? What changes in the rural economy occurred during the period under investigation?

Agricultural history cannot be separated from the history of land ownership. Many of these questions can be answered, at least in part, from the documents discussed in the previous chapter. Some of these, together with other sources, will be discussed here for the light they throw on agricultural practices. Useful guides to sources include:

- Hilton, R.H. 'The Content and Sources of English Agrarian History before 1500', *Agricultural History Review* 3(1), 1955, p.3–19.
- Thirsk, Joan. 'The Content and Sources of English Agrarian History after 1500', *Agricultural History Review* 3(2), 1955, p.66–79.
- Grigg, D.B. 'The Changing Agricultural Geography of England: A Commentary on the Sources Available for the Reconstruction of the Agricultural Geography of England', *Transactions of the Institute of British Geographers*, 41, 1967, p.73–96.

For a more detailed guide, see:

- Edwards, Peter. *Farming: Sources for Local Historians.* B.T. Batsford, 1991.

Detailed definitions of terms are provided by:

- Adams, I.H. *Agrarian Landscape Terms: A Glossary for Historical Geography.* Institute of British Geographers special publication 9. 1976.

Many farming records are held by:

- The Museum of English Rural Life
  https://merl.reading.ac.uk

Some records which throw light on agriculture have already been discussed. *Domesday Book* (p.42–3) is important for eleventh-century agricultural statistics. Tax records may be useful; for example, the 1341 inquisition of the ninths (p.114) provides useful information on matters such as flooding, dearth of seeds, and land which had ceased to be cultivated. Other records require fuller discussion here.

A. Deeds and Leases

These are primarily concerned with the ownership and occupation of land (discussed in Chapter 5). They may also provide other information. Sometimes they describe property in great detail, naming fields, identifying crops growing in them, mentioning trees, gardens, orchards, rights of way, water courses and water meadows. Some deeds include maps and are invaluable sources for the study of field systems.

Landowners expected their tenants to practise good husbandry. Most leases required tenants to maintain buildings, gates and fences. Some sought to maintain the fertility of the soil, forbade over-cropping, and protected trees. From the mid-eighteenth century, the crops to be grown, and the rotations to be followed, were increasingly specified. Local conditions underlay these clauses. On the Wiltshire chalk, for example, tenants were required to fold sheep at night on their own arable land, in order to preserve the fertility of the soil.

B. Manorial Records

Manorial records (p.59–62) provide much interesting information on agricultural practices. Customs regulated the usage of manorial resources such as open fields, water, pounds, roads, waste, the shore line, quarries, etc. Crop rotations might be specified. Stints determined how many sheep and cattle could be pastured by each tenant. Tenants might be required to undertake harvest work, to serve as carriers, and/or to give their lord a 'capon' (a chicken) at Christmas. On death, a heriot such as the 'best beast' might be taken from their heirs.

The way in which manorial customs worked out is reflected in manorial court rolls. These might record, for example, encroachments on the commons and waste, the blocking of water courses, overstocking of pastures, the breaking down of hedges and gates, the state of the common fields, the need to repair buildings, and the erection of new buildings.

Medieval ministers' accounts detail the lord's income from rents and sales of produce, and his expenses in building repairs, purchase of implements and labour. They include much information on corn, livestock and other produce.

C. Farm Accounts

Farm accounts kept by estate stewards on the home farms of large estates from the eighteenth century onwards provide much useful information. They are likely to record crops grown, acreages, livestock kept, and the labour force. They may enable profits to be determined. For a discussion of the usefulness of these accounts, see:

- Colyer, R.J. 'The Use of Estate Home Farm Accounts as Sources for Nineteenth Century Agricultural History', *Local Historian* 11(7), 1975, p.406–13.
- Jones, E.L., & Collins, E.J.T. 'The Collection and Analysis of Farm Record Books', *Journal of the Society of Archivists*, 3(2), 1965, p.86–9.

D. Toll Books

Markets and fairs are discussed below (p.146). Their clerks kept toll books recording sales of cattle, sheep, horses and other agricultural produce. Where these survive, they make it possible to study fluctuations in market activity, catchment areas, prices, and the people involved.

E. Probate Records

Probate records, (p.146), are important for agricultural history. Inventories in particular describe agricultural activities in great detail. They are one of the few sources which enable us to count and value cattle, sheep, horses, pigs, poultry – and even bees. Crops in the field and barn are valued. Acreages of growing crops may be given. Farm buildings, such as stables and barns, are mentioned. Dung carts, ploughs, harness, shovels, harrows and other agricultural equipment are itemised. The contents of the dairy, the cheese loft and the malt house are described. Cheese and malt intended for sale, together with equipment such as cheese presses and malt mills, are valued. Inventories enable us to build up a picture of agricultural activity. In doing so, the months when inventories were compiled must be noted. Crops will not be in the barn before harvest time; wool will not be shorn before the spring.

F. Commissioners of Sewers

Flood defences in areas such as the Fens, Sedgemoor and the coastal lowlands were organised by Commissioners of Sewers. The word 'sewer', historically, refers to artificial water courses. Commissioners surveyed embankments, ditches and water courses, and kept them in repair. Local landowners paid sewer rates, or undertook repairs themselves. Commissioners' records include minutes of orders and proceedings, presentments (sometimes referred to as 'verdicts'), reports, plans, accounts, rate books and a variety of other documents. In the areas where commissions operated, their records are invaluable sources for land drainage and land use. Records are generally in local record offices. TNA holds commissions and other records, in various classes. An introduction is provided by:

- Owen, A.E.B. 'Land Drainage Authorities and Their Records', *Journal of the Society of Archivists* 2(9), 1964, p.417–23.

Some Commissioners' records have been published. See, for example:

- Kirkus, A. Mary, & Owen, A.E.B., eds. *The Records of the Commissioners of Sewers in the Parts of Holland, 1547–1603*. Lincoln Record Society 54, 63, & 71. 1959–77.

G. Glebe Terriers

Glebe terriers (p.67) describe and locate each piece of glebe land, perhaps indicating whether it was arable or pasture, in open field strips or enclosed. They mention buildings on the glebe, including the parsonage house. Tithing customs are outlined. They shed much light on agricultural practices, and are likely to reflect any changes in them.

H. Enclosure Awards and Maps

Enclosure had a dramatic impact on the landscape. Its records have already been described (p.119–21). The wide open spaces of open fields and unenclosed commons ceased to exist; they were divided up amongst proprietors, and fenced. Roads were built, water courses redirected, sand and gravel pits for the highway surveyor designated, other public spaces defined. Enclosure landscape is easily recognised by its straight hedges and rectangular fields, with ruler-straight roads driven through to give access. Farmers were given a whole new world to make their mark on. The process of creating the new landscape deserves exploration. The maps which describe that (proposed) landscape are worthy of examination in their own right. Awards and maps provide information on the size of farms, and on land use.

Strips at Forrabury (Cornwall) in what is still an open field.

H. Tithe Surveys and Maps

The Tithe Apportionment Act 1836 aimed to replace the uncertainty of tithe payments with a rent charge based on the price of wheat, barley and oats. It resulted in the production of large-scale surveys and maps of parishes. Tithe maps show land use, field boundaries, woods, roads, streams and sometimes (not always) buildings. Each plot of land is numbered to facilitate comparison with surveys.

Tithe surveys (or apportionments) describe areas covered, and record acreages devoted to grass, arable and other uses. Schedules list the owners and occupiers of each piece of land. They identify houses, barns, stables, gardens and other buildings, as well as fields and plantations. Fields are usually named and described as arable, meadow, wood, or pasture. Sometimes the actual crops being grown are stated.

We have already seen the value of these documents for land ownership and occupation (p.121–2). They are obviously also important for the history of land use and agriculture. Their uses are briefly discussed by:

- Workman, Roy. 'Analysing a Tithe Map in Depth', *Local Historian*, 14(5), 1981, p.262–9.

Tithe maps and apportionments were deposited in the parish chest and the diocesan registry (both now in local record offices), and with the Tithe Commission (apportionments now in TNA, class IR 29; maps in IR 30). In theory, the three copies of maps should be identical. In practice, minor differences crept in. For a full listing, see:

- Kain, Roger J.P. & Oliver, Richard R. *The Tithe Maps of England and Wales: A Cartographic Analysis and County-by-County Catalogue.* Cambridge University Press, 1995.

TNA's tithe records cannot physically be produced but are digitised at **www. thegenealogist.co.uk/tithe**. A number of county collections of digitised maps are also available, for example, Cheshire **https://maps.cheshireeast. gov.uk/tithemaps** and Devon **www.devon.gov.uk/historicenvironment/ tithe-map**. For Wales, visit **https://places.library.wales**.

For a detailed discussion, see:

- Kain, Roger J.P., & Prince, Hugh C. *Tithe Surveys for Historians.* Phillimore, 2000.

Briefer guides include:

- Evans, Eric J. *Tithes: Maps, Apportionments and the 1836 Act: A Guide for Local Historians.* 3rd edition. British Association for Local History, 1997.
- Beech, Geraldine, & Mitchell, Rose. *Maps for Family and Local History: The Records of the Tithe, Valuation Office, and National Farm Surveys of England and Wales, 1836–1943.* 2nd edition. National Archives, 2004.

I. Tithe Files

Many documents associated with tithe surveys are held in TNA's tithe files, class IR 18. These have been heavily weeded but may still include replies to a printed questionnaire regarding areas of arable, pasture and common, courses of rotation, soil, livestock, and related matters. Sometimes there are reports by Assistant Commissioners, minutes of meetings, and notes on individual farms. Similar documents may be found in local record offices. For a useful discussion, see:

- Cox, E.A., & Dittmer, B.R. 'Tithe Surveys of the Mid-Nineteenth Century', *Agricultural History Review* 13, 1965, p.1–16.

For a detailed analysis, see:

- Kain, Roger J. P. *An Atlas and Index of the Tithe Files of Mid-Nineteenth-Century England and Wales.* Cambridge University Press, 1986.

J. Agricultural Statistics

During the Napoleonic wars, there were several attempts to collect agricultural information. In the mid-1790s, a 'crop census' was taken on an ad hoc basis through magistrates and high constables. Some returns were qualitative rather than statistical. In 1800, printed forms were used in an attempt to obtain more consistent data. Clergy were asked a series of questions on the availability of arable produce. Some provided more information than asked. Many thought that farmers were reluctant to give full details of their crops in case it led to increased taxation or greater tithes. Crop returns from both these surveys are in HO 42/53–5; they are digitised on TNA's website.

Another important survey was taken in 1801, at the same time as the first population census. The government feared that food shortages could ensue from the fact that many agricultural labourers were fighting Napoleon. It wished to discover how many people were left to cultivate the land, and how many needed the food produced. Clergy were asked to state how many acres were being cultivated, and what crops they produced. Returns are in TNA, class HO 67. They show the number of acres devoted to wheat, barley, oats, potatoes, peas, beans, turnips, rape, rye and other crops. Again, statistics may be understated due to farmers' fears of increased taxation and tithes. There are c.4,500 returns for England and almost 550 for Wales. Nottinghamshire is the only county totally unrepresented. For a complete transcript of returns, with an analysis, see:

- *Home Office: Acreage Returns (HO 67): List and Analysis.* 4 vols. List and Index Society, vols 189, 190, 195 & 196. 1982–3.

See also:

- Minchinton, W.E. 'Agricultural Returns and the Government during the Napoleonic Wars', *Agricultural History Review* 1, 1953, p 29–43.

In 1859, more detailed statistics were collected in eleven counties. These are reported in the *Reports by Poor Law Inspectors on Agricultural Statistics (England)*, in the 1854 Parliamentary papers. Annual summaries of agricultural statistics for parishes were collected from 1866; these are in TNA, class MAF 68. These record numbers of livestock and arable acreages, but should be used cautiously, as the basis of collection changed from year to year. Questions asked frequently changed. So did the size of holdings making returns. And not all returns were made. See:

- Coppock, J.T. 'The Agricultural Returns as a Source for Local History', *Amateur Historian* 4(2), 1958–9, p. 49–55.

Agricultural statistics were regularly published from 1866 as *Agricultural Statistics England and Wales*, in the Parliamentary papers series. For details of these and other TNA statistical sources, see:

- Agricultural Statistics of England and Wales
  www.nationalarchives.gov.uk/help-with-your-research/research-guides/agricultural-statistics-england-wales

Other miscellaneous agricultural statistics are in TNA MAF 7. Registers recording corn prices in various markets from 1791 until 1959 are in MAF 10. A guide to *Agricultural Statistics*, primarily covering the nineteenth and twentieth centuries, is available at **https://merl.reading.ac.uk/merl-collections/search-and-browse/databases**.

For details of waste land and commons in 1873, see the Parliamentary paper:

- *Return of the acreage of: 1. Waste lands subject to Rights of Common. 2. Common field lands in each parish of England and Wales in which the tithes have been commuted … 1874.*

K. Valuation Office Survey
This early twentieth-century survey (p.98–9) throws some light on agriculture. Its descriptions of farm buildings and acreages, for example, have been used to assess the size of dairy farms in Cheshire. See:

- Anderton, Paul. 'Milking the Sources: Cheshire Dairy Farming and the Field Notebooks of the 1910 Domesday Survey', *Local Historian* 34(1), 2004, p.2–16.

L. Forestry Commission
The Forestry Commission was established in 1919. Files on individual forests from the nineteenth century onwards are in TNA, class F 3–13. Woodland censuses of 1924, 1938 and 1944 are in F22, with maps in F 23 and 30.

M. Agricultural Executive Committees and the National Farm Survey
During both world wars, county agricultural executive committees promoted the production of food. First World War minutes are in local record offices; those for the Second World War in TNA MAF 80. In both wars, these committees conducted surveys of agricultural resources. Few returns from the 1916 survey survive. Farmers' returns from the 1941–3 National Farm Survey are in TNA, MAF 32. Maps identifying their farms are in MAF 73. The returns provide the names of farmers, details of farm sizes, labour employed, the standard of farming, the availability of water and electricity, and numbers of animals, together with comments of inspectors. See Beech and Mitchell (p.134), and:

- National Farm Survey of England and Wales 1941–1943 **www.nationalarchives.gov.uk/help-with-your-research/research-guides/national-farm-survey-england-wales-1941–1943**
- Finnegan, Oliver, Glover, Catherine, and Hoyle, Richard W., eds., *British Farm Surveys, 1941 to 1943: Reports and Statistical Analysis*. List and Index Society, 354. 2014.

For a detailed study, see:

- Short, Brian; Watkins, Charles; Foot, William; & Kinsman, Phil. *The National Farm Survey 1941–1943: State Surveillance and the Countryside in England and Wales in the Second World War*. CABI Publishing, 1999.

N. Women's Land Army
The Women's Land Army recruited land girls as agricultural labour whilst men were serving in the armed forces. It operated between 1917 and 1919, and between 1939 and 1950. Minutes of county committees

A Land Army girl ploughing during the Second World War.

and other records are in TNA MAF 59. Personal details of individual land girls are recorded on microfilmed index cards in MAF 421. See:

• Women's Land Army
  www.nationalarchives.gov.uk/help-with-your-research/research-guides/womens-land-army

O. Sale Catalogues

From the late eighteenth century onwards (and especially *c*.1880–1930), estate agents published detailed sale catalogues when estates and farms were being sold. These give detailed descriptions of the properties, sometimes listing sitting tenants. Some were annotated by auctioneers with purchasers' details. They can frequently be found amongst estate agents' and solicitors' archives deposited in local record offices and libraries. For similar information, consult newspaper advertisements and reports. See:

• Hillier, Richard. 'Auction Catalogues and Notices: Their Value for the Local Historian', *Local Historian*, 13(3), 1978, p.131–9.
• Perry, Peter. 'A Source for Agricultural History: Newspaper Advertisements', *Local Historian*, 9(7), 1970–1, p.334–7.

- Dalton, Roger. 'Farm Sale Advertisements as a Data Source in Historical Agricultural Study: Possibilities and Limitations', *Local Historian* 28(01), 1998, p.36–49.

P. Agricultural Societies

Numerous agricultural societies were founded between 1750 and 1850; there were at least 400 in 1840. Newspapers reported on their activities, and especially on their shows, which continue to this day. Their archives have sometimes been deposited in record offices. For the Royal Bath and West of England Society, visit **www.bathandwestsociety.com/about-us/library-archives**. Reading's Museum of English Rural Life **https://merl.reading.ac.uk** holds the archives of the Royal Agricultural Society. Societies' purposes, members, and influence, all deserve investigation.

Q. Published Sources

Some important sources for the history of agriculture in the late eighteenth and early nineteenth centuries are printed. Many authors described agricultural practices in particular counties and regions. Perhaps the best known of these publications are the *General Views* sponsored by the Board of Agriculture between 1793 and 1821. For most counties there are two reports, the first published in the early 1790s, the second between *c.*1805 and 1817. The latter were abstracted in:

- Marshall, William. *A Review of the Reports of the Board of Agriculture*. 5 vols. Facsimile reprint. David & Charles, 1969. Originally published 1808–17.

See also:

- *Communications to the Board of Agriculture on Subjects Relative to the Husbandry and Internal Improvement of the Country*. 2nd edition. 6 vols. G. & W. Nicol, 1802–10.

The *General Views* and many other early books on agriculture, have been digitised at:

- LIBRAL – the Library of Rural and Agricultural Literature **www.bahs.org.uk/LIBRAL**

A number of early journals may also usefully be consulted. Amongst others, these include:

- *Annals of Agriculture*. 1784–1815.
- *Farmer's Magazine*. 1800–1825.

- *Journal of the Royal Agricultural Society*. 1839–. Between 1845 and 1869 this includes a number of prize essays dealing with the agriculture of particular counties.

For the twentieth century, the reports of the Land Utilisation Survey, conducted in the 1930s, and published by county, sometimes include good surveys of agricultural history. Visit **https://en.wikipedia.org/wiki/Land_Utilisation_Survey_of_Britain**.

R. Parliamentary Papers
Many Parliamentary papers of the nineteenth century provide information on the state of agriculture. These include (amongst many others):

- *Report of the Select Committee on Agricultural Distress* 1820.
- *Report[s] of the Select Committee on Petitions Complaining of the Depressed State of the Agriculture of the U.K.* 1821–1822.
- *Report of the Select Committee into the Present State of Agriculture and of Persons Employed in Agriculture in the U.K.* 1833.
- *First, Second and Third Reports of the Select Committee on the State of Agriculture and the Causes of Distress.* 1836.
- *Report of the Select Committee of the House of Lords on the State of Agriculture.* 1837.
- *Report of the Select Committee on Agricultural Customs.* 1847–8 and 1866.
- *Report of the Royal Commission on Children and Women in Agriculture.* 1867–70.
- *Report of the Royal Commission on Depressed Conditions of the Agricultural Interests.* 1881–2.
- *First and Second Reports of the Royal Commission on the Agricultural Depression.* 1894–7.

S. The Census
The concerns which motivated the 1801 census have already been discussed. Census schedules of later years (p.36–41) also contain useful information for agricultural historians. From 1851, enumerators were required to state the number of acres each farmer farmed, and how many people were employed. The intention was to enumerate each farm's resources in terms of labour and acreages. However, the casual and part-time work of women and children was omitted, and the distinction between farmers and market gardeners is difficult to draw. Nevertheless, census data, 1841–1921, should be sufficient to gain at least a broad picture of how many local people were working in agriculture, and in what capacity.

T. British Agricultural History Society

Agricultural history is catered for by the British Agricultural History Society **www.bahs.org.uk/index.html**. Its website has much useful information for the local historian, including an online forum, notes on work in progress, the LIBRAL database mentioned above (p.139), and digitised copies of the Society's journal, *Agricultural History Review*, 1959–, which frequently covers local history topics.

Chapter 7

TRADE, INDUSTRY AND OCCUPATIONS: THE SOURCES

The study of trade, industry and occupations is an important task for local historians. What was the occupational structure of your community? Were specific industries, such as mining, fishing or transport, dominant? How was trade conducted, and with whom? Were communication links good?

A. Communications

Trade depends on communications. Improvements to rivers and roads, and the building of canals, railways and docks, had profound impacts. Road improvements enabled the Post Office to introduce fast mail coaches from 1784. A century later, railways enabled ordinary people to commute many miles to work, to have seaside holidays, and to obtain employment as railwaymen. They put canals, drovers, stage coaches and turnpike trusts out of business, and enabled fresh produce from Devon to be sold in London. At the end of the nineteenth century, the telephone enabled instant communication over long distances.

Roads were originally the responsibility of manors. The Highways Act, 1555, made parishes responsible for them. It created the office of highway surveyor, who organised 'statutory labour' (frequently a cash payment) of parishioners on them. Parish and Quarter Sessions records mention surveyors' activities. Subsequently, turnpike trusts and improvement commissioners took control of many roads. Bridges were erected and repaired by a variety of governmental and non-governmental institutions.

Since the seventeenth century, improvements to communications have frequently been made under the authority of private acts of parliament (p.26). Builders of canals, railways and docks sought Parliamentary approval before construction commenced, and submitted thousands of plans of proposed developments. Accompanying books of reference name affected property owners. See:

- Cobb, H.S. 'Parliamentary Records relating to Internal Navigation', *Archives* 9(42), 1969–70, p.73–9.

These plans are in the Parliamentary Archives **www.parliament.uk/business/publications/parliamentary-archives.** Copies are with Quarter Sessions records, and sometimes amongst estate records. Canal and railway company archives (TNA RAIL classes) include related information.

Many Parliamentary papers discuss these developments. The 1818 and 1840 reports on highways and turnpike roads, the 1836 report on turnpike trusts and tolls, reports of 1883 and 1906 on canals, the 1839 report on railways, and the decennial railway returns from 1841 onwards, should all be consulted. So should the Beeching report, *The Reshaping of British Railways* (HMSO, 1963), which initiated a drastic culling of the rail network. The Buchanan report, *Traffic in Towns: A Study of the Long-Term Problems of Traffic in Urban Areas* (HMSO, 1963), shaped the subsequent development of the urban landscape.

The earliest turnpike trust was created in 1663. Trusts maintained important routes. Records include order books and minutes, maps, plans of toll-houses, regulations regarding traffic, accounts and vouchers, details of toll charges, mortgage books, and perhaps even the day books of toll-house keepers, recording daily traffic. Surviving records are in local record offices. Newspapers reported on trust affairs, and carried advertisements relating to tolls and the leasing of tollbars. For a brief guide, see *Short Guides 1*.

Responsibility for roads was gradually transferred from parishes and turnpike trusts to highway boards under acts of 1835, 1862 and 1878. Board minutes, accounts, reports, rate books, letters and other papers may survive. For the winding up of turnpike trusts see TNA, class MH 28. Responsibility for main roads was transferred to Quarter Sessions in 1878, and to county councils in 1888. Urban and rural district councils assumed responsibility for minor roads in 1894. Their highway committee records are important sources. Changes in routes were notified in the *London Gazette*. For trunk roads and motorway construction, see TNA classes MT 39, 121, 128, 128 and 139.

For road passenger transport, see:

- Mulley, Corinne, & Higginson, Martin, eds. *Companion to Road Passenger Transport History: Public Road Passenger Transport in Great Britain, Ireland, the Channel Islands and the Isle of Man*. Roads and Road Transport History Association, 2013.

The internal combustion engine revolutionised road transport in the early twentieth century. Vehicle registration records provide details of owners, the vehicles themselves, and their uses. See:

- Riden, Philip. *How to Trace the History of your Car: A Guide to Motor Vehicle Registration Records in the British Isles.* 2nd edition. Merton Priory Press, 1998.
- Duckham, Baron F. 'Early Motor Vehicle Licence Records and the Local Historian', *Local Historian*, 17(6), 1987, p.351–7.

A few vehicle registration records are in print. See, for example:

- Hicks, Ian, ed. *Early Motor Vehicle Registrations in Wiltshire, 1903–1914.* Wiltshire Record Society, 58. 2006.

Motoring offences increased rapidly in the early twentieth century, and can be traced in court and watch committee records (see Chapter 4). Accidents also increased and were frequently reported in newspapers.

Bus and tram networks also developed in the early twentieth century. Those under local authority control can be traced in the minutes of the appropriate committees. Business records of private undertakings are scarce, but much can be learnt from trade directories and newspapers. See:

- Newman, A.G. 'Bus Services and Local History', *Local Historian*, 13(5), 1979, p.280–90.

Many road haulage companies were nationalised under the Transport Act 1947. Their records are in TNA, class AN 68.

For useful guidance on sources for canal and railway history, with a bibliography of recent publications, see:

- Railway and Canal Historical Society
  https://rchs.org.uk

See also:

- Ottley, George. *A Bibliography of British Railway History.* 2nd edition. HMSO 1983. Supplements 1988 and 1998.

Many sources are digitised at:

- Railways Archive
  www.railwaysarchive.co.uk

Pre-nationalisation records of most canal and railway companies are in TNA's RAIL classes, which also include official reports on new lines and alterations, and on accidents. For details, see:

- Railways
  www.nationalarchives.gov.uk/help-with-your-research/research-guides/railways
- Edwards, Cliff. *Railway Records: A Guide to Sources.* Public Record Office, 2001.

Encyclopedic treatment is provided by:

- Simmons, Jack, & Biddle, Gordon, eds. *The Oxford Companion to British Railway History from 1603 to the 1990s.* Oxford University Press, 1997.

Twentieth-century official correspondence and papers concerning inland waterways is in TNA, MT 52. For docks and harbours, see MT 10 and MT 19. Many archives relating to canals are held by:

- Canal and River Trust
  https://collections.canalrivertrust.org.uk/home

See also:

- Institution of Civil Engineers: ICE Library
  www.ice.org.uk/knowledge-and-resources/ice-library

For a gazetteer of waterways in 1904, see:

- De Salis, H.R. *Bradshaw's Canals and Navigable Rivers of England and Wales.* David and Charles, 1969. Originally published 1904.

Registers of barge owners 1794–9, and from 1877, were kept by Clerks of the Peace. For canal maps, see:

- Canal Maps Archive: Historic Maps and Plans of Inland Waterways
  www.canalmaps.net

Secondary works on canals are reviewed by:

- Baldwin, Mark. *Canal Books: A Guide to the Literature of the Waterways.* M.M. Baldwin, 1984.

The invention of the telephone at the end of the nineteenth century led to the construction of telephone wires, kiosks and exchanges. BT Archives **www.bt.com/about/bt/our-history/bt-archives** holds much documentation, including photographs and phone directories.

B. Markets and Fairs

Much medieval trade was conducted at markets and fairs. A few were held by prescriptive right, but most relied on charters granted by the Crown, and enrolled on the Charter Rolls (TNA C 53), the Patent Rolls (TNA C 66), or the Close Rolls (TNA C 54). See:

* Markets and Fairs
  www.nationalarchives.gov.uk/help-with-your-research/research-guides/markets-fairs

Specific markets and fairs may be identified in:

* Gazetteer of Markets and Fairs in England and Wales To 1516
  https://archives.history.ac.uk/gazetteer/gazweb2.html
  This includes a detailed discussion of the rolls mentioned above, together with information on a wide range of other sources.

Borough records and newspapers provide more recent information. The *Report of the Royal Commission on Market Rights and Tolls* (1888–91) includes lists for 1792 and 1888 taken from *Owen's New Book of Fairs*, and much other historical information. Trade directories usually give details. Correspondence relating to cattle markets, 1892–1964 is in TNA, MAF 91.

C. Trade Directories

The principal objective of trade directories was the promotion of commerce. They listed potential customers for tradesmen and shopkeepers, and enabled customers to identify businesses which could supply their needs. They also listed magistrates, clergy of all denominations, and local officials such as parish clerks and turnpike staff. Information on such matters as population, postal services, markets and fairs, carriers, transport, inns and public buildings was provided. Directories frequently included potted histories of the towns and villages they covered.

The earliest directory was published in 1677, but most date from the nineteenth and twentieth centuries. A number of specialist directory publishers, such as Pigots, Kelly's, William White, and others, published directories covering many counties. Many towns had local directory publishers; in Exeter, for example, Besley's regularly published directories between 1828 and the mid-twentieth century.

Directories were partial and selective. Only heads of households were listed. Servants, labourers, and women, were mostly excluded. There was frequently a substantial time lag between the collection of information and publication. Early directories are generally less informative than later ones. The information in them should always be compared with other directories, and with sources such as the census, newspapers and rate books.

Despite these caveats, trade directories do record information not available elsewhere, especially before the census. Town directories are generally more comprehensive than those covering rural areas. They provide both street lists and separate lists of particular trades. Both may otherwise be unrecorded. There may be no other source for carriers' timetables.

Advertisements provide useful information. Directories may be used to study topics as diverse as retailing, the coaching trade and religious history. If a run of directories is available, they offer the possibility of a study over an extended period.

Surviving directories are listed by:

- Norton, Jane E. *Guide to the National and Provincial Directories of England and Wales, Excluding London, Published before 1856.* Royal Historical Society Guides and Handbooks, 5. 1950.
- Shaw, Gareth, & Tipper, Alison. *British Directories: A Bibliography and Guide to Directories Published in England and Wales (1850–1950) and Scotland (1773–1950).* Leicester University Press, 1988. Includes a detailed history.
- Atkins, P.J. *The Directories of London 1677–1977.* Mansell, 1990.

For 689 digitised directories, visit:

- Historical Directories of England and Wales
  http://specialcollections.le.ac.uk/digital/collection/p16445coll4

Uses of directories are discussed by:

- Shaw, Gareth, ed. *Directing the Past: Directories and the Local Historian.* British Association for Local History, 2003.

In 1880, the first telephone directory was published. BT Archives substantial collection of 'British Phone Books, 1880–1984' has been digitised by Ancestry **www.ancestry.co.uk/search/collections/1025**. They perform a similar function to trade directories, and frequently include advertisements.

D. Port Books and Shipping

Many coastal communities conducted seaborne trade. Overseas' trade is best studied through TNA's port books, 1565–1798, class E 190. They record names of ships, masters and merchants, giving details of the goods carried, ships' destinations, and duties imposed. Related material, c.1272–1830, is in TNA, class E 122. See *Short Guides 1*. See also:

- Merchant Trade Records: Port Books 1565–1799
  www.nationalarchives.gov.uk/help-with-your-research/research-guides/merchant-trade-records-port-books-1565–1799

An extensive general introduction is included in:

- Hinton, R.W.K., ed. *The Port Books of Boston, 1601–1640*. Lincoln Record Society, 50. 1956.

For digitised port books, see:

- Devon Port Books
  https://search.findmypast.co.uk/search-world-Records/devon-port-books

Correspondence relating to particular ports is in CUST 50–101, reports in CUST 32, and establishment (staffing) records in CUST 19. Imports and exports 1873–99 of individual ports are recorded in CUST 23–26.

Further information on overseas trade can be found in records of the Vice Admiralty Courts (TNA HCA classes), in harbour authority, Quarter Sessions and borough records. For early customs accounts, see:

- Kowaleski, Maryanne, ed. *Local Customs Accounts of the Port of Exeter, 1266–1321*. Devon & Cornwall Record Society New Series 36. 1993.

Local record offices hold shipping registers from 1786. Some are in TNA, BT 107–11 and BT 145. For crew lists, see:

- Crew lists and agreements and log books of merchant ships after 1861
  www.nationalarchives.gov.uk/help-with-your-research/research-guides/crew-lists-agreements-log-books-merchant-ships-1861

Some crew lists are available online at **www.findmypast.co.uk** and **www.ancestry.co.uk**.

E. Work

Occupational information of a general nature is found in many sources discussed elsewhere in this book, for example parish registers, poll books, eighteenth-century militia lists, census returns, probate records, apprenticeship indentures and trade directories. Deeds occasionally mention workshops where trades and crafts were carried on. Most sources mentioned in this book provide some information. For a general discussion of early occupational sources, see:

- Glennie, Paul. *Distinguishing Men's Trades: Occupational Sources and Debates for Pre-Census England*. Historical Geography Research Series, 25. 1990.

Many sources are specific to particular occupations. Trade guilds, trade unions and professional organisations recorded the names of members involved in the occupations they catered for, and perhaps published journals. Government, both secular and ecclesiastical, licensed particular occupations such as alehouse keepers, medics and schoolmasters, and conducted investigations into practices in specific occupations. Biographical dictionaries relating to specific occupations should be explored for the biographies of local people. Records of individual businesses contain much information on the industries in which they engaged.

It is important to recognise that many people had two or even three occupations. Even the upper tier of local society could take casual work: schoolmasters, for example, frequently also served as parish clerks or census enumerators. Most rural dwellers – and some urban ones – kept a pig or a cow, even if they were blacksmiths, carpenters, or even clergymen. Their wives and daughters spun wool. Husbandmen with insufficient land to earn a living served as casual labourers. It is frequently difficult for the researcher to discern whether craft activities or agricultural labour were more important sources of income to particular individuals.

The life cycle is also important. In the nineteenth century, children increasingly went to school. The census identifies them as 'scholars'. Many became living-in servants[1] or apprentices, before marrying and perhaps setting up their own businesses, and/or undertaking casual labour. In times of war, many young people were pressed for the army or navy. At the end of their working lives, many became paupers.

F. The Census

The most important general source for studying nineteenth-century occupations are the returns of the decennial census from 1801 (p.36–41).

Early census enumerators were only expected to provide statistics. In 1801, one of the six questions asked 'what number of persons in your parish, township or place, are chiefly employed in agriculture; how many in trade, manufactures, or handicraft, and how many are not comprised in any of the preceding classes?' This was revised in 1811 to relate to families rather than individuals. In 1831, much more detailed questions were asked. The answers were analysed in the published census reports; see **www.histpop.org**.

From 1841, household returns record not just the occupations of householders and family members, but also the presence of servants, employees and lodgers. Until 1891, each individual's 'rank, profession, or occupation' had to be recorded. The mingling of status and occupational information does not make it easy to disentangle the two, even at the lowest level. Some agricultural labourers, for example, insisted on being described as shepherds or horsemen.

Male employment is fairly accurately recorded in the census. Difficulties may, however arise. The occupational descriptors used are occasionally ambiguous or obscure. For example, a bank manager might be working in finance, or equally could be superintending at a pit head. A tingle maker made small tacks.

A more serious difficulty is the use of terms such as 'labourer', which do not indicate the relevant industry. Such occupations were, however, sometimes qualified by noting the materials worked on, such as metals or animals. This was intended to ensure the data was entered in the correct occupational categories when compiling statistics.

Even more problematic is the fact that census schedules make no provision for the fact that many men had multiple or seasonal occupations. The dates when they were taken (mostly between 30 March and 5 April) were chosen to avoid the summer months, when substantial sections of the population were mobile, perhaps hop-picking, fishing, or getting in the harvest. Schedules completely ignore summer seasonal work.

The recording of women's work is similarly problematic. Many housewives worked on a casual, seasonal, or part-time basis, whilst also engaged in housework. Their domestic work was ignored. Frequently, so was their part-time work. However, from 1851, farmers' wives and their daughters, as well as their sons, were recorded as such; the assumption was that they worked on the farm.

Children too found casual or part-time work, usually ignored in the census. Many were described as 'scholars'. That reflects the presence of a school. But when education became compulsory, some parents wished to hide the fact that their children worked.

Institutional schedules were used for large institutions (from 1851, those with over 200 inmates). These are useful for studying the staffing of prisons, hospitals, workhouses and other establishments. Census returns for soldiers in barracks, and Royal Navy seamen living in shore establishments, enable the local historian to evaluate the impact they had on local communities.

Occupational statistics in census reports are based on occupational classifications which changed between censuses. They must therefore be studied in conjunction with the occupational tables for each census,[2] and are not directly comparable decade by decade.

G. Parish Registers

Parish registers (p.33–4) are worth checking for occupational information. Some clergy included much detail, including occupations; others provided minimal information, not mentioning occupations. Hardwicke's 1753 act made no provision for the entry of occupations in marriage registers, although occasionally[3] that information was provided. Rose's 1812 act required the occupations of the fathers of baptised children, and of the deceased, to be recorded.

The introduction of civil registration in 1837 did not immediately affect the compilation of baptism and burial registers. Ecclesiastical marriage registers, however, did change. Clergy were required to state the occupations of both bride and groom.

The absence of occupational information from marriage registers between 1753 and 1837 can be partially compensated for by marriage licensing records. In order to marry, couples were required to either have banns called in church, or to obtain a marriage licence. Licensing records (p.34) record the status or occupations of the parties.

H. Probate Records

Most testators stated their occupation or status in their wills (p.49–51). Tools of their trades and trade goods were frequently bequeathed. Fathers frequently left funds to pay for sons to be apprenticed. Occupations may be stated on the administration bonds of intestates.

Probate inventories and accounts also record the status or occupation of the deceased. This information is not necessarily identical with accompanying wills. Wills give the opinions of testators; inventories the opinions of neighbours who valued the goods. Inventories and accounts frequently list the anvils of the blacksmith, the fabric and groceries of the mercer, the nets and boats of fishermen, the vats and barrels of the innkeeper, the shoes of the cobbler.

I. Apprenticeship Records

Apprenticeship was the means by which boys (and, to a much lesser extent, girls) were trained in specific trades and occupations. In the twelfth century, the custom of London was for boys in their early teens, represented by their parents, to contract with a master to learn his trade over a period of seven years. The boy would live with his master, who usually (not always) provided food, clothing, housing and medical care. The master obtained a valuable but cheap assistant. The contract was recorded in indentures – one for the master, one for the apprentice, and, from the sixteenth century, one for any charity prepared to pay premiums to apprentice poor children. Premiums were not originally demanded, but became frequent by c.1700.

Indentures specified the respective duties of master and apprentice. The duties of the latter were harsh: he had to be totally obedient to his master, could not marry, and was expected to seek permission even to leave his master's house. The wording of apprenticeship indentures remained almost identical – apart from the switch from Latin to English – from c.1200 until c.1900. The 'custom of London' gradually spread from London to provincial cities, and was adopted as the national norm by the 1563 Statute of Apprentices.

Apprenticeship indenture of William Spencer, 1766.

Private indentures frequently do not survive. They were private documents. Town clerks sometimes kept them when former apprentices applied for the freedom of the borough (p.82). Charities retained their counterparts. Indentures are occasionally found in solicitor's collections, amongst estate, business and private papers, and in parish chests, which effectively served as safe deposit boxes.

The loss of indentures does not necessarily mean the loss of information in them. Boroughs and guilds registered indentures. Registers provided the evidence needed when apprentices completed their terms and became eligible to apply for freedom. Some borough registers have been published. See, for example:

• Barlow, Jill, ed. *A Calendar of the Registers of Apprentices of the City of Gloucester, 1595–1700.* Gloucestershire record series 14. Bristol & Gloucestershire Archaeological Society, 2001.

London's apprentices came from far afield; most English local historians will find useful information by searching:

• London Apprenticeship Abstracts 1442–1850
  https://search.findmypast.co.uk/search-world-records/london-apprenticeship-abstracts-1442–1850

Between 1710 and 1804, stamp duty was imposed on apprenticeship premiums. Registers in TNA, class IR1, digitised by **www.ancestry.co.uk**, record the names and places of residence of masters and apprentices who paid the duty. Original registers, without indexes, are digitised at **www.nationalarchives.gov.uk/help-with-your-research/research-guides/free-online-records-digital-microfilm**.

Other apprenticeship records can be found amongst the records of guilds and charities. In Exeter, for example, the Weavers' Company ran the Crispin Charity, which regularly paid premiums for the sons of its poorer members.[4] The overseers of St Stephens, Exeter, administered the charity of Lady Pembroke, using it to fund poor apprentices who might otherwise have claimed poor relief. In London, the Foundling Hospital apprenticed its children, and assisted them financially when they completed their terms – on condition that masters provided them with testimonials. These testimonials, now in London Metropolitan Archives, are valuable sources of evidence.

Pauper apprenticeship was a perversion of traditional apprenticeship. Its aim, theoretically, was to provide pauper children with a trade by which they could earn their own living. In practice, many overseers sought to rid their parish of an immediate drain on the rates. Pauper apprentices

Elizabeth Brownrigg flogging her charity apprentice, 1776.

were placed with a master at age 10 or 11 – sometimes much earlier. Originally, they served until age 24 for boys, and 21 for girls. Parents and apprentices had no say in choosing masters; that was decided by the overseers, supervised by Justices of the Peace. Some overseers required householders to take apprentices in rotation, or by lot, and imposed a fine if they refused to do so. Others sought masters in other parishes; the apprentice would in due course become 'settled' in his new parish, and cease to be eligible for poor relief in his home parish. A premium might be paid in such cases. Masters chosen by overseers were not always suitable; the trades they taught did not always offer long-term prospects. In rural areas, boys were frequently apprenticed to 'husbandry', and girls to 'housewifery', both of which could merely mean drudgery. Many late eighteenth-century apprentices were sent to work in the new industrial factories of northern England, and totally removed from their home environment. But some did learn skills useful in later life.

Pauper apprentice indentures differ from those of both private and charity indentures. The parties are the master and the overseers. Apprentices' names, and sometimes their ages, are recorded, with the 'trades' to be learnt. But parents were not named. The latter omission resulted in the introduction of pauper apprenticeship registers in 1812. These were compiled from the indentures, but also recorded the names of parents. Vestry minutes, overseers' accounts, and other parish records (p.62–7) also provide evidence on apprenticeships, as can the records of Quarter Sessions and borough courts which heard disputes.

After 1834, the Poor Law Commissioners were dubious about apprenticing paupers. The concept did not fit the principle of 'less eligibility' on which the new poor law was based (p.84–5). Nevertheless, some pauper apprenticeship continued; documentation may be found amongst Poor Law Union records.

For a detailed guide, see:

- Raymond, Stuart A. *My Ancestor was an Apprentice: How Can I Find Out More About Him?* Society of Genealogists, 2010.

J. Licensing and Governmental Regulation

Government has always sought to regulate or license a variety of different trades and occupations. The purpose of licensing has varied. Religion motivated the granting of licences to schoolmasters, midwives and surgeons in the seventeenth century. The perceived need to control the lower orders meant that alehouse keepers and badgers (pedlars) had to obtain licences. In the eighteenth century, the protection of game required licensed gamekeepers. In recent centuries, the maintenance of professional standards has led to the regulation of medical professionals, teachers and others. More recently, local councils have acquired powers to regulate a wide range of occupations, such as grocers, taxi drivers, tram drivers and conductors, and pharmacists.

Various records of governmental regulation survive. Licensing records enable public house histories to be traced, and the links between local licensees to be examined.[5] Registers of badgers' licences, kept between 1563 and 1772, provide an important source for retailing history.[6] Gamekeepers and their masters are recorded in registers of gamekeepers' deputations from 1710 and in Game Duty registers between 1784 and 1807. Printers' notices record printers between 1799 and 1869. Registers of cow keepers, barge owners, grocers, pedlars, chimney sweeps, hackney cabs, slaughter houses, dentists, pharmacists and nursing homes have all been kept by Clerks of the Peace at various times.

Diocesan registrars also kept much occupational information. Midwives and, to a lesser extent, surgeons, played important roles in local society; they can be traced in the licences issued to them by bishops. That also applies to early schoolmasters, and to curates. For curates' licences and other clergy records, see p.159–60.

K. Tax Records
Tax lists (p.44–6 & 113–17) occasionally include occupational information, especially the poll taxes of 1377 and 1379. The Shop Tax returns of 1785–9, in TNA, class E182, do not record the names of taxpayers but could be used to identify the presence of retailers in particular communities. See:

- Mitchell, Ian. 'Pitt's Shop Tax in the History of Retailing', *Local Historian* 14(6), 1981, p.348–51.

L. Trade Guilds, Professional Associations, and Trade Unions
Governmental regulation has frequently run hand in hand with the activities of trade guilds and professional bodies. Trade guilds (livery companies in London) became important in medieval times, and continued to exercise influence over trade and commerce until the nineteenth century. They were associations of urban tradesmen formed to regulate particular trades, and usually controlled admission to that trade through the apprenticeship system. They frequently had monopoly powers within their borough boundaries, and could prevent non-members from trading. They provided for their members in sickness and old age, and for their children. Some ran schools. In some cities, freemen of the guild were also freemen of the city.

Guilds were the forerunners of the many professional and trade associations established in the nineteenth century. Many of them published journals and yearbooks, which included lists of officers, and/or members, biographical notices, obituaries, death notices, advertisements, and much professional/trade related information. The *Library Association Record*, for example, regularly listed new appointments, and noted the opening of new libraries. A trawl through such publications may be rewarding.

Trade unions also sprang into existence in the nineteenth century. Their role included not only protecting members' rights at work but also insuring them against sickness and death. Many had branches throughout the country. Records include minutes, lists of members, financial records and other documents. Many published journals, which may include local information.

The Modern Records Centre at the University of Warwick **https://warwick.ac.uk/services/library/mrc** holds many of their archives; its website includes a useful guide to 'Local Labour Records'. See also TNA's guide to 'Labour history records held by other archives' **www.nationalarchives.gov.uk/help-with-your-research/research-guides/labour-history-records-held-by-other-archives**. TNA itself holds annual returns of registered trade unions, 1872–1958, which may include branch information, in class FS 12.

For useful guides, see:

- Southall, Humphrey; Gilbert, David; & Bryce, Carol. *Nineteenth Century Trade Union Records: An Introduction and Select Guide.* Historical Geography Research Series 27. 1994.
- Crail, Mark. *Tracing your Labour Movement Ancestors: A Guide for Family Historians.* Pen & Sword, 2009.

M. Business Records

Business archives include minutes, accounts, letters, personnel records, and a wide range of other documents. Many are in local record offices or with university archives. For example, Reading University holds the archives of Huntley and Palmers, the biscuit manufacturers. Other business archives remain with the firms concerned, or with their successors. For example, Post Office archives (including details of all postmen, and of local post offices) are now held by the Postal Museum **www.postalmuseum.org**. For the records of over 250 banks, visit NatWest Heritage Hub **www.natwestgroup. com/heritage.html**.

From 1844, joint-stock companies were registered with the Board of Trade. Registers 1844–60 are in TNA, BT 41. Files for dissolved companies, 1855–1955 are in BT 31. For later information about registered businesses, visit **www.gov.uk/get-information-about-a-company**. In-depth guides include:

- Orbell, John. *Tracing the History of a Business.* Phillimore, 2009.
- Armstrong, John, & Jones, Stephanie. *Business Documents, Their Origin, Sources and Uses in Historical Research.* Mansell, 1987.

Useful reference works include:

- Orbell, John, et al. *Business History Explorer: Bibliography of UK Business and Industrial History.* Business Archives, Council, 2012. Also available by subscription at **www.businesshistoryexplorer.co.uk**.
- Jeremy, D.J., ed. *Dictionary of Business Biography: A Biographical Dictionary of Business Leaders Active in Britain in the period 1860–1980.* 5 vols. Butterworths, 1984.

Major collections of business archives are listed in:

- Company and Business History Records held by other Archives **www.nationalarchives.gov.uk/help-with-your-research/research-guides/business-history-records-held-by-other-archives**

For banking archives, which can provide much information on customers, see:

- Orbell, John, & Turton, Alison. *British Banking: A Guide to Historical Records.* Routledge, 2001.

The journal *Business Archives* **www.businessarchivesjournals.org.uk** includes much information on source materials.

N. Manorial Records
Wind- and water-mills, forges, quarries, mines, and similar plant are frequently mentioned in manorial court rolls and surveys. Individuals' occupations (including dual occupations) may also be revealed.

O. Tithe Maps and Apportionments
These documents (p.133–4) record land use. That includes, of course, industrial use. Workshops, factories, dye-houses, bakeries, boiler houses, and a whole range of other industrial uses may be recorded.

P. Accidents and Safety
Reports on accidents in mining, shipping, transport and other industries, are scattered throughout the archives of TNA, and in the Parliamentary papers. Safety in factories and mines was a prime concern of the Factories Inspectorate, whose entry books 1836–1921 are in HO 87, and which regularly published reports in the Parliamentary papers' series.

Q. Specific Occupations
There are numerous sources for specific occupations. They cannot be treated comprehensively here. For published sources, see:

- Raymond, Stuart A. *Occupational Sources for Genealogists.* 2nd edition. Federation of Family History Societies, 1996.

See also:

- Raymond, Stuart A. *Trades and Professions: The Family Historian's Guide.* Family History Partnership, 2011.

A variety of sources, and/or guides to sources, are available for clergymen, gypsies, lawyers, medical professionals and publicans. These ought to be of particular interest to local historians, and are discussed below.

Clergymen

The Anglican clergy[7] have always been at the centre of village life. It is therefore particularly important to identify them. Since 1835, *Crockford's Clerical Directory* (online from 1968 at **www.crockford.org.uk**) has regularly published details of clergymen.

Many of the diocesan sources required to identify earlier clergy – bishops' registers, ordination papers, subscription books recording clergy oaths, licensing books recording licences to preach, curates and other appointments, *liber cleri* or call books listing those required to attend visitations, and various other records – have been brought together in a new database, which enables the viewer to see the succession of clergymen for the period 1540–1835 at a glance. See:

- CCEd: Clergy of the Church of England database
  http://theclergydatabase.org.uk

This only covers diocesan sources systematically. A variety of other clergy records are also available. For the medieval period, bishops' registers (p.70) must be consulted. Manorial court rolls occasionally record payments to lords for boys who entered the church. Crown presentations to livings may be found on the Patent Rolls (p.104–105). The *Calendar of Entries in Papal Registers Relating to Great Britain and Ireland* (19 vols. to date. HMSO, 1893–), covering 1198 to 1513, and the *Calendar of Petitions to the Pope, 1342–1419* (Eyre & Spottiswoode, 1896) record dispensations for pluralities and illegitimacy, petitions for preferment and non-residence, and various other matters. They are digitised at **www.british-history.ac.uk**. Wills (p.49–57), and some of the records discussed below, may also help, as may the records of clerical subsidies. The latter are either in TNA class E 179, or amongst diocesan archives. They began in 1253, and were regularised by direction of Pope Nicholas IV in 1288–91; see:

- Taxatio Database
  www.dhi.ac.uk/taxatio

For abbots and priors, see:

- Knowles, David, Brooke, C.N.L., & London, Vera C.M. *The Heads of Religious Houses, England and Wales.* 3 vols. Cambridge University Press, 1971.

From the sixteenth century, clergy can be traced in parish registers and other parish records, and in the Oxbridge listings of alumni (p.55). The CCEd has not necessarily tapped even all diocesan records; for example, letters testimonial and benefice papers recording personal details of clergy may not be included.

During the Civil War and Interregnum, many Church of England clergy were ejected. For details, see:

• Matthews, A.G., ed. *Walker Revised, being a Revision of John Walker's Sufferings of the Clergy during the Grand Rebellion. 1642–1660.* Clarendon Press, 1948. This is separately indexed in Surman, C.E. *A.G. Matthew's Walker Revised: Supplementary Index of Intruders and Others.* Occasional Paper 2. Dr Williams' Library, 1956.

Many ejections were carried out under the aegis of the Parliamentary Committee for Plundered Ministers (subsequently the Committee for Scandalous Ministers), whose records are in TNA class SP 22–3. The papers of local committees are held by the British Library, the Bodleian Library, and possibly elsewhere. An example of their records is provided by:

• Hart, Graham, ed. *The Cambridgeshire Committee for Scandalous Ministers 1644–45.* Cambridgeshire Records Society, 24. 2017.

For dissenting clergy ejected after the Restoration, see p.195.

Between 1544 and 1912, bishops returned certificates of institution to the Exchequer; these are in TNA E 331. After the Reformation, clergy were required to pay first fruits and tenths to the Exchequer; these are recorded in classes E 331–48. This revenue was diverted to the augmentation of clergy incomes in 1704; the records of Queen Anne's Bounty can be found in QAB 1, and also amongst the records of the Office of First Fruits and Tenths. There are many Bounty records in Lambeth Palace Library. Bounty correspondence with local clergy is frequently met with amongst parish records.

For a detailed guide to sources for clergy, see:

• Towey, Peter. *My Ancestor was an Anglican Clergyman.* Society of Genealogists Enterprises, 2007.

Gypsies

Gypsies were regularly seen in most English villages, and local historians should pay more attention to them. Their itinerant status, however, means that they are particularly difficult to trace. For a basic introduction, see:

• Floate, Sharon Sillers. *My Ancestors were Gypsies.* 2nd edition. Society of Genealogists, 2005.

Lawyers

The numerous legal documents that local historians use were written by local attorneys, whose names are frequently written on them. The registers of the Inns of Court identify legal students. See:

- Foster, Joseph. *The Register of Admissions to Grays Inn, 1521–1889, Together with the Register of Marriages in Grays Inn Chapel, 1695–1754.* Hansard Publishing Union, 1889.
- Inner Temple Admissions Database **www.innertemplearchives.org.uk**
- Baildon, William. *Records of the Honourable Society of Lincolns Inn: Admissions 1420–1893, and Chapel Registers.* 2 vols. Lincolns Inn, 1896. Digitised at **www.lincolnsinn.org.uk/library-archives/digitised-records**
- Sturgess, H.A.C. *Register of Admissions to the Honourable Society of the Middle Temple from the Fifteenth Century to the Year 1944.* Butterworth & Co., 1949. Available online at **www.middletemple.org.uk/archive/ archive-information-access/sources-resources/digitised-records/ registers-admissions**

A comprehensive guide is provided by:

- Brooks, Brian, & Herber, Mark. *My Ancestor was a Lawyer.* Society of Genealogists Enterprises, 2006.

Medical Profession

Who cared for the health of local people? Qualified doctors are likely to be mentioned in the trade directories mentioned above (p.146–7). They are also listed in the *Medical Directory* (from 1846) and in the *Medical Register* (from 1859).

In earlier centuries, surgeons and midwives needed bishops' licences to practise. See:

- Willis, Arthur J. 'Bishop's Licences to Laymen in the Eighteenth and Nineteenth Centuries', *Amateur Historian* 5(1), 1961, p.2–6.

For licences issued by the Archbishop of Canterbury, see:

- Lambeth Palace Library Research Guide: Medical Licences Issued by the Archbishop of Canterbury 1535–1775 **www.lambethpalacelibrary.org/sites/default/files/Medical_ Licences.pdf**

Higgs discusses many other sources:

- Higgs, Michelle. *Tracing your Medical Ancestors: A Guide for Family Historians*. Pen & Sword, 2011.

Publicans

Alehouse keepers, innkeepers, victuallers, call them what you will, played important local roles. Licences were issued annually by Quarter Sessions, petty sessions, and (from 1729) special Brewster Sessions. Registers were mandated in 1753. For a detailed listing of licensing records, see:

- Gibson, Jeremy. *Victuallers' Licences: Records for Family and Local Historians*. 3rd edition. Family History Partnership, 2009.

For detailed guidance, see:

- How to Research the History of a Pub
  www.pubhistorysociety.co.uk/research.html
- Fowler, Simon. *Researching Brewery and Publican Ancestors*. Family History Partnership, 2009.
- Jennings, Paul. 'Liquor Licensing and the Local Historian', *Local Historian* 39(1), 2009, p.24–37; 40(2), 2010, 136–50, & 41(2), 2011, p.121–36. These articles cover 'the 1904 Licensing Act and its administration', 'inns and alehouses 1753–1828', and 'The Victorian Public House'.

In 1686, and again in 1756, surveys of accommodation for men and horses in inns were conducted on behalf of the army. Returns are in TNA WO 30/48–50. See:

- Hartley, John S. 'The 1756 War Office Survey: A Source for Local Historian', *Local Historian* 46(1), 2016, p.47–56.

Chapter 8

LIVING CONDITIONS, EDUCATION, RELIGION AND LEISURE: THE SOURCES

Human beings need shelter, clothing, food, good health, and space to work, relax and sleep. The ways in which these were provided in the past are important concerns for local historians. Many sources provide information about housing, furniture, clothing and diet.

Religion is also well documented. It permeated all life, including both education and leisure activities. The word 'holiday' derives from the 'holy days' in the church's calendar. Until the nineteenth century, most schools operated under ecclesiastical auspices. The state's gradual assumption of educational responsibility can be traced in TNA sources, and amongst local government records.

A. Daily Life: Diaries

Since the Reformation, many people have kept diaries. Pepys' diary **www.pepysdiary.com** is a classic. Clerical diaries such as those of Ralph Josselin **wwwe.lib.cam.ac.uk/earls_colne/diary/index.htm**, Parson Woodforde[1] and Rev Kilvert **www.thekilvertsociety.org.uk** are full of information on parish life. Diaries are Invaluable sources for daily life in particular places. For lists, see:

- Matthews, W. *British Diaries: An Annotated Bibliography of British Diaries written between 1442 and 1942.* University of California Press, 1950.
- Havlice, P.P. *And so to Bed: A Bibliography of Diaries Published in English.* Scarecrow Press, 1987.
- Batts, J.S. *British Manuscript Diaries of the Nineteenth Century: An annotated Listing.* Centaur Press, 1976.

B. Housing

How many houses were there in your locality? When were they built? Who built them? Do they show local characteristics? How many rooms did they have? Who lived in them – owners or tenants? Were mortgages easily available? When were amenities such as running water and electric lighting installed? For these and other questions, see:

- Crosby, Alan G. 'Housing and the Local Historian: Some Approaches and Research Agendas', *Local Historian*, 47(3 & 4), 2017, p.227–43 & 298–316.

For the various sources available to answer these questions, see:

- Bailey, Keith. 'The Richest Crop that it Can Grow: Building Estate Development in Nineteenth Century Battersea', *Local Historian*, 47(1), 2017, p.13–28.

There is a huge variety of houses in England. Until the seventeenth century, only the houses of the gentry and aristocracy were built to last. Most medieval houses were impermanent and have disappeared. Many were replaced with 'vernacular' buildings, built by local builders using traditional methods during the sixteenth and seventeenth centuries. The nineteenth-century middle classes built their architect-designed villas in the leafy suburbs. In the twentieth century the lower middle classes bought semi-detached houses in the less leafy suburbs. For the working classes, there were nineteenth century 'back to backs', followed, in the twentieth century by council houses.

The task of recording standing buildings is outside of the scope of this book. Some general guidance may, however, be useful. See:

- Barley, M.W. *The English Farmhouse and Cottage*. Routledge and Kegan Paul, 1961.
- Brunskill, R.W. *Illustrated Handbook of Vernacular Architecture*. 3rd edition. Faber & Faber, 1987.
- Mercer, Eric. *English Vernacular Houses: Study of Traditional Farmhouses and Cottages*. HMSO, 1975.

The Vernacular Architecture Group **www.vag.org.uk** provides much useful information, including its digitised *Bibliography of Vernacular Architecture*. The Royal Institute of British Architects **www.architecture. com/about/riba-library-and-collections** holds an extensive collection of archival sources:

- Mace, Angela. *The Royal Institute of British Architects: A Guide to its Archive and History*. Mansell Publishing, 1986.

Ownership of houses can be traced by consulting the sources listed in Chapter 5. *VCH* general volumes describe local architecture. The inventories of the former Royal Commission on Ancient and Historical Monuments (now English Heritage) provide authoritative reports on historic buildings in specific places. Nickolaus Pevsner's *Buildings of England* series should be consulted for surviving gentry houses. Sale catalogues (p.138–9) provide detailed descriptions of houses, buildings and fields, together with maps. Newspaper advertisements are useful too. Many buildings, especially churches, were drawn in the early nineteenth century by John Buckler, whose drawings can be found in repositories such as the British Library, Oxford's Bodleian Library, the Wiltshire Museum in Devizes, and the William Salt Library in Stafford. Most institutions discussed in Chapter 2 hold relevant photographic and print collections. The Historic England Archive **https://historicengland. org.uk/images-books/archive** has 12 million+ photographs, including over a million available online.

For listings and detailed descriptions of surviving historic houses and other monument, see:

- Heritage Gateway
  www.heritagegateway.org.uk

Surviving houses provide a clue as to what once existed. Archaeological evidence is also important, but is outside of the scope of this book. The sources discussed below frequently provide detailed descriptions of particular houses. See (p.124) for fire insurance policies, which record features of houses relevant to insurers, and for manorial court rolls (p.59–62), which frequently mention houses.

Deeds
Deeds (p.101–13) can be used to trace the development of housing and urban sprawl. They frequently record houses and other buildings 'newly erected', or possessing 'workshops' where some craft was practised. For the nineteenth and twentieth centuries, deeds used in conjunction with building plan registers, wills and rate books can be very informative about the building process. See:

- Green, Geoffrey. 'Title Deeds: a Key to Local Housing Markets', *Urban History Yearbook*, 7, 1980, p.84–91.

Builders' Records and Tradesmen's Bills
The papers of individual builders and craftsmen infrequently survive. Those which do may include contracts, correspondence, accounts and other records. Banks sometimes preserved customers' accounts (p.158), which may also provide information. Bills of builders, glaziers, plumbers, plasterers and others are frequently found amongst estate and family papers, telling us who worked on particular developments, and where materials came from. For medieval documents, see:

• Salzman, L.F. *Building in England down to 1540: A Documentary History.* Corrected ed. Clarendon Press, 1967.

Architectural Journals
The Builder, and other architectural journals, reported on many new buildings throughout the country. For indexes, see:

• *The Builder; The Building News*: An Index to *The Builder* (London) and to *The Building News* (London)
  www.builderindex.org

Building Society and Freehold Land Society Records
Building societies enabled their members to pool funds and build their own homes. By 1900, they were a major source of housing finance. Annual reports and rule books record many housing developments. Mortgage registers record individual owners. See:

• Gaskell, Martin. 'Self-Help and House Building in the Nineteenth Century', *Local Historian* 10(2), 1972, p.65–9.

Nineteenth-century freehold land societies, formed by the lower middle and upper working classes, were similar to building societies. They purchased land which was then sold to members, who paid for it by instalments over many years. Records rarely survive, but sometimes newspapers report their activities.

Glebe Terriers
Glebe terriers (p.67) include detailed descriptions of rectories. Eighteenth- and nineteenth-century fire insurance policies found with them provide complementary information.

Maps
Houses are sometimes recorded on estate, enclosure and tithe maps. Maps of the Valuation Office (p.98–9) and National Farm Surveys (p.137),

with their associated documentation, frequently include detailed information on housing. Mid-twentieth-century maps in TNA, class IR 90, show how plots subject to tithe redemption annuities under the Tithe Act 1936 were sub-divided. Maps and associated documents offer clues to the dates and history of particular estates.

Probate

Probate inventories (p.122–3) frequently enumerate the goods of the deceased room by room, revealing how rooms were used, and how many there were. Care does, however, have to be taken. Decedents did not always occupy entire houses. Shared occupation may mean that not all the goods in a particular room were enumerated. Houses are occasionally also mentioned in wills.

Taxation

Tax records occasionally throw light on housing. Hearth tax schedules (p.45) tell us how many hearths houses had, although it is not easy to match returns against specific houses. Land tax assessments (p.115–16) occasionally provide useful information, although mostly they just name taxpayers. More information may be given in post-1826 assessments. See:

• Noble, Margaret. 'Land-Tax Returns and Urban Development', *Local Historian*, 15(2), 1982, p.86–92.

Window tax was originally a flat-rate tax on houses, supplemented by a tax on windows where there were more than ten. In 1747, the tax on houses was separated from the tax on windows. The few surviving returns, which list taxpayers, count windows, and record tax paid, are listed by Gibson & Medlycott (p.116).

Rate lists are another important source. New houses and streets can be identified in successive lists, and the development of suburbs can be traced. See:

• Daunton, M.J. 'House-ownership from Rate Books', *Urban History Yearbook*, 3, 1976, p.21–7.

The Census

Information about houses in census returns (p.36–7 and p.39–40) enable us to track the way in which urban areas developed in the nineteenth and twentieth centuries. From 1891, the number of rooms was recorded, revealing the incidence of overcrowding. Later censuses asked more probing questions; in 1951, for example, there were questions concerning water taps, baths and toilets.

Counting census houses is not always as easy as it might seem. Instructions to enumerators on the definition of a 'house' varied between censuses, and enumerators' interpretations of those instructions also varied. For early censuses, see:

- Sheppard, June. 'Inhabited Houses, 1801–1851: Evaluation of Census Figures', *Local Historian*, 18(3), 1988, p.106–11.

Planning Records

Late eighteenth-century improvement commissioners paved the way for the development of town planning. Legislation began in the mid-nineteenth century with various public health acts. Enforcement of planning legislation became the responsibility of local councils. Local medical officer of health reports from 1849 (p.172–3) include much information on working-class housing. Planning permission was increasingly required for new housing; applicants submitted detailed plans, which have frequently been preserved. Registers recorded details of applications. The information in Southampton records is discussed by:

- Dedman, M.J. 'Documents and Urban Growth: Southampton 1878–1914', *Local Historian* 12(7), 1977, p.353–9.

Central government was deeply involved in planning. Many relevant records are in TNA classes MH and HLG. For example, details of local authority planning schemes are in HLG 4; related maps and plans in HLG 5; rehousing schemes in HLG 24; correspondence in HLG 1 and 47, consents in HLG 13–14 and 95. Parliamentary papers such as those on the *House Accommodation of Rural Labourers* (1864) and the *Royal Commission on the Housing of the Working Classes* (1885) provide much evidence.

The Housing of the Working Classes Act 1890 paved the way for the development of council housing. Councils built over 1.1 million houses between the two world wars, radically transforming the lives of those who occupied them. The minutes of local authority housing committees, with officers' reports, provide much information. Administrative records may mention tenants, rents and repairs. There may be detailed specifications and plans for individual houses.

In 1934, the government undertook a major survey of overcrowding in working-class homes. Local authorities conducted the survey, recording addresses and occupiers, giving descriptions of property and compiling registers of unfit houses. The original surveys, covering 10 million houses, are now in local record offices. TNA holds administrative records in HLG 52/795–803, and local files in HLG 49. Aggregate results were reported in:

- *Housing Act 1935: Report on the Overcrowding Survey in England and Wales 1936.* HMSO, 1936.

For a detailed discussion, see:

- White, Jerry. 'When Every Room was Measured: The Overcrowding Survey of 1935–1936 and its Aftermath', *History Workshop Journal*, 4(1), 1977, p.86–94.

Another housing survey was conducted in 1978. Returns do not seem to have been deposited, but statistics for local areas were published in:

- *National Dwelling and Housing Survey.* HMSO, 1978.

Further Reading:
The best guides to documentary sources for tracing the history of houses are:

- Alcock, N.W. *Documenting the History of Houses.* Archives and the user series 10. British Records Association, 2003.
- Blanchard, Gill. *Tracing Your House History.* Pen & Sword, 2013.

For TNA sources, see:

- Barratt, Nick. *Tracing the History of Your House.* 2nd edition. National Archives, 2001.

Thom describes London records:

- Thom, Colin. *Researching London's Houses: An Archives Guide.* Historical Publications, 2005.

C. Furniture and Clothing
In the sixteenth century and earlier, the average yeoman's house was bare of furniture; sometimes the pillow was merely a good round log, and bedding was straw. In the seventeenth century most people had a proper bed, and houses began to fill up. Probate inventories (p.122–3) provide detailed descriptions of furniture, and reveal how standards improved.

Inventories (with wills) are also our prime source for the history of clothing. Admittedly, this is frequently described merely as 'wearing apparell'. But sometimes descriptions are very detailed. The inventories of those involved in the clothing trade may describe their stock.

Increasing comfort levels and conspicuous expenditure amongst the will-making classes can be easily traced in probate inventories between *c.*1600 and *c.*1750. By the mid-eighteenth century, there were so many goods to be described that space in probate registries ran out, and inventories ceased to be preserved.

D. Food

Most food consumed by our ancestors was produced by farmers. The sources described in Chapter 6 provide the evidence for their produce. There are fewer sources for consumption. Two important sources come from opposite ends of the social scale, and reveal how consumption was socially determined. The household accounts of the gentry reveal that they ate much meat. For inmates of workhouses, dietaries found amongst Poor Law Union records (p.84–5) show that bread and cheese, and gruel, frequently featured, although meat was provided occasionally. Between these extremes, the best (although limited) evidence we have for food are probably probate inventories (p.122–3). See:

• Trinder, Barrie. 'Food in Probate Inventories, 1660–1750', *Local Historian*, 38(1), 2008, p.35–48.

For a useful bibliography on food history, see:

• Food and Nutrition
  https://merl.reading.ac.uk/merl-collections/search-and-browse/databases
  Scroll down and click 'food and nutrition'.

E. Health

In past centuries, poor medical knowledge meant that ill health frequently had more devastating impact than it does now. Good health was of vital concern to all, and the health of communities is therefore an important topic for local historians to investigate. Reference has already been made to the use of parish registers in investigating epidemics, to the means by which local medics may be identified, to the nineteenth-century Boards of Health, and to the collections of the Wellcome Library. The latter's website **https://wellcomelibrary.org/collections/digital-collections** includes digitised versions of some of the documents referred to below. Vestry minutes and overseers' accounts (p.66) include useful information. Diaries may also be useful: Pepys' diary, for example, provides much information on the 1665 London plague.

Many voluntary hospitals were established in the eighteenth and nineteenth centuries. For these, see the early nineteenth-century reports of the Charity Commission (p.127). Most eventually became NHS hospitals. Many hospital archives are held by the Wellcome Library, which also has many digitised records from psychiatric institutions. Admission records for one Glasgow and three London Hospitals, 1852–1921, are digitised at:

- Historic Hospitals Admission Records Project
  http://hharp.org

Voluntary hospitals did not have a monopoly on care. Many Union workhouses gradually morphed into infirmaries for the poor, eventually becoming NHS hospitals. Records prior to 1929 are amongst Guardians' records (p.84–5).

Hospital records are catalogued by:

- Hospital Records Database
  www.nationalarchives.gov.uk/hospitalrecords

Bethlem Hospital, the oldest lunatic asylum, dates back to 1247. Few others were founded prior to the eighteenth century. Before then, the principal evidence for the mentally ill are the commissions and inquisitions of lunacy in TNA C 211.

Private asylums were licensed by Quarter Sessions from 1774. Applications for licences, registers of admissions, visitors' report books and other records are amongst Quarter Sessions records. A register of private asylums is in TNA, MH 51/735. MH 51 also includes many late nineteenth- and twentieth-century files on individual asylums.

Until the nineteenth century, most pauper lunatics were confined in workhouses or houses of correction. Better provision began under the County Asylums Act 1808, which permitted Quarter Sessions to erect asylums. They were required to do so from 1845. Reports from county asylums are digitised at **archive.org/details/wellcomelibrary**.

Admission registers, minutes and reports of visitors, personnel records, case books, registers of deaths and burials, and a variety of other documents survive. Applications for admission was made to Justices of the Peace by overseers, or, after 1834, by Union officers. Parish and union records should therefore also be consulted. From 1815, overseers made returns of pauper lunatics to Clerks of the Peace. Similar returns were made by Unions to the Poor Law Commissioners from 1842; these are in TNA MH12.

The Lunacy Commission collected copies of both county and private admission registers from 1845; these are now in TNA, class MH 94 (digitised at **www.ancestry.co.uk**). Asylum building plans are in

MH 83. The *Report of the Metropolitan Commissioners in Lunacy to the Lord Chancellor* (1844) is a detailed account of every asylum in England and Wales. Notes on the histories of all asylums are included in:

* County Asylums
  www.countyasylums.co.uk

For a detailed guide to lunacy records, see:

* Chater, Kathy. *My Ancestor was a Lunatic*. Society of Genealogists Enterprises, 2015.

The health implications of poor sanitation was another governmental concern. The landmark report on this topic was originally published in 1842, but has been republished as:

* Chadwick, Samuel. *Report on the Sanitary Condition of the Labouring Population of Great Britain*, ed. Michael W. Flinn. Edinburgh University Press, 1984.

Chadwick obtained reports on sanitary conditions in many places, and provided much information on public health, mortality and housing. The subsequent reports of the Royal Commission on the State of Large Towns and Populous District provide similar information.

These reports led to the appointment of the first local authority medical officers of health. Their reports include statistical information on matters such as infant mortality and diseases, together with condemnations of noxious trades, inadequate water supply, sewerage arrangements and other health-related matters. Reports are held both locally and in TNA MH 30. Many have been digitised by the Wellcome Library **wellcomecollection.org/collections**

The cholera outbreak of 1848 forced national action. The Public Health Act 1848 established a central General Board of Health, and elected local Boards of Health. Local boards played major roles in improving public health. The Salisbury Board, for example, spent £27,500 in 1853/4 on mains drainage and water supply, leading to a steep fall in the death rate.[2] Minutes, accounts, letters, personnel files and other records of local boards are in local record offices. Large-scale maps sometimes show building densities, water supply, sewerage and other sanitary arrangements.

Reports to the General Board of Health between 1848 and 1857 (TNA class PRO 28/125) describe local sanitary conditions, and present well-argued cases for implementing their recommendations.

METROPOLIS LOCAL MANAGEMENT ACT, BER 6

18 and 19 Vic., cap. 120.

Report

AND

ACCOUNTS OF THE VESTRY

OF THE

PARISH OF BERMONDSEY,

SURREY,

FOR THE YEAR ENDING LADY-DAY, 1864,

AND

REPORT OF THE MEDICAL OFFICER OF HEALTH

FOR THE YEAR 1863.

(1862 not Pub.)

Bermondsey:

ALFRED BOOT, STEAM PRINTING WORKS, 10 & 18, DOCKHEAD, S.E.

1864.

Bermondsey Vestry and Medical Officer of Health reports, 1863–4.

Correspondence between General and local Boards is in TNA, class MH 13. The General Board was abolished in 1858 and replaced by the Local Government Board. From 1872, local boards became 'urban sanitary authorities', whilst Poor Law Guardians became responsible for 'rural sanitary districts'. From 1894, urban and rural district councils took over their work.

Meanwhile, in 1869, the Royal Sanitary Commission was established. Its reports provide much evidence on sewerage, housing and disease, and include (in its 3rd report) answers to a questionnaire on public health and housing from many borough authorities. Later Parliamentary papers provide much useful local information, but are too numerous to be listed here; reference may be made to Powell (p.26)

In the nineteenth century, a number of private individuals conducted extensive surveys of social conditions which included much health-related information. Henry Mayhew's *London Labour and the London Poor*, originally published in 1851, but considerably extended in 1861, provides much invaluable information. Some decades later, Charles Booth's inquiry into the life and labour of the London Poor resulted in a massive archive ripe for exploration by local historians:

- Charles Booth's London: Poverty Maps and Police Notebooks
  https://booth.lse.ac.uk

Similarly, the Borthwick Institute holds the archives of Benjamin Seebohm Rowntree's inquiry into poverty in York, which resulted in the publication of *Poverty: Study of Town Life* in 1901.

Further Reading

- Lane, Joan. *The Making of the English Patient: A Guide to Sources for the Social History of Medicine*. Sutton Publishing, 2000.

The local reports to the General Board of Health have been published on microfilm. See:

- Pidduck, William. *Urban and rural social conditions in industrial Britain: the local reports to the General Board of Health, 1848–1857: a complete listing and guide to the Harvester Press microfilm collection.* Harvester Press, 1978. A second series, edited by M. Thomas, covers 1869–1908.

These reports are briefly introduced in *Short Guides 1*. For other sanitary authorities, consult:

- Public Health and Epidemics in the nineteenth and twentieth centuries **www.nationalarchives.gov.uk/records/research-guides/public-health-epidemics.htm**

F. Education

Educational records are scarce in medieval and early modern times. Few schools existed. The presence of a school or teacher in a community may, perhaps, be inferred by studying literacy. A crude estimation of the extent of literacy in a parish can be made by counting and comparing signatures and marks in collections of documents such as wills, post-1753 marriage registers, oath rolls, marriage bonds and allegations, depositions from ecclesiastical courts, and signed protestation returns. Methods of assessing literacy are discussed by:

- Cressy, David. *Literacy and the Social Order: Reading and Writing in Tudor and Stuart England.* 2nd edition. Cambridge University Press, 2006.

Early schools were frequently founded by will or trust deed. Between 1597 and *c.*1820, their activities were sometimes investigated by Commissioners for Charitable Uses, whose inquisitions and decrees are in TNA, class C 93. Local charities frequently named parish and borough officers as trustees. Many records can therefore be found amongst parish and borough records. Trust deeds for schools (and other charities) were enrolled on the Close Rolls (TNA C 54) between 1735 and 1903. See:

- Land and Property for Charitable Use: Trust Deeds, 1736–1963 **www. nationalarchives.gov.uk/help-with-your-research/research-**guides/**conveyances-of-land-charitable-uses-trust-deeds-1736–1963**

Firmer checks on charities were established in the nineteenth century. The reports of Brougham's Charity Commission, 1819–40 (in the Parliamentary papers) provide much information on endowed schools. The Commission ceased in 1837, but a new Charity Commission was established in 1853. Between 1867 and 1913, it published a series of *Digests of Endowed Charities*, which are as useful as its predecessor's reports.

Before 1870, most schools were run by charities, although state support was increasing. After 1870, the state aimed to fill in the gaps left by voluntary schools, eventually creating the present state system.

The starting point for researching schools is the *VCH*, which has, since the 1950s, endeavoured to identify every elementary school. The questions to be asked primarily concern staffing, pupils, curriculum and effectiveness.

A number of major national institutions – all connected with the church – played important roles in the establishment of local schools. Their records provide us with much information.

The Society for the Promotion of Christian Knowledge was at the forefront of the eighteenth-century charity school movement. It helped to establish some 1,500 schools before 1735. Printed *Reports* for 1705–32 (from 1720, *Reports and Accounts*) include lists of schools connected to the Society, together with information on numbers of pupils, curriculum and finance. Its 'in letters', (1699 to 1729), 'out-letters' (1711–29), minutes, and other archives, held by Cambridge University Library, provide much information. The papers of local committees, and of schools which they supported, can frequently be found in local record offices. See:

- Tate, W.E. 'S. P. C. K. Archives, 1, with special reference to their value for the history of education (mainly 1699–*c.* 1740)', *Archives* 3(18), 1957, p. 105–15.

The National Society was founded in 1817. It aimed to establish a Church of England school in every parish. Local clergy frequently served as trustees. Many older schools became National schools. Its archives include *c.*15,000 files for individual schools, which contain applications for grants, trust deeds, and plans for new buildings, amongst other documents. The Society's annual reports, 1812–1900, digitised at the fee-based British Online Archives **https://microform.digital/boa**,

Walter Scott's Charity school at Ross (Herefordshire).

provide much local information; those for the 1830s and 1840s (especially 1838) include various surveys of school provision. Society archives are held by the Church of England Record Centre. See:

- Lambeth Palace Library: Education Sources
  www.lambethpalacelibrary.org/content/education

Nonconformist education (theoretically non-denominational) was promoted by the British and Foreign School Society **https://bfss.org.uk/ archive**, founded in 1808 as the Society for Promoting the Lancasterian System for the Education of the Poor. Annual reports 1814–1900 are digitised at British Online Archives **https://microform.digital/boa**.

The society's archives, held by Brunel University **www.brunel. ac.uk/about/Archives/British-and-Foreign-School-Society-BFSS-Archive**, contain much correspondence regarding individual 'British' schools, together with inspectors' reports, trust deeds and applications for admission to BFSS training colleges. The website includes a list of British schools in 1897, together with various lists of teachers trained at the Society's college. For more detail, see:

- Bartle, G.F., & Collins, G.P. 'The British and Foreign School Society Archives Centre', *History of Education*, 10(3), 1981, p.179–81.
- Bartle, G.F. 'The Records of the British and Foreign School Society', *Local Historian*, 16(4), 1984, p.204–6.

The Wesleyan Committee of Education produced similar documentation, now held in the Methodist Archives and Research Centre. Annual reports cover 1837–1932.[3]

The education of Roman Catholic poor was promoted by the Catholic Poor School Committee and its successors. Its archives are held by St Mary's University, Twickenham, and are described on Aim25 **https:// aim25.com** (see Catholic Education Council). Its 1849 annual report includes a survey of Catholic schools in 1845. Other annual reports also contain useful information, and have been published on microform as:

- Catholic Poor School Committee. *Annual Reports*. 71 fiche. EP Microform, 1979. Also digitised, 1848–1900, at British Online Archives **https://microform.digital/boa**.

A range of other ecclesiastical sources detail educational provision. Late nineteenth- and twentieth-century parish magazines frequently include information on schools associated with the church. Sermons delivered on occasions such as the founding of a school were frequently printed, or reported in newspapers. After 1571, replies to bishops' visitation queries (p.70–1 and p.73) provide useful information. Bishops frequently acted as visitors to educational charities, and retained relevant papers (mostly post-1700) in diocesan archives. In the nineteenth century, bishops supported local affiliates of the National Society, and instituted diocesan education committees.

Schoolmasters required bishops' licences until the early nineteenth century. Diocesan archives include nomination forms and testimonials. Schoolmasters presented their licences at visitation and were recorded in call books and visitation act books. Licensing fees may be recorded in archdeacons' fee books. Subscription books record schoolmasters' subscriptions to oaths promising loyalty to church, and/or state. Some schoolmasters were university graduates, and may be identified in university alumni lists (p.55).

The government became increasingly interested in education in the nineteenth century, and published many reports in the Parliamentary papers series. The *Abstract of the Answers and Returns ... relative to the expence and maintenance of the Poor in England ...* 1804 gives number of children in parochial schools, with other information. A Select Committee on the Education of the Lower Orders in the Metropolis produced reports in 1817 and 1818, and a *Digest of Parochial Returns* in 1819, detailing educational provision in every parish. The *Abstract of Education Returns 1833* provided more detailed information. It was compiled under the auspices of the Select Committee on the State of Education of the Poor, which produced a separate report in 1834.

The 1851 census was accompanied by a census of educational provision. Returns were published in 1854 as *Census of Great Britain 1851: Education: England and Wales: Report and Tables*. These returns provide statistics for areas rather than for particular schools. Most original returns were destroyed, but a very few can be found with the ecclesiastical census returns in TNA, class HO 129. The main census itself (p.36–41) may be used to identify pupils (described as 'scholars').

Ten years later, in 1861, the Royal Commission on Education produced its report (known as the Newcastle report). It included very detailed evidence from many localities. Another survey, *Returns relating to Elementary Education (Civil Parishes)* was published in 1871, followed by *Returns for each Public Elementary School Examined (Inspected) in England and Wales*, in 1894 and 1900. The *Minutes of the Committee of Council on Education* run from 1840–41 (described as *Reports* from 1858–9). They provide much detailed information, including, in the early years, inspectors' reports on individual schools. Between 1870 and 1879 they include information on the newly established school boards.

A substantial number of other Parliamentary papers deal with education. They are listed by:

- Argles, Michael. *British Government Publications in Education during the Nineteenth century.* Guides to Sources in the History of Education, 1. History of Education Society, 1971. A similar volume deals with the twentieth century.

Many educational records are in TNA ED classes. For example, files containing returns, inspectors' reports, plans, correspondence and other documents 1872–1904, are in ED 2, 3, 4 and 16. Preliminary statements seeking funding for new buildings, 1846–1924 are in ED 7, and grant applications 1839–99 in ED 103. Files concerning attendance post-1870 are in ED 6 and ED 18. Public and endowed elementary school files 1853–1945 are in ED 21 and ED 49 respectively. The responses of local education authorities (LEAs) to the Second World War, including evacuation activities, are detailed in ED 134. Post-1944 files for individual primary schools are in ED 161. See:

- Elementary and Primary Schools
  www.nationalarchives.gov.uk/help-with-your-research/research-guides/elementary-primary-schools
- Education Inspectorate Reports
  www.nationalarchives.gov.uk/help-with-your-research/research-guides/education-inspectorate-reports

From 1834, Poor Law Unions were required to employ schoolmasters/mistresses, and to provide at least three hours of tuition per day for their children. Registers of children in workhouse schools are with other Union records (p.84–5). Inspectors' reports are in MH 12, early twentieth-century files on poor law schools in ED 132.

A few reports on schools were published in the *Reports* of the Poor Law Commissioners before 1847, and thereafter in the irregularly issued *Minutes of the Committee of Council on Education (Schools of Parochial Unions)* between 1847 and 1859. The 1851 *Report of the Poor Law Board on the Education and Training of Pauper Children* was followed by similar reports in 1862 and 1878. From 1867, information on poor law schools can be found in the *Reports* of the Poor Law Board, and subsequently the Local Government Board. These are all Parliamentary papers.

Industrial schools complemented Workhouse schools. These were originally voluntary institutions, designed to help destitute children by removing them from bad influences. From 1857, magistrates were empowered to sentence children aged from 7 to 14 to a period in one of these institutions. Schools set up in factories for young employees were also styled 'industrial schools'. Records can be found in various TNA classes and in local record offices.

In London and a few other cities, the Ragged School Union, founded in 1844, brought together several hundred schools for the poor. The Union's minutes and magazines provide much information on these schools. See:

- *Victorian Philanthropy and Social Problems. Series 1: Archives Of The Shaftesbury Society, Parts 1–3. 1844 To 1944.* 8 microfilm reels + 219 fiche. Harvester Press, 1980.

Sunday schools, started by Robert Raikes in 1785, were important for the poorer classes. They aimed to reach every child, but were riven by denominational rivalry. The few surviving records are found amongst parish and nonconformist records. Numbers attending were recorded in the 1851 ecclesiastical census (p.192).

School Boards were established in 1870, originally to run government-funded elementary schools in areas where there was inadequate provision. See:

- Everett, B.G. 'The School Boards: an Exercise in Participation', *Local Historian,* 9(3), 1970, p.130–34.

For the period 1870–1902, school board records are important. They include minutes, correspondence, election posters, salary books, attendance committee minutes, and a range of other documentation. Board members are named in board minutes, in the *School Board Chronicle and Review* (from 1870), and (annually from 1877) in the *Municipal Corporations Companion.* Newspapers (p.26–7) reported elections to school boards and their activities. For voting papers, see TNA ED 9/22.

The records of both board and voluntary schools were similar. They include minutes, punishment books, plans, photographs and accounts. Two records were particularly important: registers and logbooks. A few early registers of pupils survive.[4] From 1870, they had to be kept. They name children, including dates of birth, admission and leaving, give parents' details, and identify previous schools. Sometimes they record what children did on leaving.

From 1862, schools which received grant support were expected to keep school log books, recording day-to-day life. See:

- Drake, Michael, ed. *School and Community: Family and Community History through the Prism of School Logbooks.* FACHRS Publications, 2018.

For logbooks in print, see:

- Brown, Ruth, ed. *Littlehampton School Logbook 1871–1911*. Sussex Record Society, 95. 2012.
- Horn, Pamela, ed. *Village Education in Nineteenth-Century Oxfordshire: The Whitchurch School Log Book (1868–93) and Other Documents*. Oxfordshire Record Society, 51. 1978.

National School registers and logbooks are digitised at:

- National School Registers 1870–1914
  www.findmypast.co.uk/page/school-registers

School boards were abolished by the Education Act 1902 and replaced by LEAs, which kept similar records. See:

- Ottewill, Roger. 'Education, Education, Education: Researching the 1902 Education Act', *Local Historian*, 37(4), 2007, p.258–72.

'History sheets', providing summary information on each LEA school, *c.*1920–1983 are in TNA ED 185. Many schools were built by School Boards and LEAs. The plans of some school buildings were printed in *The Builder* (p.166). General sources for primary school history are discussed by:

- Pugh, R.B. 'Educational Records 1. Sources for the History of English Primary Schools', *British Journal of Educational Studies*, 1, 1952, p.43–51.

The records discussed above relate primarily to elementary schools. Secondary schooling before the twentieth century was provided by the old endowed grammar schools. Many of these were founded under the auspices of institutions such as cathedrals, monasteries and Oxbridge colleges. For their records, see:

- Tate, W.E. 'Some Sources for the History of English Grammar Schools', *British Journal of Educational Studies* 1(2), 1953, p.164–75; 2(1), 1953, p.67–81; 2(2), 1954, p.145–65.

Many school histories (not all) have been recounted in the *VCH*. A much older work is provided by:

- Carlisle, Nicholas. *Concise Description of the Endowed Grammar Schools in England and Wales*. 2 vols. Baldwin, Cradock & Joy, 1818.

For sixteenth-century schools, see:

- Leach, Arthur F. *English Schools at the Reformation, 1546–8.* Archibald Constable & Co., 1896.

Mid-seventeenth-century schools are listed in:

- Vincent, W.A. *The State and School Education, 1640–1660, in England and Wales: A Survey Based on Printed Sources.* Church Historical Society (Great Britain), 1950.

In the 1670s, Christopher Wase undertook a survey of grammar schools. His papers in the Bodleian Library list 704 schools, with details of their foundation and governance. See:

- Wallis, P.J. 'The Wase School Collection', *Bodleian Library Record* 4(2), 1952, p.78–104.
- Oakeshot, A.M.d'I. 'The Education Inquiry Papers of Christopher Wase', *British Journal of Educational Studies* 19(3), 1971, p.301–32.

Nineteenth-century secondary schools are listed in the *Digest of Parochial Returns* (1819) and the *Abstract of Education Returns* (1835) mentioned above. The *Digest of Schools and Charities for Education* (1843) is a consolidation of

The schoolroom at Hawkshead (Lancashire).

Schoolmasters at Hawkshead (Lancashire).

the earlier Charity Commission reports, which are indexed in the *Report of the Schools Inquiry Commission* of 1868–9 (the Taunton Commission), a mine of information in its own right. In 1865, the Committee of Council on Education published a *Return of Endowed Grammar Schools*. Useful information is also included in the *Educational Register*:

- Wallis, P.J. 'The Educational Register, 1851–5', *British Journal of Educational Studies* 13(1), 1964, p.50–70.

The stream of Parliamentary papers continued after the Taunton Commission, and cannot all be listed here. The *Reports of the of the Endowed Schools Commission* for 1872 and 1875, the *Reports of the Select Committee on the Endowed Schools Acts*, 1873, 1886 and 1887, and the *Reports of the Charity Commissioners' Proceedings on Endowed Schools*, 1894, all include useful information. So does the *Return of Scholarships and Endowments* (the Fortescue return) of 1884 and the *Reports of the Royal Commission on Secondary Education* (the Bryce Commission) of 1895. The *Return of the Pupils in Public and Private Secondary and other Schools in England* (1897) gives much information on the numbers of schools and pupils, the ages of pupils and the qualifications of teachers.

Government increasingly involved itself in the affairs of endowed schools in the late nineteenth century. Reports of the Endowed Schools Commission have already been mentioned; its role was to ensure that endowments were being properly used. Its work was continued by the

Charity Commission and, subsequently, by the Department of Education. Endowment files in TNA, class ED 27, include c.6,700 files of correspondence and other papers relating to individual schools, c.1850–1903. See:

- Gordon, Peter. 'Some Sources for the History of the Endowed Schools Commission, 1869–1900', *British Journal for Educational Studies*, 14, 1966, p.59–73.

A 'directory of masters in secondary schools', with listings of public and grammar schools, regularly appeared in:

- *Schoolmasters' Yearbook and Directory*. 1903–1933.

TNA holds much other information on secondary schools. Files (mainly twentieth century) for every school are in TNA, ED 35 and 162. A variety of records are discussed by:

- Secondary Schools **www.nationalarchives.gov.uk/help-with-your-research/research-guides/secondary-schools**

Endowed school records usually include deeds and accounts. There may be governors' minutes, school registers, punishment books and, perhaps, school magazines. Schools such as Eton College **www.etoncollege.com/CollegeArchives.aspx** retain their own archives. For printed public school registers, see:

- Jacobs, Phyllis May. *Registers of the Universities, Colleges and Schools of Great Britain: A List*. Athlone Press, 1966.
- *School, University and College Registers in the Library of the Society of Genealogists*. 2nd edition. The Society, 1996.

Information may also be found amongst the records of the institutions under whose auspices schools were founded or operated. For example, foundation deeds of church schools might be found in bishops' registers (p.70), chapter act books and monastic cartularies. After 1391, they may also be on the Patent Rolls (p.104–105). Oxbridge colleges hold records of schools created under their auspices. Many early schools were connected with chantries; chantry certificates (p.191) may mention them. Some became 'Edward VI' grammar schools; particulars of grants to them and other schools are in TNA classes E 319, E 123, LR 6, 7 and 12, and DL 29. Exchequer special commissions of inquiry sometimes investigated educational provision made from former chantry property;

see TNA E 178. Newspapers reported school activities, and carried advertisements seeking both pupils and staff. For published histories of particular schools, see:

- Wallis, P.J. *Histories of Old Schools: A Revised List for England and Wales*. University of Newcastle upon Tyne Dept of Education, 1966.
- Cunningham, Peter. *Local History of Education in England and Wales: A Bibliography*. Museum of the History of Education, University of Leeds, 1976.

Adult and higher education are more specialist topics, which cannot be dealt with in-depth here. Mechanics Institutes played an important role in the early development of adult education, and should attract the attention of the local historian. Minute books, membership lists, committee reports and account books, provide the basic evidence for their history. Adult education was promoted by public libraries, whose history should be of interest to local historians as well as to librarians.[5] So should the history of the parochial libraries.[6] TNA class ED 64 includes files relating to public libraries. The dissenting academies will be mentioned on p.198.

For more detailed guidance on sources for educational history see:

- Stephens, W.B., & Unwin, R.W. *Materials for the Local and Regional Study of Schooling, 1700–1900*. Archives and the User 7. 1987.
- Purvis, J.S. *Educational Records*. St Anthony's Press, 1959.
- Morton, Ann. *Education and the State from 1833*. PRO Publications, 1997.

A variety of education records are discussed by:

- Education History Records held by other Archives
  www.nationalarchives.gov.uk/help-with-your-research/research-guides/education-history-records-held-by-other-archives

A number of essays are included in:

- Cook, T.G., ed. *Local Studies and the History of Education*. Methuen & Co., 1972.

Useful websites include:

- Exe Libris: the UK History of Education Society's Online Bibliography
  http://projects.exeter.ac.uk/hoebibliography
- History of Education Society
  https://historyofeducation.org.uk

For a detailed history of schooling, together with a gazetteer listing all known schools, see:

- Cannon, John. *Schooling in England 1660 to 1850*. 2 vols. List and Index Society, Special series 54–5. 2016.

A basic historical outline is provided by:

- Chapman, Colin R. *The Growth of British Education and its Records*. 2nd edition. Lochin Publishing, 1992.

G. Religion: Monastic Life

Monasteries were important in medieval England. Histories of individual monasteries are in *VCH*. For a detailed listing of monastic and other ecclesiastical institutions, see:

- Knowles, David, & Hadcock, R. Neville. *Medieval Religious Houses, England and Wales*. 2nd edition. Longmans, 1971.

Useful sources are printed in the *Calendar of … Papal Registers* and the *Calendar of Petitions to the Pope, 1342–1419* (p.159). Numerous other documents are in:

- Dugdale, William, Sir. *Monasticon Anglicanum: A History of the Abbies and Other Monasteries, Hospitals, Frieries, and Cathedral and Collegiate Churches, with their Dependencies, in England and Wales …*, ed. J. Caley, H. Ellis, & B. Bandinel. 6 vols. Record Commission, 1817–30.

Individual monks at the Dissolution can be identified in the surrenders (in TNA E322) they signed. For other useful sources, see p.102.

H. Religion: the Church of England

Parish churches tell us much about the history of the communities they serve. Local historians must read their architectural styles, their monuments, and their furniture, and understand the evidence of destruction during the Reformation. The significance of church buildings is outside the scope of this book. Numerous guides are available; a useful introduction is provided by:

- Taylor, Richard. *How to Read a Church: An Illustrated Guide to Images, Symbols and Meanings in Churches and Cathedrals*. Rider, 2004.

For encyclopedic treatment, see:

- Friar, Stephen. *The Companion to Churches.* History Press, 2011.

Photographs of most churches are online:

- The Churches of Britain and Ireland
  www.churches-uk-ireland.org

Anglo-Saxon churches are sometimes recorded in early charters (p.103–104), and in *Domesday Book* (p.42–3), although they are only mentioned in the latter if they affected payments due to the Crown. Their presence may also be inferred from place names. Otherwise, prior to the twelfth century, written evidence is scarce. Thereafter, bishops' registers record institutions of incumbents. Two thirteenth-century tax

Minster Church (Cornwall).

lists record the presence of churches. The 'valuation of Norwich' was a levy imposed on the English clergy by the Pope in 1256. Unfortunately, only eight dioceses are covered by surviving returns. See:

- Lunt, W.E., ed. *The Valuation of Norwich*. Clarendon Press, 1926.

The taxation of Pope Nicholas, 1291–2, mentions some 8,500 churches. It formed the basis for subsequent clerical taxation. See:

- University of Sheffield: Taxatio
  www.dhi.ac.uk/taxatio

Two centuries later, in 1535, the *Valor ecclesiasticus* (p.95), made for reformation purposes, provided a much more detailed valuation.

The church exists primarily to worship God. That is reflected in parish and diocesan records (p.62–8 & p.70–3). It is difficult to study the spiritual life of a parish. The reality of spiritual experience, ultimately, is unknowable except to the Deity. Historians can only examine the mostly fairly minimal surviving surface evidence, and should refrain from making personal judgements on underlying motives. Evidence for such judgements rarely exists.

Such written evidence as does exist is found in bishops' registers, churchwardens' accounts, visitation documents, the records of the church courts, and wills, all of which have already been discussed. Formal statements of piety in wills or on monumental inscriptions tell us something – but usually not a lot.

Other relevant documents include, amongst others, chantry certificates, significations of excommunication, sermons, tracts, diaries, letters and registers of services. Nonconformist and Roman Catholic records are discussed below.

Sources for worship during the Reformation are particularly interesting. In that period, altars, rood-lofts, screens and statues were condemned as papist and torn down; the glorious wall paintings of medieval times were whitewashed. In their place were erected tables of the Ten Commandments, and the royal arms. Foxe's *Book of Martyrs* and Bishop Jewell's *Homilies*, were purchased. Payments for such items are recorded in churchwardens' accounts (p.64–6). Unfortunately, most accounts for this period have been lost. The few which have survived have been used extensively. For a particularly valuable study using them, see:

- Duffy, Eamon. *The Voices of Morebath: Reformation and Rebellion in an English Village*. Yale University Press, 2003.

Right: *Plaque commemorating Sir John Trelawny at Pelynt (Cornwall).*

Below: *Doom painting in St. Thomas's, Salisbury (courtesy Nassino, Wikimedia).*

For an edition of churchwardens' accounts particularly relevant to the Reformation, see:

- Mattingly, Joanna, ed. *Stratton Churchwardens' Accounts 1512–1578.* Devon & Cornwall Record Society, new series 60. 2018.

Church goods are recorded in the inventories of church goods drawn up in 1552, preparatory to seizure by the Crown. Seizure was, however, interrupted by the accession of Queen Mary, who ordered goods already seized to be returned. The inventories record all manner of 'goodes, plate, juells, vestyments, bells and other ornyments within every paryshe belonging or in any wyse apperteying to any churche, chapell, brotherhed, gylde or fraternytye'. Occasionally, details of the parish armouries kept within churches are given. Inventories, with related documents, are now in TNA, classes E 117 and E 315/495–515. London certificates are in LR 2, and those for the Duchy of Lancaster in DL 38. See:

- Knightbridge, A.A.H. 'Documents in the Public Record Office, IV: Inventories of Church Goods', *Amateur Historian*, 7(7), 1967, p.219–22.

Many are in print; see, for example:

- Snell, Lawrence S., ed., *The Edwardian Inventories of Church Goods for Cornwall.* Documents towards a History of the Reformation in Cornwall, 2. 1956.

For background, see:

- 'The End of it All: the Material Culture of the Late Medieval English Parish and the 1552 Inventories of Church Goods', in Duffy, Eamon. *Saints, Sacrilege and Sedition: Religion and Conflict in the Tudor Reformation.* Bloomsbury, 2012, p.109–32.

Evidence for pre-Reformation worship is also found amongst chantry records. Chantries funded the payment of priests, the erection of side chapels, the provision of lights before the altar, the funding of obits and bede rolls.[7] Their primary purpose was to secure prayers for the dead. They also funded sermons, schools, poor relief and other charitable ends. From the thirteenth century, many were founded by will. Licences for the 'alienation' of land required to support them is on the Patent Rolls (TNA, class C66) from 1279. They are sometimes mentioned in bishops' registers. The chantry certificates of 1546–8 (TNA class E 301) give details of original foundations, list landed property, plate and other valuables, and name priests and other dependants. See *Short Guides 1*. For a printed edition, see:

• Kitching, C.J., ed. *London and Middlesex Chantry Certificates, 1548.* London Record Society, 1980.

The course of the Reformation can also be traced through religious preambles in wills. Before *c*.1800, it was conventional to bequeath the soul to Almighty God. Pre-Reformation bequests of the soul are likely to mention the Virgin Mary, the whole company of heaven, and/or purgatory. The standard post-Reformation formula limits the bequest to 'Almighty God my maker and redeemer', perhaps also mentioning the elect. Such bequests are frequently formulaic, and likely to reflect the views of the scribe rather than those of the testator. Used with care, however, they may be used to identify those who clung to the old religion, and early protestants. Non-standard wording is more likely to reflect the views of testators.

Pre-Reformation testators frequently required their executors to organise masses for their souls; indeed, as already noted, some founded chantries. Others funded 'lights' before altars in their parish churches, or bequeathed vestments, mass books and other items used in worship.

Post-Reformation testators continued to make bequests to parish churches. Bequests may provide useful information concerning the refurbishment of churches. Wills specifying texts for funeral sermons clearly reflect the religious beliefs of testators. Charity sometimes extended beyond the church: schools, almshouses, workhouses, bridges and other charitable institutions attracted many bequests. Doles for the poor at funerals were frequently mandated.

Post-Reformation worship continued to need funding. Communion bread and wine had to be purchased. So did service books, Bibles and vestments for the clergy. Fonts, altars, pulpits and organs needed refurbishment or replacement. So did church buildings. These costs continued to be recorded in churchwardens' accounts (p.64–6).

Religious issues are also recorded in visitation documents. Churchwardens made presentments (p.71 and p.73) on such matters as the lack of prayer books and coverings for the altar, and on the activities of their clergy, as well as on the morals of parishioners. Incumbents' replies to bishops' queries (p.71 and p.73) dealt with such matters as the regularity of services, teaching the catechism, and numbers of communicants, nonconformists and Roman Catholics.

For recent centuries, more sources are available. The 1851 ecclesiastical census identified every place of worship in the country, Anglican, Nonconformist and Roman Catholic, giving denominations, dates of erection, the number of free and 'other' sittings, details of endowments and the names of ministers. Worshippers at morning, afternoon and evening services were counted (those who attended twice were double-counted), together with children in Sunday schools. This census revealed that less than half of the population attended church, and that half of those were nonconformists. Downloadable returns are in TNA, class HO 129. Published returns are listed by:

- Field, Clive Douglas. 'The 1851 Religious Census of Great Britain: A Bibliographical Guide for Local and Regional Historians', *Local Historian*, 27(4), 1997, pp. 194–217. Updated at **www.brin.ac.uk/commentary/drs/appendix2**

For useful guides, see:

- Thompson, David M. 'The Religious Census of 1851', in Lawton, Richard, ed. *The Census and Social Structure: An Interpretative Guide to Nineteenth-Century Censuses for England and Wales*. Frank Cass, 1978, p.241–88.
- Ambler, R.W. 'The 1851 Census of Religious Worship', *Local Historian*, 11(7), 1975, p.375–81.

The religious census is analysed in detail by:

- Snell, K.D.M., & Ell, Paul S. *Rival Jerusalems: The Geography of Victorian Religion*. Cambridge University Press, 2000.

For other religious statistics, see:

- Religion in Numbers
  www.brin.ac.uk

Trade directories (p.146–7) usually provide information on religion. Addresses and denominations of churches and chapels, names of clergy, and times of services, may be mentioned.

The lack of seats in churches was a major issue in the nineteenth century. In 1801, there were just 58 seats for every 100 persons in England. By 1851 that had declined to 45,[8] despite the fact that many buildings had been erected or renovated. The census led to a redoubling of effort, reflected in the number of faculties (p.71) granted. Much information on

] 16 CENSUS, 1851 :—RELIGIOUS WORSHIP. [ENGLAND

TABLE F.—continued.

RELIGIOUS DENOMINATION.	Number of Places of Worship.	Number of Sittings.			Number of Attendants at Public Worship on Sunday, March 30, 1851 [including Sunday Scholars].			Number of Places of Worship.	Number of Sittings.			Number of Attendants at Public Worship on Sunday, March 30, 1851 [including Sunday Scholars].		
		Free.	Appropriated.	Total.	Morning.	Afternoon.	Evening.		Free.	Appropriated.	Total.	Morning.	Afternoon.	Evening.
	CARLISLE. (Municipal Borough.) Population, 26,310.							CHATHAM. (Parliamentary Borough.) Population, 28,424.						
TOTAL -	18	4629	3989	11,078	5152	674	3376	31	3949	7325	11,962	7558	2283	5007
PROTESTANT CHURCHES:														
Church of England -	5	763	1816	4039	1678	390	948	10	2220	3702	6610	4013	1440	1994
Church of Scotland -	1	..	750	750	160	..	116	..	..	..	..	..	..	..
United Presby. Church	1	100	370	470	452	..	..	..	..	..	..	..	..	..
Independents -	3	1217	153	1370	439	..	402	3	270	950	1220	915	138	893
General Baptists -	..	..	..	..	..	..	..	1	123	163	286	94	..	85
Particular Baptists -	1	1000	..	1000	30	..	60	2	264	644	908	665	..	873
Society of Friends -	1	360	..	360	94	64	..	..	..	..	..	..	..	..
Wesleyan Methodists -	2	200	800	1000	415	..	463	6	420	1112	1532	1246	340	1140
Primitive Methodists -	1	..	..	..	120	..	200	..	..	..	..	..	..	..
Bible Christians -	..	..	..	..	..	..	..	4	231	466	697	220	151	324
Wesleyan Association -	1	900	100	1000	680	..	700	2	231	138	369	95	14	98
New Church -	..	..	..	..	..	..	..	1	70	..	70	20	..	40
OTHER CHRISTIAN CHS.:														
Roman Catholics -	1	..	..	1000	1060	180	456	1	..	150	150	250	200	100
Cath. and Apos. Church	..	..	..	..	..	..	..	1	120	..	120	40	..	60
Latter Day Saints -	1	89	..	89	24	40	31	..	..	..	..	..	..	..

RELIGIOUS DENOMINATION.	Number of Places of Worship.	Number of Sittings.			Number of Attendants at Public Worship on Sunday, March 30, 1851 [including Sunday Scholars].			Number of Places of Worship.	Number of Sittings.			Number of Attendants at Public Worship on Sunday, March 30, 1851 [including Sunday Scholars].		
		Free.	Appropriated.	Total.	Morning.	Afternoon.	Evening.		Free.	Appropriated.	Total.	Morning.	Afternoon.	Evening.
	CHELTENHAM. (Parliamentary Borough.) Population, 35,051.							CHESTER. (Municipal Borough.) Population, 27,766.						
TOTAL -	27	6942	12,123	19,065	10,900	4248	8067	35	4612	8517	13,529	7112	4022	4801
PROTESTANT CHURCHES:														
Church of England -	7	3398	7457	10,855	6866	3338	3200	15	2378	5069	7547	4242	2830	1540
Presby. Ch. in England	..	..	..	..	..	..	..	1	..	50	50	60	60	..
Independents -	4	680	1350	2030	1031	45	804	4	580	880	1400	776	40	899
Particular Baptists -	3	800	1400	2200	1190	..	1600	1	88	162	250	71	16	102
Scotch Baptists -	..	..	..	..	..	..	..	1	..	..	..	8	12	..
Baptists (not otherwise defined)	1	100	..	100	30	..	30	..	..	..	..	..	..	..
Society of Friends -	1	100	..	100	21	9	..	2	300	..	600	34	26	..
Unitarians -	1	300	..	300	72	..	35	1	..	250	250	102	..	57
Wesleyan Methodists -	4	489	926	1415	805	107	756	3	428	941	1369	872	357	999
Methodist New Connex.	..	..	..	..	..	..	..	1	350	620	970	146	..	156
Primitive Methodists -	..	..	..	..	..	..	..	1	200	180	380	177	224	180
Wesleyan Association -	2	130	110	240	44	49	42	..	..	..	..	..	..	..
Calvinistic Methodists	..	..	..	..	..	..	..	1	100	265	365	120	125	179
L'Huntingdon'sConnex.	1	200	550	750	350	..	700	..	..	..	..	245	..	200
Isolated Congregations	..	..	..	..	..	..	..	1	150	..	150	89	32	29
OTHER CHRISTIAN CHS.:														
Roman Catholics -	1	100	260	360	325	400	400	1	38	100	138	190	270	210
Latter Day Saints -	1	630	..	630	150	300	500	1	..	..	..	30	30	250
Jews - -	1	15	70	85	16	..	..	..	..	..	..	..	..	..

CARLISLE.—The returns omit to state the number of *sittings* in one place of worship belonging to the WESLEYAN METHODISTS, attended by a maximum number of 63 persons at a service; and in one place belonging to the PRIMITIVE METHODISTS, attended by a maximum of 200 at a service.—The number of *attendants* is not given for one place of worship belonging to the CHURCH OF ENGLAND.

CHATHAM.—The returns omit to state the number of *sittings* in one place of worship belonging to the CHURCH OF ENGLAND, attended by a maximum of 600 at a service.—Neither *sittings* nor *attendants* are given for one place of worship belonging to the CHURCH OF ENGLAND.

CHELTENHAM.—The number of *attendants* is not mentioned for two places of worship belonging to the CHURCH OF ENGLAND.

CHESTER.—The returns omit to state the number of *sittings* in one place of worship belonging to the INDEPENDENTS, attended by a maximum of 55 persons at a service; in one belonging to the SCOTCH BAPTISTS, attended by a maximum of 12 at a service; in one belonging to LADY HUNTINGDON'S CONNEXION, attended by a maximum of 200 at a service; and in one belonging to the LATTER DAY SAINTS, attended by a maximum of 250 at a service.

Extract from the 1851 religious census.

Victorian church buildings was published in *The Ecclesiologist*, 1841–67 and in the *Transactions of the St Pauls' Ecclesiological Society*, 1881–1905, both digitised at **http://ecclsoc.org/resources**. Files and surveyors' reports for the churches built by the Church Building Commission between 1818 and 1850 are held by Lambeth Palace Library. Its annual reports are in the Parliamentary papers series. See:

- Port, M.H. *600 New Churches: The Church Building Commission 1818–1856*. Spire Books, 2006.

Sixteen thousand files relating to applications for grants from the Incorporated Church Building Society are held by Lambeth Palace Library. Over 13,000 images of church building plans are available at **http://images.lambethpalacelibrary.org.uk/luna/servlet**. These archives are discussed by:

- Mackinnon, Ann Dolina. 'The Files of the Nineteenth-Century Incorporated Church Building Society as a Means of Reconstructing the Past: The Example of St Andrew's Church, Earls Colne, Essex', *Local Historian*, 27(2), 1997, p.91–105.
- Yates, Nigel. 'The Historical Value of Church Building Plans', *Archives*, 18(78), 1987, p.67–75.

Religious periodicals became important in the nineteenth century. A number are available online; visit **https://biblicalstudies.org.uk/articles. php** and **www.britishnewspaperarchive.co.uk**. For a full listing, see:

- Altholz, Josef L. *The Religious Press in Britain, 1760–1900*. Greenwood, 1989.

Parish magazines began regular publication. They included service times, flower-arranging rotas, baptisms, marriages and burials, letters from the rector, obituaries, details of prayer groups, and much other local information. See:

- Platt, Jane. *Subscribing to the Faith? The Anglican Parish Magazine, 1859–1929*. Palgrave Macmillan, 2015.
- Lawton, Ann. 'Parish Magazines as a Source of Village History', *Local Historian*, 16(8), 1985, p.457–66.

Parish magazines were complemented by diocesan handbooks, which included the names of diocesan officers, lists of recent ordinations, details of local church charities, and much information on individual parishes.

Clergy also began to keep registers of services. These reveal changes in the patterns of services, and identify clergy who presided and preached. Other potential sources include the records of Sunday schools, youth clubs, and a variety of other parish organisations.

I. Religion: Nonconformity and Roman Catholicism

The doctrines and practices of Christianity have been much disputed, ever since New Testament times. In England, serious divisions within the church began with the Lollards in the late fourteenth century. Evidence (relatively rare) of local Lollardy is primarily found in bishops' registers. Throughout the Reformation, the English church almost managed to remain a single institution, although Roman Catholics established their own (secret) organisation in Elizabeth's reign, and some Puritans were persecuted. The Civil War, however, removed restrictions on religious belief, and nonconformist (originally known as dissenting) denominations were founded. The attempt to reimpose uniformity after the Restoration failed.

Most early records of nonconformists and Roman Catholics are records of their persecution. The State Papers (p.91–2) are full of information on both groups. Attendance at church became a statutory duty in 1558. Churchwardens were supposed to name recusants (those who refused to attend church) in their presentments (p.191). Incumbents' replies to bishops' queries include much information on dissenters.

Recusants could be tried in the church courts, or at Quarter Sessions and Assizes. Estreats of recusant fines (TNA classes E137 and E 362) were compiled by Clerks of the Peace for the Exchequer. They were copied into the Pipe Rolls (TNA E 372/426–36) between 1582 and 1591, and, thereafter, into separate recusant rolls (TNA E 376, duplicates in E 377). Before 1662, the great bulk of entries in the recusant rolls relate to Roman Catholics; thereafter, many dissenters are also mentioned. See *Short Guides 1*. More detail is included in:

• Bowler, Hugh, ed. *Recusant Roll no.2 (1593–1594): An Abstract in English*. Catholic Record Society 57. 1965.

In 1662, a fifth of the clergy refused to conform to the *Book of Common Prayer*. They were ejected from their livings, and serious persecution of nonconformists commenced. See:

• Matthews, A.G. *Calamy Revised: Being a Revision of Edmund Calamy's Account of the Ministers and Others Ejected and Silenced, 1660–2*. Clarendon Press, 1934. Calamy's original work should also be consulted.

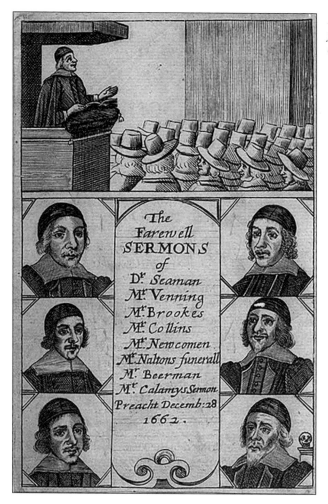

*Farewell sermons
from ministers
ejected in 1662.*

In 1669, Archbishop Sheldon surveyed nonconformist 'conventicles' (see *Short Guides* 2). In 1672, Charles II issued his 'Declaration of Indulgence', providing for the licensing of preachers and meeting houses. Sheldon's survey and the 1672 licensing records, are printed in:

• Turner, G.L., ed. *Original Records of Early Nonconformity under Persecution and Indulgence*. 3 vols. T. Fisher Unwin, 1911.

Charles's 'Indulgence' attracted much Parliamentary hostility and was soon withdrawn. However, William of Orange's 1688 invasion meant increased toleration for nonconformists. From 1689, they were again able to licence their meeting houses. Licences could be granted by Quarter Sessions, bishops and archdeacons. But nonconformists remained barred from public office or attending university.

The right to meeting house licences was extended to Roman Catholics in 1791. In 1852, licensing was transferred to the Registrar General, who began the (still ongoing) worship register, and obtained returns of all former registrations (TNA, class RG 31). See:

• Welch, Edwin. 'The Registration of Meeting Houses', *Journal of the Society of Archivists* 3, 1966, p.116–20.

Many registration records are in print. See, for example:

• Chandler, John, ed. *Wiltshire Dissenters' Meeting House Certificates and Registration, 1689–1852.* Wiltshire Record Society, 40. 1985.

Chapel building required the purchase of land in trust. Trust deeds may be held with chapel records. Over 40,000 were enrolled on the Close Rolls (TNA, class C 54) between 1736 and 1890. See:

• Ambler, R.W. 'Enrolled Trust Deeds: A Source for the History of Nineteenth-Century Nonconformity', *Archives*, 20(90), 1993, p.177–86.

A number of surveys of dissenters and Roman Catholics have been conducted by both state and church. Reference has already been made to 'censuses' of 1603 and 1676, and to the 1851 ecclesiastical census (p.48 & 178). The latter should be compared with the 1829 survey of non-Anglican places of worship. See:

• Ambler, R.W. 'A Lost Source? The 1829 Returns of Non-Anglican Places of Worship', *Local Historian* 17(8), 1987, p.483–9.

The range of records available to nonconformist historians is vast, and it is not possible here to give more than a brief summary. The records of the more important denominations are discussed below. The many splits within them have been barely mentioned, nor have the records of many smaller denominations, for example, the Huguenots,[9] the Christian Brethren, the Pentecostalists, the Free Church of England, the Salvation Army, all of which may have been important locally. So may the Jews, at least in cities.[10]

A brief introduction to nonconformist archives is provided by:

• Field, Clive D. 'Preserving Zion: The Anatomy of Protestant Nonconformist Archives in Great Britain and Ireland', *Archives*, 2008, Vol. 33, Issue 118, 2008, p.14–51.

For more detail, see:

- Raymond, Stuart A. *Tracing your Nonconformist Ancestors: A Guide for Family & Local Historians*. Pen & Sword, 2017.
- Mullet, Michael. *Sources for the History of English Nonconformity 1660–1830*. Archives and the User 8. British Records Association, 1991.

Baptists

Baptists are defined by their insistence on the need for adult rather than infant baptism. Each congregation is governed by its church meeting, open to all members. Meeting minutes are the key documents for the history of each church, and frequently include full lists of members. Baptist sources are described by:

- Mills, Susan J. *Probing the Past: A Toolbox for Baptist Historical Research*. Baptist Historical Society, 2009.

The Baptist Historical Society **https://baptisthistory.org.uk** publishes the *Baptist Quarterly*. The Baptist Union has published its annual handbook since 1832 under a variety of titles; it lists member churches and their ministers, and includes obituaries. Other Baptist sources are held by the Angus Library in Oxford **https://theangus.rpc.ox.ac.uk**.

Congregationalists (Independents), Presbyterians and Unitarians

Denominational boundaries between early dissenters were fluid, and many of them came together for a time in the 'Common Fund', established in 1690 in consequence of the 'Happy Union'. For its survey of nonconformist strength, see:

- Gordon, Alexander. *Freedom after Ejection: A Review (1690–1692) of Presbyterian and Congregational Nonconformity in England and Wales*. Manchester University Press, 1917.

Many sources are held by:

- Dr Williams's Library
  https://dwl.ac.uk

This includes the Surman Index **https://surman.english.qmul.ac.uk**, listing about 32,000 Congregational and other dissenting ministers. The Library supports the Dissenting Academies Project, whose database of student ministers is online at **www.qmul.ac.uk/sed/religionandliterature/dissenting-academies**. Another survey of ministers is indexed in:

- Creasey, John. *Index to the John Evans List of Dissenting Congregations and Ministers, 1715–1729, in Dr Williams's Library*. Dr Williams Trust, 1964.

Congregational churches and ministers were listed in the *Congregational Yearbook* (1847–1972), which also included obituaries. All independent churches in England were listed in 1855; the 1901 yearbook included a consolidated listing of all nineteenth-century ministers.

Most of the older Presbyterian churches eventually became Unitarian; however, Scottish Presbyterians founded many new congregations in the nineteenth century. Both Congregational and Presbyterian churches ran their own affairs, although Presbyterians tended to be dominated by their ministers. The records of individual Presbyterian churches tend to be concerned with ministerial matters, buildings and finance. Church meetings were more central to the life of Congregational churches; their church books frequently begin with their founding covenant. The two denominations joined together in the United Reformed Church in 1972. Before the union, each denomination had its own historical society, which published, respectively, the *Journal of the Presbyterian Historical Society of England* (1914–72) and the *Transactions of the Congregational History Society* (1901–72). The two societies merged in 1973, forming the United Reformed Church History Society **www.urchistory.org.uk**. It publishes *The Journal of the United Reformed Church History Society* (1973–).

The Unitarian History Society **www.unitarianhistory.org.uk** publishes the *Unitarian History Society Transactions* (1917–). Its website includes an index to Unitarian ministers since 1800, together with other helps to research.

Friends

The Society of Friends was founded during the religious anarchy of the Interregnum. Friends sought the 'inner light', rejecting formal religion; they are frequently referred to as Quakers. From their beginnings, they infuriated the authorities by refusing to pay tithes, or to remove their hats in the presence of their social 'superiors'. They were much persecuted, and fill the pages of both secular and ecclesiastical court records. They kept detailed records of their 'sufferings'. Abstracts are published in:

- Besse, Joseph. *Sufferings of Early Quakers in Yorkshire, 1652–1690: Facsimile of part of the 1753 edition*, with new introduction by Michael Gandy. Sessions Book Trust, c.1998. Further volumes cover other regions.

The Society was organised in a heirarchy of 'meetings', at the apex of which was the annual London Meeting, consisting of representatives from Quarterly Meetings. These in turn consisted of representatives from Monthly Meetings. Most business was administered by Monthly Meetings, which were responsible for ensuring that the directives of the London Meeting (now termed the Britain Yearly Meeting) were implemented. Each Monthly Meeting had responsibility for a number of Preparative Meetings, most of which were formed by single Particular Meetings, that is, congregations. There were many variations from this basic pattern. All meetings kept detailed minutes and accounts; the quality of their marriage records persuaded the government that they could be exempted from the requirement to be married by an Anglican priest under Hardwicke's 1753 Marriage Act. Friends only began to record 'convictions', that is, admissions to the Society, in the late eighteenth century.

The records of most 'meetings' are in local record offices. Those of the London Meeting, and the records of 'Sufferings' mentioned above, are held by Friends House Library **www.quaker.org.uk/resources/library**. It also holds the archives of a number of other Quaker organisations and an extensive library. Its website has a number of useful subject guides.

The denominational historical journal is published by the Friends Historical Society **https://friendshistoricalsociety.org.uk**. The Quaker Family History Society **www.qfhs.co.uk** publishes *Quaker Connections*. For guidance on Quaker records, see:

• Milligan, Edward H., & Thomas, Malcolm J. *My Ancestors were Quakers: How Can I Find Out More About Them?* 2nd edition. Society of Genealogists, 1999.

Methodists

Methodism arose from the preaching of John Wesley and others in the mid-eighteenth century. Its denominational structure was established by its first annual conference in 1744. Each congregation became a 'society' within a 'circuit', which generally consisted of a dozen or so societies. Preachers were appointed to the circuit. Districts consisted of a number of circuits.

'Leaders' meetings' ran the local society. Their minutes are the prime source for the history of individual chapels. Chapel trustees, responsible for the building, met separately and kept their own minutes. Accounts of society stewards provide many details. Pew rents were an important source of income and may be recorded separately. Class books record the names of members who attended weekly classes for Bible study and prayer, one of the major features of early Methodist activity.

Circuits were governed by their quarterly meetings, whose minutes record their deliberations and name attendees. Much of their business was concerned with finance and property, as they owned the manse, and had some responsibility for chapel buildings. There are also membership lists, class books, accounts and other documents. Printed circuit plans (usually quarterly) named preachers scheduled to conduct services in each chapel. Most were local preachers, rather than ordained ministers. Minutes of local preachers' meetings provide much information on the men and women who offered themselves for this ministry. For circuit plans, see:

• Leary, William. *Methodist Preaching Plans: A Guide to their Usefulness to the Historian*. William Leary, 1977.

Methodist Districts coordinated the work of Methodism regionally. Much of their business was taken up by doctrinal and ministerial matters, although they also involved themselves with new Methodist schools and chapels. District minutes and other records are usually found with the connexional archives, in:

• Methodist Archives and Research Centre (MARC) **www.library.manchester.ac.uk/search-resources/special-collections/guide-to-special-collections/methodist**

In the nineteenth century, Methodists split into a number of different denominations. In the twentieth century, most of them came together to form the Methodist Church. MARC holds the connexional archives of all of these denominations. They all had the same basic structures, and created similar documentation. They were governed by their annual conferences, and the 'journals' of their conferences provide the definitive records of proceedings. They are closed for seventy-five years. Published Conference minutes record decisions, and provide much information on preachers (including obituaries). The records of some divisions, e.g. Property Division, Home Missions Division, Education and Youth Division, contain much local information.

MARC also holds the papers of prominent evangelicals, such as the Wesleys, the Countess of Huntingdon and George Whitfield, together with over 4,000 small collections of personal papers from prominent Methodists. It also holds many Methodist journals, some of which are online:

• Wesleyan and Primitive Methodist periodicals, 1744–1960 **https://microform.digital/boa/collections/3/wesleyan-and-primitive-methodist-periodicals-1744–1960**

The Bible Christian chapel at St Ives (Cornwall): a typical nonconformist chapel.

Encyclopedic treatment of Methodism, together with valuable guidance on tracing sources and links to 'Online Books: Lists of Ministers and their Circuits', is provided by:

- Methodist Heritage
  www.methodistheritage.org.uk

The Wesley Historical Society **www.wesleyhistoricalsociety.org.uk** regularly publishes its *Proceedings*. It has a substantial library in Oxford, and its website includes a bibliography of Methodist history.

Useful guides to sources include:

- Swift, Wesley F. *How to write a Local History of Methodism*. 5th edition, revised by Thomas Shaw & E.A. Rose. Wesley Historical Society, 1994.
- Leary, William. *My Ancestors were Methodists: How Can I Find Out More About Them?* 4th edition. Society of Genealogists Enterprises, 2005.
- Ratcliffe, Richard. *Methodist Records for Family Historians*. Family History Partnership, 2014.

Roman Catholics

For two centuries following the Reformation, Roman Catholics were subjected to penal legislation. Property, as has been seen, was liable to confiscation, and indeed, priests could be executed. Most sixteenth- and seventeenth-century sources for Roman Catholics are therefore to be found in governmental records. Those records relating to both nonconformists and Catholics have already been described. A number of others relate specifically to Catholics. A variety of Catholic censuses and name lists are identified by Raymond (p.204). The most substantial include:

- Ryan, Patrick, ed. 'Diocesan Returns of Recusants for England and Wales, 1577', in *Miscellanea*, 12. Catholic Record Society, 22, 1921, p.1–114.
- Worrall, E.S., ed. *Returns of Papists, 1767*. 2 vols. Catholic Record Society Occasional Publications, 1–2. 1980–89.

Roman Catholics were subjected to heavy taxation. From 1628, convicted recusants liable to the subsidy were required to pay double. Those not liable to the subsidy nevertheless had to pay poll tax. Returns in TNA, class E179, record their names. Double taxation was also imposed with certain other direct taxes.

Roman Catholics may also be identified in the records of continental institutions, which attracted many English and Welsh students, monks and nuns. Many registers and other records have been published (and in some cases digitised) by the:

- Catholic Record Society
  www.crs.org.uk

Roman Catholic priests can be identified in:

- Bellenger, Dominic Aidan. *English and Welsh Priests 1558–1800: A Working List*. Downside Abbey, 1984.
- Fitzgerald-Lombard, Charles. *English and Welsh Priests, 1801–1914: A Working List*. Downside Abbey, 1993

For biographies of priests trained in the continental seminaries, see:

- Anstruther, G. *The Seminary Priests 1558–1850*. 4 vols. 1968–77.

Many exiled religious communities and seminaries returned to England during the Napoleonic era. Innumerable Irish Catholics followed in the nineteenth century. The hierarchy was re-established in 1850, and many new parishes were created. The process is described in a variety of parish and diocesan records. Priests regularly reported the *Status Animarum* of their congregations to their bishops. Bishops made *ad limina* reports to the Pope every five years. Priests compiled separate listings of converts, confirmations and communicants. Obit lists recorded the dead who were to be prayed for. Some congregations charged pew rents, recorded in their accounts. Roman Catholic bishops conducted regular visitations of their dioceses, which may be well documented. Efforts have been made to collect these records in Roman Catholic diocesan archives. The most important collection of official Roman Catholic archives is held by Westminster Diocesan Archives **https://rcdow.org. uk/about-us/archives**. Its holdings include bishops' papers, diocesan administrative archives and parish records, as well as many records pre-dating the restoration of the hierarchy. That includes the papers of the 'Old Brotherhood', which unofficially governed the secular clergy in the seventeenth and eighteenth centuries.

Much evidence of local Catholicism is held by monasteries such as Downside and Douai, by the Jesuits, and even in the Vatican Archives. Catholic archives are listed by:

• Religious Archives Group: Roman Catholic Church
https://religiousarchivesgroup.org.uk/advice/directory/christianity/ catholic

For a detailed discussion of Catholic sources, see:

• Raymond, Stuart A. *Tracing your Roman Catholic Ancestors: A Guide for Family and Local Historians*. Pen & Sword, 2018.

A narrower focus is taken by:

• Williams, J.A. *Recusant History: Sources for Recusant History in English Official Archives*. Catholic Record Society, 1983.

J. Leisure

Holy days – holidays – were feast days in the Christian calendar, when parishioners were given a day off work in order to attend worship. In practice, such days frequently involved feasting, dancing, sports and drama. Plays on both religious and secular themes were laid on by the church; church ales were held to raise money; Rogationtide processions 'beat the bounds' to mark parish boundaries. Pre-Reformation churchwardens' accounts make many references to such events. They were gradually curtailed in the century before 1660, as puritanism took its hold, and as parish elites tired of the associated rowdyism. Sixteenth- and seventeenth-century churchwardens' presentments, and the records of both ecclesiastical and secular courts, frequently mention the (increasingly frowned upon) leisure activities of the lower orders.

Leisure activities can be traced in a variety of sources. Between c.1550 and c.1750, sporting equipment, musical instruments, books and card tables may be mentioned in probate inventories. Estate accounts record sums laid out for prizes in sporting activities at fairs. Bowling greens are occasionally mentioned in deeds. Chancery depositions sometimes mention sporting activities, even if only in passing. Justices of the Peace licensed alehouses and theatres, exercised control over wakes and gaming, and closed down 'suspect' events such as fairs, bull baiting and cock fighting.

Some popular entertainment did, however, survive. Evidence for drama prior to 1642 has been collected by the Records of Early English Drama project, and published in a series of twenty-seven local volumes. See:

- REED Online
  https://ereed.library.utoronto.ca

Nineteenth- and twentieth-century newspapers advertised leisure activities, and reported on them. Since 1880, much information on drama has been printed in *The Stage*, available at **www.britishnewspaperarchive. co.uk**. Sources for musical history are discussed by:

- Mackerness, E.D. 'Sources of Local Musical History', *Local Historian*, 11(6), 1975, p.315–20.

Much evidence for fairs and circuses is provided by:

- National Fairground and Circus Archive
  www.sheffield.ac.uk/nfca/index

Leisure time for the working classes steadily increased after the 1833 Ten Hour Act. Their leisure activities, however, continued to be regarded with suspicion. It was increasingly channelled into sporting clubs, whose rules were devised to control behaviour. These rules applied not just to plebeian sports such as football, wrestling and boxing, but also to more gentlemanly pursuits such as cricket and hunting. Sporting clubs created many records. Some are deposited in record offices; others are still held by clubs, which occasionally have their own museums. The annual handbooks of sports governing bodies are likely to list local organisations. Publications such as *Wisden's Cricketers' Almanac* (published annually since 1864) provide much information of interest.

Outdoor sports required playing fields. In rural areas, these were frequently provided by parish councils, whose minutes may provide useful information on their acquisition and use. Parish councils sometimes also provided halls, where clubs could raise funds by organising dances, whist drives and other social gatherings. Twentieth-century leisure activities are included in the Mass Observation archives (p.25).

A variety of sources for sporting history are discussed by:

• Huggins, Mike. 'The Local History of British Sport: Approaches, Sources and Methods', *Local Historian*, 42(2), 2012, p.90–106.

For sources at TNA, see:

• Paley, Ruth. 'Sources for the History of British Sport in the National Archives', *Archives*, 50(130–1), 2015, p.47–65.

Many people preferred to spend their leisure time at home, in the garden, perhaps hoping that they could feed themselves.[11] That interest can be traced in trade directories. They record nurserymen, whose business records may also be useful. Interest in gardening was also reflected in the growth of allotments for the working classes. These were originally provided by landowners, but the Allotments Act 1887 encouraged local authorities to provide them as well; there were *c.*1.25 million by the 1920s. Records of allotments amongst council archives provide useful details.

These activities were accompanied by a growing interest by antiquarians in folklore. The customs they recorded included many details of leisure activities, for example, squirrel hunting, hurling, and the Abbots Bromley horn dance, although perhaps adding much that was fanciful. See:

• Simpson, Jacqueline, & Roud, Steve. *A Dictionary of English Folklore.* Oxford University Press, 2003. Online at **www.oxfordreference.com**
• The Folklore Society **https://folklore-society.com**

The middle classes also supported attempts to establish new cultural traditions. The village fete began its career in the late nineteenth century and is likely to be mentioned in the minutes of vestries and parish church councils, in parish magazines, and in newspapers. Many twentieth-century communities organised pageants, frequently involving large numbers of people.

Extensive details of over 400 pageants, together with a *Local History Study Guide*, are included in:

• The Redress of the Past: Historical Pageants in Britain
  www.historicalpageants.ac.uk

The brass band, public lectures, book clubs, lantern shows, concerts and plays, all flourished in the late nineteenth and early twentieth centuries. The pub provided a venue for these activities. So did the Temperance Hall.[12] Organisations such as Mechanics Institutes, the Townswomen's Guild, the Women's Institute and the Mothers' Union, were popular. Their minutes, membership lists and accounts enable their histories to be written.

Tourism began with pilgrimages, and developed with visits to spa towns, such as Bath, where visitors hoped to cure their diseases. The modern holiday is closely associated with the seaside. The coming of the railways changed the whole concept of what a holiday should be. Successive editions of *Bradshaw's Guide* may be used to trace the development of resorts. Statistics of arrivals were printed in the local press; annual statistical returns were published as Parliamentary papers from 1845. For information on train excursions, see TNA's AN and RAIL classes. Guide books to resorts issued by publishers such as John Murray and Ward Lock & Co are important sources for holiday history. Trade directories are also useful. Nineteenth-century local newspapers frequently listed visitors. The 1921 census was taken in June, and therefore records the presence of many holidaymakers. Sources for holiday history are reviewed by:

• Walton, John K., & McGloine, P.R. 'Holiday Resorts and Their
  Visitors: Some Sources for the Local Historian', *Local Historian*, 13(6),
  1979, p.323–332.

On guidebooks, see:

• Vaughan, J.E. 'Early Guide Books as Sources of Social History',
  Amateur Historian, 5(6), 1963, p.183–8.
• Vaughan, J.E. *The English Guide Book, c.1780–1870: An Illustrated
  History*. David & Charles. 1974.

For the background, see:

• Walton, J.K. *The English Seaside Resort: A Social History 1750–1914*.
  Leicester University Press, 1983.

Nailsworth (Gloucestershire) subscription rooms.

ENDNOTES

Introduction
1. Most of the sources discussed also relate to Wales, but not to Scotland or Ireland.

Chapter 2
1. So was the Duchy of Cornwall, but it retains its own records.
2. It also has a 'special series', listing documents in other repositories.
3. Digitised at **www.hathitrust.org**.
4. For a detailed list and discussion of nineteenth-century administrative units, see Higgs, Edward. *Making Sense of the Census Revisited: Census Records for England and Wales, 1801–1901: A Handbook for Historical Researchers*. Institute of Historical Research / National Archives, 2005, p.189–95.
5. Crosby, Alan G. 'The Historical Geography of English and Welsh Dioceses', *Local Historian*, 37(3), 2007, p.171–92.
6. See Christie, Peter. 'The Gentleman's Magazine and the Local Historian', *Local Historian*, 15(2). 1982, p.80–4; Hearl, Trevor. 'The Gentleman's Magazine: A Nineteenth-Century Quarry', *Local Historian* 16(6), 1985, p.346–50.

Chapter 3
1. See Benton, T. *Irregular Marriage in London before 1754*. Society of Genealogists, 1994.
2. On studying local epidemics, see Barker, Rosalin. 'The Local Study of Plague', *Local Historian* 14(6), 1982, p.332–40.
3. A useful substitute, albeit compiled over a century later, is provided by Austin, David H., ed. *Boldon Book: Northumberland and Durham*. Domesday Book 35 supplementary volume. Phillimore, 1982.
4. Hoskins, W.G. *Local History in England*. 3rd edition. Longman, 1984, p.51–2.

5. For example, Darby, H.C., & Finn, R. Welldon. *The Domesday Geography of South-West England*. Cambridge University Press, 1967.

6. Moore, John S. *Counting People: A DIY Manual for Local and Family Historians*. Oxbow Books, 2013, p.32–4.

7. Moore, op cit, p.31.

Chapter 4

1. Chapman, Colin. *Sin, Sex and Probate: Ecclesiastical Courts, Officials and Records*. Lochin Publications, 1997.

2. For these, see King, Peter. 'Pauper Inventories and the Material Life of the Poor in the eighteenth and early nineteenth centuries', in Hitchcock, Tim, King, Peter, & Sharpe, Pamela, eds. *Chronicling Poverty: The Voices and Strategies of the English Poor, 1640–1840*. Macmillan, 1987, p.155–91; Harley, Joseph, ed. *Norfolk Pauper Inventories c.1690–1834. Records of Social and Economic History* new series 59. Oxford University Press, 2020.

3. For a 'Gazetteer of Improvement Acts and Municipal Incorporations', see West, John. *Town Records*. Phillimore & Co., 1983, p.194–205.

4. For these organisations, see Raymond, Stuart A. *The Home Front, 1939–45: A Guide for Family Historians*. Family History Partnership, 2012.

Chapter 5

1. Thompson, F.M.L. *English Landed Society in the Nineteenth Century*. Routledge & Kegan Paul, 1963, p.332.

2. Except for those covering London and Paddington, in TNA, class IR 91.

3. For a full list, see Alcock, Nat. *Tracing History Through Title Deeds: A Guide for Family and Local Historians*. Pen & Sword, 2017, p.60–2.

4. Listed by ibid, p.51–3.

5. See Martin, G.H. 'The Registration of Deeds of Title in the Medieval Borough', in Bullough, D.A., & Storey, R.L., eds. *The Study of Medieval Records: Essays in Honour of Kathleen Major*. Clarendon Press, 1971, p.150–73.

6. Sources for the Jacobite rebellions are discussed by Oates, Jonathan. 'Sources for the Study of the Jacobite Rebellions of 1715 and 1745 in England', *Local Historian*, 32(3), 2002, p.156–72.

7. Hoyle, Richard W. *Tudor Taxation Records: A Guide for Users*. Public Record Office readers guide 5. 1994, p.42–7 & 50–2. Hoyle lists the few surviving returns.

8. Edwards, Peter. *Rural Life: Guide to Local Records*. B.T. Batsford, 1993, p.60.

9. For the importance of sub-tenants, see Harrison, C J. 'Elizabethan Surveys: a Comment', *Agricultural History Review*, 27(2), 1969, p.82–9.

10. For their history, see Polden, Patrick. *A History of the County Court, 1846–1971*. Cambridge University Press, 1999.

Chapter 6

1. The living in farm servant gradually disappeared in the nineteenth century.
2. For a detailed discussion of these, see Higgs, Edward. *Making Sense of the Census Revisited: Census Records for England and Wales, 1801–1901: A Handbook for Historical Researchers*. Institute of Historical Research / National Archives, 2005, p.153–64.
3. Moore, op cit, p.93, claims that many celebrants inserted occupations, despite the lack of a column for them.
4. Raymond, Stuart A. 'The Crispin Apprentices', *Devon & Cornwall Notes & Queries* 42, 2017–18 , p.25–33, 57–64, 89–96, 117–25 & 152–7.
5. For the national context, see Clark, Peter. *The English Alehouse: A Social History, 1200–1830*. Longman, 1983; Hailwood, Mark. *Alehouses and Good Fellowship in Early Modern England*. Boydell Press, 2014.
6. For an interesting study of badgers – or 'chapmen' – see Spufford, Margaret. *The Great Reclothing of Rural England: Petty Chapmen and their Wares in the Seventeenth Century*. Hambledon Press, 1984.
7. For nonconformist and Roman Catholic clergy, see p.195–204.

Chapter 7

1. Winstanley, R.L., & Jameson, P., eds. *The Diary of James Woodforde*. 17 vols. Parson Woodforde Society, 1977–2007. Many other editions.
2. Ward, W.R. 'County Government since 1835', in Pugh, R.B., & Crittall, Elizabeth, eds. *A History of Wiltshire*, vol.V. Oxford University Press, 1955, p.257.
3. Digitised 1838–1901 at British Online Archives **https://microform.digital/boa**.
4. See, for example, Redshaw, Ann. 'Education in an Eighteenth-Century Northamptonshire Village: The Rockingham School Register, 1764–1773', *Local Historian*, 46(3), 2016, p.220–8.
5. For background, see Kelly, Thomas. *History of Public Libraries in Great Britain, 1845–1975*. 2nd edition. Library Association, 1977. See also the Library History and Information Group of CILIP **www.cilip.org.uk**
6. Hastings, Paul. 'Parish Libraries in the Nineteenth Century', *Local Historian* 15(7), 1983, p.406–13. For their earlier history, see Kelly, Thomas. *Early Public Libraries*. Library Association Publishing, 1966.
7. On bede rolls, see Norton, Elizabeth. 'Parish Bede Rolls during the English Reformation', *Local Historian*, 48(1), 2018, p.19–29.
8. Rogers, Alan. *Approaches to Local History*. 2nd edition. Longmans, 1977, p.133.
9. Huguenot Society of Great Britain and Ireland **www.huguenotsociety.org.uk**.
10. Jewish Historical Society of England **https://jhse.org**; Jews and Jewish Communities in the 18th–20th centuries **www.nationalarchives.gov.uk/**

help-with-your-research/research-guides/jews-and-jewish-communities-18th-20th-centuries.

11. Floud, Roderick. *An Economic History of the English Garden*. Allen Lane, 2019, p.278–9.

12. For these, see Harrison, Brian. 'Temperance Societies', *Local Historian* 8(4), 1968, p.135–8. See also 8(5), 1969, p.180–6.

SUBJECT INDEX